BON AMOUR

Ken McAdams

Bon Amour

Published by Central Park South Publishing 2021
www.centralparksouthpublishing.com

Copyright © Ken McAdams, 2021

All rights reserved. No part of this publication may be reproduced, stored in a retrieval system, or transmitted in any form or by any means, electronic, mechanical, photocopying, recording or otherwise, without the prior written permission from the publisher.

Typesetting and e-book formatting services by Victor Marcos

ISBN: 978-1-956452-05-1

> "Yesterday, all my troubles seemed so far away,
> now it looks as though they're here to stay
> oh, i believe in yesterday…"
>
> **THE BEATLES**

Contents

Chapter One	1
Chapter Two: The Listing	29
Chapter Three: A New Place	43
Chapter Four: Like Being Kids Again	53
Chapter Five: Tenting Under the Stars	65
Chapter Six: Garvey, His Board & We the People	77
Chapter Seven: A Good Man	81
Chapter Eight: Cranking Up	91
Chapter Nine: So, Where Is the Book?	107
Chapter Ten: On the road	121
Chapter Eleven	135
Chapter Twelve: Pulling it all Together	143
Chapter Thirteen: By the Side of the Road	157
Chapter Fourteen: Don't Mess with A Union	163
Chapter Fifteen: It Should not be So	173
Chapter Sixteen: The Day Later	177
Chapter Seventeen: Skunk in Glass	189
Chapter Eighteen: Who?	197
Chapter Nineteen: Swaps For a Friend	223
Chapter Twenty: Trips from, Hell	227
Chapter Twenty-One: Backfilling	233
Chapter Twenty-Two: Bombs, Bowling Balls and a Yam	237
Chapter Twenty-Three: A Drill Weekend	253
Chapter Twenty-Four: An Editor?	259
Chapter Twenty-Five: Another Down	277
Chapter Twenty-Six: He Comes	285

CHAPTER ONE

My "Yesterday" truly had all my troubles seeming far away, but now I fear they truly are back to stay... In the early Sixties I was a Marine fighter pilot stationed at Kaneohe Bay, Hawaii. That certainly was a plus since my squadron was the same 214 "Black Sheep" of top American Pacific theatre ace, "Pappy" Boyington, who was big trouble for The Corps from day one of his time there.

In the beginning, as Scripture liked to phrase it, Lieutenant Boyington couldn't keep his mouth shut and had a strong tendency to elbow and shoulder his way into discussions conducted by far higher ranks, winning him highly negative fitness reports and gaining attention all the way to the Commandant of the Marine Corps. Appearing back in Washington before this man with many stars on his uniform shoulders, Boyington was challenged to defend his personality, conduct, and seeming disregard for the long established and respected Chain of Command.

Boyington had prepared his answer well, and led off with this frank response, "Yes sir, it is obvious that I am a loose cannon and without question a true pain in the ass for any and all of the C.O.'s I have served under, but let me offer the following respectfully submitted proposal. Though I am a true loud-mouthed pain in the ass, I am still an excellent fighter pilot. We are at war. The Japanese are kicking our ass in the Pacific right now. What we need is to turn that around so we kick theirs instead…and here is how we can do it.

"The Corps has lots of good pilots who are not with it militarily. I am the perfect example of the type, but I am proposing a solution to this problem. Put me in charge of assembling a Black Sheep squadron of misfits who can really fly, and we'll go out and turn around the air war in the Pacific. No bullshit. What do you think, sir?"

The Commandant was quiet for a moment, though honestly impressed with what the brash young lieutenant had to say. The general let his non reply hang in the air for another long moment… until he put out his large gnarly hand, making it a deal, and said, "I'm giving you the chance to put up or shut up back here in D.C flying a desk. It's up to you. No bullshit, son. From now on it's going to be nothing but performance. I want your list of 40 tough guy pilots on my desk by 0800 hours tomorrow morning. On my approval you will start training them to be the best in air-combat. Any questions? No, good. So, get the hell out of here and put your butt in gear. Build me a squadron…a hard-flying, tough, straight-shooting squadron that will take down these Jap bastards, one we all can be proud of. And I am kicking you up a rank to do the job."

"Aye, aye sir."

"Dismissed."

And with that exchange, the Pacific air war did begin to turn around. Boyington's squadron of butt-kickers became number one in the theatre and Pappy rose to become our top Pacific ace there as well.

Decades later, considering all the troubles and similar slights of hand I'd used to get myself into and through flight school and into the seat of a Marine fighter aircraft, I believed I had found my rightful home there in the Corps. All of which was ironic because in college I had flunked the Navy physical for getting into Officer Candidate School, (OCS), much less the pilot program and its officer's gold bar at graduation. As a matter of fact, my failure defined the only slot open to me at graduation which would have been as an enlisted rifle-carrying Infantryman.

This, however, sorted itself out in my favor, following an incredible fistfight at the Cannon Club at Princeton University my senior year at Yale. After having been beaten half to death for 15 rounds by a larger Golden Gloves champion, I connected with my only hit of the night, in the last round of this bare-knuckle battle, knocking my opponent out cold.

It turned out the referee over-seeing this match was a Quantico Marine who was so impressed with my battling-back that he felt the Marine Corps needed me as an officer. I told him I had no future as such because I'd flunked the color test a couple of years earlier. He said no problem. They could train me to pass it ,which they did and then upward I would go onto flight school and amazingly enough, as it worked out, into VMA 214, the very squadron Pappy Boyington founded and named as the historic, Black Sheep Squadron. Appropriately so, since my career in life turned out to be much like another chapter in Boyington's autobiography, *Bah Bah Blacksheep*.

Initially my era's combat record in Hawaii bore only the battle ribbons of an occasional brass-rail shoving match or a sailing surfboard retrieval. Our country was at peace then, no wars, just the sun to fight on the many beaches on the islands of Hawaii. In general, my compatriots zeroed in their sights on the cocoa-skinned Waheenies of Hnauma Bay, or on the sun-streaked Howlie girls parading Waikiki. They invested in the sports cars, surfboards, speedboats, sailboats, and cement grass shacks necessary for waging such war.

For many servicemen then and now, Hawaii is known as The Rock. It is such an irony that in this lush paradise, replete with lovely ladies everywhere, a young man can still find himself so lonely. The fact is that there are simply too few ladies to go around considering all the military bases on the Rock, and too few service dollars to pay the price of a Waikiki beach head if a lovely young thing should smile in his direction. I found this true anyway, so I quit looking. And wouldn't you know that after I quit the race, while I was out on one of my lonely walks on the beach one morning, I practically stepped on, tripped over a fascinating, and amazingly beautiful lady.

Isn't that often the way? To find someone or something, is to stop looking for them. To find success is to stop pursuing it. Could this be true of everything in life?

Anyway, running into this young lady on that beach was much the same thing. I had given up looking and then I practically tripped over her... and what an extraordinary find she was.

During this period our First Lady, Jackie Kennedy, was the beauty and class package leader for all the women of the world. She was the liberation of the brunettes, bane of blondes. So, as I trudged down Waikiki, bleary-eyed, pale and a bit wasted from a week's leave on the outer islands with another fighter pilot friend, I spotted ahead of me, sitting sweetly on a large beach blanket, a deeply tanned, brunette whose highlighted hair was cut exactly in Jackie's Pan Am flight-attendant fashion. "Good Lord," I whispered, "what is the First Lady doing here?" Though I was in uniform, my brass was not sparkling nor had the sand done nice things to my normally glistening "Marine Green" dress shoes.

I wanted to execute a one-eighty reversal out of there, at least until the young woman stopped me dead with a very sweet smile. Her teeth were so white. Her brown eyes were so golden and flecked with green. Though even my tired eyes realized it was not actually Jackie Kennedy, my heart still skipped a beat from the impact of that smile.

Marines take beaches. Always have. I was on a beach, and I was a Marine. Clearly, I had to show my stuff.

"Hi, my name's Ken. What's yours?" I asked, keeping it short and sweet.

She looked up at me almost elegantly, much as if she actually was the wife of the President of the United States and said, "I'm Bobbye, Bobbye with a Y... E. Bobbye Menefee from Tennessee."

"My father was born in Tennessee," I announced meaninglessly, nodding to make my inane point all that much stronger. Bobbye raised her hand to deflect the sun from her eyes.

She had a smile on her face without any wrinkling of her brow. I took that as a good sign. Actually, the fact that she hadn't scooped up her beach towel and ran into the ladies' changing room was an even better sign.

"Would you like a swim?" I asked, not really thinking that through.

"Sure, but your outfit looks kind of problematic, the tie and wings and all."

"If you'll wait a couple of minutes, I'll run into the shop there and buy some trunks," I said, wishing I'd had time to pump up my weight-lifter's arms before I'd wandered down the beach. She looked terrific, so anything I might have going for me would be important.

She smiled again and followed that with a nod which I took as clearance to do the trunks number in the shop.

"I'll be right back," I said, turning and churning through the sand to the Fort Derusy beach shop.

All they had in my size was purple. Marines don't wear purple, but at least they weren't pink.

Perfect in purple, with an oversized towel over my shoulders, I jogged back to where beautiful Bobbye was still stretched out. Needless to say, I hardly knew how to handle a beach confrontation with a drop-dead look-a-like of Mrs. J. F. K. So, I punted.

"Would you mind if I took a short nap before we swim, surf or whatever?" I asked, my bleary eyes squinting through the halo around her head caused by the sun directly behind her.

"I'll do the same," she said. "I had a final dress rehearsal last night that went on forever. I need a rest myself."

"A rehearsal? Are you an actress?"

"I teach English and drama at a high school outside of Nashville. I am staying at my uncle's house here and taking a couple of graduate theater courses for my masters. Our final is our own adaptation of the play 'Picnic.' I was lucky enough to get the Kim Novak lead."

"So, who is your William Holden costar from the movie?" I asked, already feeling a bit jealous.

"Another Nashvillian, Pat Boone's brother who is warming up for his debut on Broadway," she said, her gorgeous eyes flickering down and away from mine.

"Is he as good-looking as Holden?" I asked with a mildly growing concern.

"He is and his name is Nicky, Nicky Boone. But he has problems of his own," she said, with a slow nod of her head.

"How's that? What do you mean?"

"First, as I said, he is very handsome, but he looks exactly like his brother, Pat. And his singing voice is the same as Pat's, too. They used to sing and play their guitars together on a Nashville radio station. The result of that was the record company telling the two that there was room for only one Boone. Pat is older and he got the nod. So, Nicky is trying out for Broadway, but if that doesn't work, I think he'll go into social work or teach."

You know him pretty well?" I asked, unconsciously bracing myself for bad news.

"I do. But that's the way Nashville is. The singing celebrities are like anybody else there. They aren't full of themselves as the Hollywood people seem to be. They're just folks, so I've met and know a lot of them," she said with a smile that made my heart skip several beats.

"As a matter of fact, Nicky asked me to marry him," she added, looking down at the sand she was pushing around with her big toe.

I started to ask her if she had accepted his offer, but my diaphragm seemed to have quit working properly leaving me airless as well as speechless. I looked away feeling kind of like the Big Bad Wolf, ready to huff and puff to blow Nicky Boone's house down, if only I could get some air into my lungs to do it.

But Bobbye volunteered her answer to my unasked question anyway.

"I refused him. Not that I don't like him, it's just that I don't love him. And from rehearsing opposite him here, I don't think Broadway will be right for him either. Or the other way around. I don't believe he'll be right for the stage. So, we will continue to be friends, but nothing more than that."

I could breathe again, but not wanting to push my luck any further, I fluttered my eyes shut and flopped down onto my towel and napped, dreaming of living in the White House with this incredibly beautiful and charming Bobbye Menefee from Tennessee.

About an hour later I awoke. Jackie Kennedy was gone, though Bobbye Menefee had taken her place. I was delighted. Though I adored the First Lady, I dreaded tangling with the President, Commander-in-Chief of my very own service.

We swam some. We had sandwiches together. We chatted, smiled at each other, and laughed a lot. She was totally delightful. Which I found kind of shocking. I mean the young ladies I'd met before there, in Hawaii, had seemed dull and focused primarily on emptying my tiny wallet, and as soon as that was done, they were gone. Which was most of my reason for settling down to write a novel.

But this Bobbye was pretty, pleasant, warm, genuinely open, and agreeable…and all of that on Waikiki. Though she was from Tennessee she didn't have a Grand Ole Opry accent. I liked that.

I liked her. Suddenly I felt, I mean all-over-really felt…she was my girl. Had to be.

After sandwiches and cokes we ate ice cream. Hell, I knew it was shabby of me, but I just couldn't stop showering her with extravagance. She even accepted my dinner invitation. We ate just down the beach at Chuck's Steak House. The wine re-incarnated me. We walked over to the Ala Moana hotel for some dancing to live music. It was Tex Beneke and the Glenn Miller orchestra. He played the sax and sang. I used to play the sax, but couldn't sing. Memories flooded in from the Totem Pole Ballroom in Newton, outside of Boston. Sweet memories from high school, dancing to any number of these big bands. Bobbye could really dance. I could really dance. With her in my arms, that wonderful music guiding us around the dance floor, more memories flooded into my parched spirit…I found myself falling powerlessly in love.

I walked her home. We stopped to stand on her uncle's lanai, on his low fieldstone veranda overlooking Waikiki beach below, with Diamond Head's exclamation mark beyond Hanauma Bay where its rugged outcropping of land tumbles into the sea.

We said goodnight. Then we said goodnight to each other again. And again. Then I held her. I kissed her. In my arms she was exactly the right height. We kissed again and as I held her in my arms, I tilted my head back and was overwhelmed by the sky full of gorgeous stars. They paraded across the deep purple panorama above us, just touched by the gathering morning light of Diamond Head on the edge of the eastern horizon. It all was another version of Van Gogh's Starry Night.

My head was swimming. An undertow was pulling me down deeper and deeper still. No more goodnights. Suddenly my heart shouted, "She can't leave me." I couldn't allow it. I held her close and begged her to stay out on the beach with me instead of going into her uncle's house.

It must have been the assurance of her uncle being only a door away that allowed her to stay there with me. I wanted the two of us to share the incredible sunrise I knew was only minutes away. That sun, just peeking up over the horizon, would further silhouette Diamond Head. It would be stunning. It would be the travel poster of a lifetime. Something just the two of us would share for the rest of our lives. And I am proud to report that I timed it to the second as I asked, "Will you marry me?"

She seemed surprised. But I pressed on with, "You have to marry me."

"But I'm not sure I even remember your name," she said in total honesty.

"No problem," I countered, "our names will be the same." Whatever that meant.

"But we just met. What makes you think that in the little time we have had together qualifies for us to marry?"

I was momentarily stumped, but then, looking over her shoulder, it all became clear to me.

"Bobbye, you must marry me," I said, still looking over that shoulder.

"Why must I marry you?" she asked, but I noted without any negativity in her voice.

"Because... " and I paused, putting both my hands on her shoulders ,and slowly turning her so as to face to the east... "You must marry me because... you cannot deny that sunrise."

And at that very instant the sun peeked up from the horizon, and in all its golden glory, Diamond Head was presented to the two of us, but more specifically to Bobbye as if a very gift from God.

She gasped. I stopped breathing. It all was so totally breathtaking, and I must add, perfectly timed.

After, I don't know how many seconds, minutes, but not hours passed before she turned her face back to me and said... "Yes, I will marry you."

And that is truly how it happened. So, with her promise ringing in my ears, I knew it was time to act. Enough procrastination. Action! I bundled her into my little TR-3 sports car and off we went to Tripler Army Hospital for blood tests. Sure, she looked like she was going into shock, but what the hell, we were headed to a hospital anyway. The sun was now up with enthusiasm determinedly lighting our way. Omens everywhere!

Okay, some might call me impulsive, but I reject that out of hand. All of this was carefully painstakingly thought out. I just like to feel that I think faster than most, so I'd asked myself, why dilly-dally?

Speed was necessary for other reasons too. My squadron C.O. was holding a full-uniform pilot and aircraft inspection at 1300 hours of that new day. I was officially off leave at 0000 hours. I had to be by my aircraft, in uniform, and of course, married. There were only four hours left. If they made it snappy with the blood business, the license probably would take just a minute or two, then to the chaplain's office at the base across the Pali mountains, into uniform and then the dash to my aircraft. It would be tight, but the Marine Corps has always faced the impossible and pulled it off. Right?

The corpsman said the tests would take something like thirty-six hours to complete, which was nonsense. But then the hospital's commanding officer confirmed they would take about thirty-six hours to complete. Yes, damn it, we would lose a day or so on my carefully drawn up schedule, but hell man, building Rome and all that.

We crossed the Pali mountain range heading to the windward side. I couldn't let Bobbye out of my sight for fear she would evaporate or melt or somehow disappear. I set her down in a somewhat bedraggled state on Kailua Beach to rest while I hurried to the base and to my aircraft. I made it just as the colonel reached my plane, executing a perfect movement to face me and demanding, "Where the hell have you been, lieutenant?"

I crisply replied, "Trying to get married, sir."

"Did you complete your mission?" he hissed.

"No sir, I ran out of time."

"All right, Marine, get your ass out of here and don't come back until you are married," he snarled.

I was already at attention, so I snapped a sharp salute and shouted back with equal volume to his, "Aye, aye sir."

The colonel returned my salute and did a facing movement turning to the next pilot and aircraft as I ran across the tarmac to my car, jumped over the door, cranked up the engine and roared off to retrieve my bride-to-be back at Kailua Beach. I thought we should get to Waikiki to meet and brief her uncle. I thought he, as her family, should know something about all this. And I could not have come across a more off-the-charts kind of guy than Bobbye's Uncle Hugh. Another Pappy Boyington sort of guy. A true gem.

I learned that at age fifteen, he'd run away from home. His father, a brilliant man, was also a deaf mute, in an era that ignored, mistreated and generally looked down upon such people as defective. All of which turned him into an abusive father whom his son, Hugh, wanted only to get as far away from him as he could. All of which led to his running away.

But young Hugh was resourceful. He found jobs along the Tennessee River, and was so good at all he pursued on those waters, the Coast Guard noticed and enlisted him, and finally set him up for their officer candidate program at the academy in New London, Connecticut. It was late 1941 and the whole world was falling into various states of war.

Having already been in the Coast Guard four or more years, Hugh was a tough kid who, in the Guard/Naval jargon, was known as "Salty." Which led to his undoing on his very first day in the Officer's Candidate Program. There, totally unexpectedly, a D.I. (drill instructor) got in his face as if Hugh was nothing more than a wet-behind-the-ears timid cadette. Which Hugh Menefee was not by any means. So, when the D.I. got nose-to-nose with him and shoved Hugh's shoulder, Hugh simply unloaded a roundhouse right, knocking him flat and out. Which ended his career as a potential officer in the U.S. Coast Guard.

After Pearl Harbor, Hugh was sent to school to control and captain landing barges, the primary wartime role of the Coast Guard. Those who designated this salty tough guy to landing-barge school primarily had in mind to leave this smart-ass kid dead on a Pacific beach somewhere, certainly out of the hair of the Guard admirals who already had enough on their hands with the war itself.

For three years Menefee controlled the first landing barge of the first wave on every island attacked by U.S. forces in the Pacific theatre. And he did it all with such skill, daring, and guts, they promoted him to Warrant Officer, the highest enlisted rank, to command the training of those who followed him.

As Hugh came up to his retirement, he was offered any station in the world to run out his two-year clock. He chose

Waikiki where the peacetime demands were not that great. Being resourceful, on the side, Hugh formed an island band and featured a rising local star by the name of Don Ho. And daytimes he dabbled in real estate, so, when his retirement came about, Hugh had made his first of several million dollars and was an entertainment personality in the islands as well.

Once I'd gotten together with Hugh and told him how I was trying to complete a meeting-to-marriage with his niece, all in twenty-four hours, he thought that was a terrific program. He became solidly behind it and from then on acted much like my big brother while I was still in the Corps there in Hawaii.

Back during that first morning, once I'd picked up Bobbye on Kailua Beach and we'd chatted with Hugh, she fell asleep. All I could do at that point was promise Hugh I would be back the next day to marry her. I asked him to handle whatever details I'd missed so we could finish it all up by cocktail time the next day. He signed on to the whole program, including his band and Don Ho, for the big-time luau he'd be putting together in our honor.

But then, that very next day, Bobbye left Oahu, cancelled her picnic performance, and set off for Nashville. She called me from the airport to say a very small goodbye. Oh, such fluttery unpredictable women. I would not throw my fighter pilot stability away on such fluff. I would write novels, damn it, and become a giant amongst writing men. That poor capricious kitten, how she would pine; how she would suffer.

And I did write, but not sad love letters launched toward Tennessee. No, for several months I wrote what turned out to be a good start on a bad novel. Yes, some even said of my writing that I seemed only to be learning how to type. And yet, in time, Bobbye came back to haunt my every moment. I'd pass Waikiki and she would be there. I even ran into her uncle and had dinner with him several times. And I decided he was one hell of a guy who knew how to deal with whatever came at him. He was a master at turning misfortune into grand accomplishment. I hoped the two of us were on the same page in the book of life.

Though I had only seen Bobbye for less than twenty-four hours in my life, I somehow knew she had to be my wife. I knew this as I knew I could vouch for the sunset and the sunrise.

Eventually, oh loneliness, heart-rending love-sick loneliness, bittersweet yet still bitter, so painful still. I broke down and phoned her. I really didn't think she ever expected to hear from me again. I questioned, from the panic of our encounter, whether she was totally sure I even existed; that we had really met; that we had chased all over that island on our first day trying to get married. Who could believe such a fantasy anyway?

Yes, I did call her. I called her and wrote to her and called her some more and wrote to her endlessly. By playing hard to get in this fashion…I calculated she would soon give up the ghost and call my name.

Christmas. I took leave to go to Nashville, to meet her family and then to drive with her to Boston to meet mine. I chose New Year's Eve as my zero hour to re-ask the question.

My biggest fear was, as I got off the plane and walked through the terminal, would I be able to recognize her? I comforted myself, nevertheless, with the assurance of 20/15 eyesight and a mind like a bear trap. I was a Marine!

She wasn't anywhere in sight. Nowhere in the airport. There were only a few women in the terminal of about the right age, whatever that was, and only two who looked to be the right height. I knew I'd look foolish holding them, one by one, in my arms, even one at a time, to run the infallible kiss goodnight test. A lesser man might have panicked. Could she have said Memphis? Then a woman approached me, calling my name. Right height, yes, but white hair. Some confusion.

"I am Mrs. Menefee," (the name was familiar), "Bobbye's mother."

Of course! The steel jaws of my incredible mind slammed shut. This woman could well lead me to Bobbye!

The story of our first Christmas together is an unspectacular one. It is enough to say that I did pass the first hurdle by recognizing Bobbye when she entered her family's living room, and that the same electricity was there, the old assurances for us both returned. The history of our drive to Boston was something else, however, and is much too involved to cover in this brief volume. I will venture, however, that the Book of Exodus had little on this journey. Moses never had a generator fall out of his TR-3 on a winding West Virginia mountain road at midnight during a snowstorm; nor did his plastic side windows blow out, to be followed by drifts of the downy stuff blowing inside shortly thereafter. Nor, I am sure, did his front end vibrate apart and his SU carburetors dismantle themselves in the wilderness either. Despite the fact Bobbye had the same model sports car as I had, hers turned out to be in horrible shape. Something we learned piece by falling piece during our drive to Boston.

Despite all these mishaps, our love came through stronger for it all. Stronger, perhaps, in the sense that it weathered my strongest language which, during times of stress, reaches Herculean proportions. I am frankly miserable under pressure. Low, loud, vulgar, and sometimes even vicious.

Finally reaching Boston, Bobbye somehow still loved me. And, while off the road, having skidded off it, hood deep in a snowbank, nearly out of gas, well-after midnight, she again promised, I believe seriously this time, to marry me. I hadn't waited for New Year's Eve; I was sure we were going to die in that damned car that night, so I at least wanted to go to my frozen grave with that issue settled.

My military discharge became final the following August and I was about one hundred pages into the novel. It was somewhat herky-jerky, but I had great hopes. Bobbye already had a teaching position lined up in Lynnfield, Massachusetts, and added to that, all on her own, an apartment in nearby Wakefield. We'd tried for Rockport on Cape Anne and a flat on colorful old Bearskin Neck, but it wasn't to be. My writing would have to go on in the more plebeian surroundings of Walnut Street, Wakefield, Massachusetts.

Of the wedding, the only out-of-the-ordinary thing was my best man, and my brother Alan's confusion with the local southern accent there. Though a senior and brilliant Cornell University professor, he had never met Bobbye and did not know that her middle name was "Lou." In southland, U.S.A., a girl either had "Lou" as a middle name, or "Lee." One or the other. So, when the deeply accented minister advised that the best man (brother Alan) should hand him the ring when he said, "Baabaloo;" Alan, as a Yankee, was naturally thrown off stride. What on earth did this Cab Calloway howl of "Baabaloo" have to do with getting married in that church? When I told him that that was her name, he looked even more distressed.

Once settled in Wakefield, following a less harrowing trip northward, this time in my little TR-3, one complete with all the nuts and bolts the factory originally had in mind, we put together the schedule that was to guide us for the next two years. And good years they surely were. My deal with Bobbye was that she would bring home the bacon with her teaching job while I wrote. If I couldn't make it as a writer in that time, well, maybe, I wasn't meant to be a writer and I'd have to find some other kind of job. It seemed a fair deal to me and to her.

We got the first-floor apartment of a two-family house. And as legend had it, all the houses on the street had been built by one man, his own two feet and ten swollen thumbs. This early-day Levitt finished the block strong, admittedly, but our place must have been one of his earliest efforts. What I mean is that the living room floor, for instance, sloped toward the front of the house. But what really caused problems was when looking the length of the living room toward the bay window at the far end. Since the floor sloped down, right to left, it came as a great confusion that the ceiling sloped in exactly the opposite direction – high left to low right. This was emphasized by the nine inches from the top of the level cornice to the ceiling on the left but six inches on the right. An extra cocktail in that place could turn you into a drunken sailor on a pitching deck.

But it was delightful. Not only were we secure in knowing we could hose down our living room at any time with complete runoff, but there was also a winterized front porch for my writing station, tax deductible.

Then there was the issue of our landlord. Some might say he looked Cro-Magnon to them, but we didn't have to look at him much. He never came around to fix anything. The lawn, his responsibility, didn't get cut much, but we didn't have to worry about him hanging around our bathroom window either.

Our day was clockwork. Bobbye had freshman English and coached the drama group. This meant we got up at 6:30 AM and while she dressed, I'd put breakfast together. After a kiss goodbye, I'd get down to work.

The whole day, every day was totally organized. Following my early morning deliberations, I would head to my typewriter on the porch. My goal was 2,500 words per day. I used a word count for two reasons. I didn't want to just sit down and stare at a blank page, nor did I want to work off a clock that could be overly depressing or falsely encouraging. If I was having a very good day, I might finish the count early as a reward. On a bad day, I would finish up late or never, but whatever the case, the word count called the shot. Don't forget, it's possible to run off at the brain just like one might run off at the mouth.

Though Bobbye, as the schoolteacher, brought in most of our money each week, I was bringing in a little by flying with a Marine reserve squadron out of Navy South Weymouth, about fifty miles south of our apartment in Wakefield.

Though pretty-well organized, there were also distractions to my day. We bought a dog. A Scottish border collie we named MacIntosh. Super smart. He was a black and white attention-demanding hound who would chew my toes to get me away from the typewriter.

But the neighborhood around us applied a subtly distracting pressure too. I was the only at-home, daytime male on the street. Our block was blue collar which caused some to look at me askance. Why was I there? Why didn't I have a job? Was I some kind of a hippie or what? Over the two years we were there, I doubt I ever got off some of the curtain-peeking folk's questionable list. Was he even an American? Whatever he was, they felt he (me) wasn't regular. For sure.

When Bobbye got home from her high school job, I might chase her around the house, which became the breakpoint of our day, shaking out the cobwebs for an evening of research, reading or, on Fridays, a movie. We were so organized. We shopped grocery specials, calculating every unit price to the ounce, penny, or pound. It was a great battle of wits. The McAdamses vs. Brand X. But it paid off. Though it is ages of inflation later, we lived on eight to twelve dollars a week for food. Sure, we didn't buy our first steak for four years, but it was a hell of a lot more fun than just walking into a market and grabbing anything, price be damned. The challenge was there. We felt we were beating the system.

Shortly after settling down in Wakefield that August, I tore up the first one hundred pages of my great American novel and started all over again. By the end of December, the new draft was finished. Through January I rewrote and reworked it, and finally finished the manuscript for submission in February.

The next part of the drama revolved around the submission itself. On my way from Hawaii to Nashville the winter before, bouncing across the country in a beat-up military C-47, I happened to sit next to an older gentleman who turned out to be a most interesting fellow indeed.

He was dressed in East Village smart—the dark navy turtleneck, elbow-patched jacket, and an old gas mask knapsack thrown over his shoulder. At one point I'd given him a hand up the steps onto the plane, so we'd ended sitting together and chatting, chatting up a storm.

After I told him of the romantic nature of my journey and how I was working on my first novel, he mentioned that he had some connections in the publishing world and might assist me in getting my book to the right people. His name was Marcus Aurelius Goodrich, a novelist himself who had written a bestseller in the late thirties. His name had meant nothing to me, but Bobbye knew of him as Olivia DeHavilland's first husband. So, when my book was finished, I mailed it to his address in Virginia. Much to my surprise and great joy, he acknowledged its arrival and later critiqued it quite favorably. Since Marcus had been a critic at one time as well, I was sailing on Cloud Nine.

I made the few small changes he recommended, and then we sent it to John Farrar of Farrar and Straus. Marcus had already prepared the way.

Another few weeks went by, then Farrar's airmail letter came, saying only nice things and that I could expect something firm shortly. He said not to worry.

I was young. Goodrich had been enthusiastic, then, in Farrar's letter he even said, "Mr. McAdams, you are obviously a brilliant novelist, so I am taking this early opportunity to welcome you to the Farrar Straus family and affirm that I anticipate many years of mutual profitability publishing your work."

Reading that, Bobbye and I felt like F. Scott and Zelda. So, rather than sit around and needlessly worry, we took the publisher's advice, and did just what the Fitzgerald's would have done. We bought plane tickets to Europe, sold my TR-3 to pay the way, and even arranged for a VW beetle for pick-up at the factory in Germany. So, off we went to jump into all the fountains America's leading novelist and his bride should jump into. It truly was a memorable trip. Less plush than the way the Gatsby's might have done it, but on Arthur Frommer's $5 a day, done rather well.

Nearly two months later we returned, only to find our soap bubble had burst. The manuscript was there waiting... *Refused*.

Thank the Lord, Bobbye was with me at that moment. Having had a theatre background, she well knew the ups-and-down struggles writers, playwrights, artists, all the creative types go through in their efforts trying for a place at the top or at least a rung or two higher up the ladder of life. Few others know what they all go through during those moments of failure. It's as if a part of one's soul has been inspected and found wanting, then stamped UNSATISFACTORY. If one feels himself close to a higher mark, only to be rudely dumped like I was, it was as if I'd been kicked in the groin. All I could do was double up, hold tight, and gasp. Oh God, what would I do?

But Bobbye was there wrapping her arms around me, hugging me hard and whispering in my ear, "Kenny, you are a writer. You have a voice, a voice that readers want to listen to. This is only one refusal. My stars," she threw in as her country mother would have, "Think of those hugely successful writers who have stacked up scores of refusals. There's one author I recently read about who was refused fifty-seven times! but she still ended up with a huge bestseller and a movie contract. I heard she now throws an annual party for all those publishers who refused her before. My goodness, with only this one black mark, you couldn't offer more than a coke and a pretzel. So, my darling, put this behind you, behind *us* and move on. We are young and we have nothing but our lives ahead of us."

Bobbye ended this by nuzzling her nose just below my ear, kind of down my neck a bit which got my mind off sad things, kind of nudging me toward happy things, snuggling with growing enthusiasm as we turned the lights down low.

The next morning, after a great struggle with what seemed a rural and ancient backwoods telephone system, I was finally able to reach Goodrich. My struggle wasn't totally with the Bell system, Marcus was working on a novel of his own and had gone into a sort of seclusion. He'd taken a room in some kind of a boarding house, or maybe a flophouse, in Richmond, Virginia. The place had only one pay phone in the lobby, so it was hell to get anyone to answer my call in the first place, then to persuade whomever to trudge to Marcus' room to boot. After many tries, however, I did make contact. Bobbye finally broke the code for me offering, "Kenny, Marcus is in hiding trying to write another book. He's run off to his version of nowhere, where there aren't even telephones in the rooms. And whoever answers the one in the lobby gets to run up, what, three floors to his room to tell him you are on the phone way downstairs? The place is probably full of men. Women would probably have taken beds in the YWCA. Right?"

I nodded and she went on saying, "It sounds like an old west flop house for men only."

I gave a shrug and added an affirmative nod.

"So, it strikes me that a woman's sweet voice, actually mine, asking for Marcus will get a heck of a lot more attention and cooperation than your Marine Corps growl. My voice," Bobbye continued, might even make Goodrich somewhat of a celebrity down there in Richmond, giving whomever answers and does the runup the stairs to his room... cachet. He'd have loads of cachets."

Once Bobbye got Marcus got on the line, she smiled and handed me the phone. After a moment of getting my thoughts together, I asked him what had happened at Farrar and Straus after all the supportive words John Farrar had laid on me? Since the book was about Boston and had presented the reality of an American melting pot that never melted, I had characters representing the various ethnic, racial, and religious elements I had grown up with and knew were there. Marcus said that Straus had been in Europe, and though Farrar had given the book a green light, the financial end of the firm belonged to Straus, and his reading of my story had convinced him I was anti-Semitic and therefore he would not publish it.

I couldn't believe what I was hearing. In high school one of my girlfriends was Charlotte Deitche, whose mother made Mrs. Deitche's strictly kosher blintzes. And I was the Sabot Goy who made the blintzes on Saturday mornings because rabbinical law forbade a Deitche working on the sabbath. How's that for an anti-Semite? And my senior prom date was another eastern beauty named Bagriansky who, with her mother and father had escaped the Holocaust, having joined partisans in the Caucasus Mountains, escaping the Nazi's tracking them for months on end. Hardly the Cabots or the Lodges for sure.

But when you get tagged with a blackball like that, you're dead. Nevertheless, John Farrar was good about it all and promised to give my next work a personal look. He left out that Straus would still be there and there was no way an anti-Semite was going to go to press as long as he was there. But Farrar would still do what he could. And Marcus Goodrich jumped in promising he'd move the manuscript around to some other contacts he had. Send it down. He'd handle it. No sweat.

So, I decided to hold off on the suicide. The book was in the mail that afternoon.

I had thought we were back in business. I thought that once again it was just a matter of time. I could be such a child. Faith and hope were so much easier than reason and reality. But it took a long time to even begin to understand that. Five or six months in the case of my mentor, Marcus Aurelius Goodrich. By December, I again thought it time to see how things were going. Of course, I had been a perfect ass waiting so long before checking, but you know, faith and hope. Besides I was cranking along in, I thought, great style on my next book. When producing fiction all the time anyway, why clutter one's life with facts?

Well, through December and January, Marcus was missing... off in Texas, Africa, some place nobody had the faintest idea where. Merry Christmas. Then, in February, when I finally did reach him, he confessed that he hadn't done a damn thing with the manuscript. He was working on his own. What had I done with it? Me? Nothing? Only one presentable copy? Dear me. Shit. Another groin shot. Happy New Year.

And would you believe that next, my single and last manuscript, got lost in the mail. But then I heard of Harper and Row's "First Novel Contest." It closed that June. Enough time for me to enter, but my entry was wandering somewhere off in postal limbo-land. Nor did it comfort me to suddenly discover that my second book, now completed in first draft, was in truth a laboriously long, tedious piece of crap. At least that was the verdict after my first read.

I felt whipped. What could I do? Time was running out on our two-year deal. That promise had become a precipice, one I was teetering on, I was about to fall far and deeper into... two years wasted.

Suddenly Bobbye's high school offered me a teaching job for the entire spring semester. I had been subbing and the school system thought I had promise. Their teacher of Medieval History had accepted six months in Anchor Watts. I would now have advanced placement kids along with nine-g's. The latter being thugs just waiting around to have their eighteenth birthday which would set them free from any further education. I'd also have regular curriculum types too. Quite a challenge, but I was ready and accepted.

I'd thought I'd be able to teach and write at the same time. Hah. I became like Charlie Chaplin in a cookie factory – running classes, researching, correcting papers, preparing the next day's classes and quizzes... oh man, I was only a day ahead of the kids at best. Exhausting.

Then Bobbye said, "Kenny you always have brought up F. Scott and Zelda when we thought we had an acceptance on your first book, and we'd flown off to Europe. You couldn't stop talking about our thoughts on one of those wee cottages off in Scotland near Inverness we'd seen. Well, why can't we just move those thoughts to New England? The lay of the land is not that different and Boston is not all that much unlike Edinburg. We might find a little place like one of those wee cottages somewhere around there, close enough to Weymouth for your Reserve flying and the income it brings in, and... I guess I could start door-to-dooring-it for Avon or somebody. I know it probably would be a struggle, but we'd be together. You'd be writing and we would be out of the ticky-tacky world with its grubbing for dollars like so many of our friends seem caught up in." And she did say she believed the first book would hit.

"Yeah, that's if anybody can find the damn thing to read," I said, shaking my head, my eyes going to the floor.

But Bobbye wasn't having any of that. She reached over to me, putting both hands to either side of my face, tilting my head up, and kissing me so sweetly, so tenderly I could almost have cried.

"So, Kenny," she said with a gentle smile, "enough of that. You're going to make it and I'll be there guarding your backside," which she emphasized by pressing all of herself against my front side, causing some youthful distractions to chase all our sad thoughts to run far, far away.

So, a couple of days later, in search of that wee cottage we went. And that led to some funny times and some sad times too, but at least we were always looking up that hill of hope, looking for the house where we would put together our futures of fame and fortune.

CHAPTER TWO
The Listing

A three-bedroom masterpiece for the discriminating buyer seeking privacy. A decorator eat-in kitchen, formal dining room, salon style living room with colonial foyer. Single convenient bath, luxurious master bedroom with assorted outbuildings all on 10 lush New Hampshire acres overlooking the Connecticut River and convenient to urban centers. An absolute steal at $7,500. Contact Mrs. Nurney, Box 1234 Lebanon, New Hampshire.

"Kenny, this is it!" Bobbye burst out over the breakfast table as she read the whole listing. "It has to be it! Lebanon, a big town—libraries, theatres, things to do outside our own little enclave and yet within striking distance of Boston. Perfect. Dartmouth College is up there too. We could borrow the extra money. Our own little castle. And our kids would be born there, clean and fresh in that fantastic piney New Hampshire air with snow and babbling brooks and fishing in the Connecticut River and hunting and swimming. And those autumns. Absolutely breathtaking.

"We've got to touch base with this Nurney lady. She doesn't list a phone number. Just an address. Let's do a special delivery to her. Right now. Oh Kenny, this is so exciting."

And I've got to say, I had never heard Bobby so excited about anything. Even when she agreed to marry me on our first date, she wasn't like this. So, breathlessly we Special Delivered our inquiry to Mrs. Nurney. Mrs. Nurney wrote back. She would be delighted to show us the property. She suggested a date. We agreed and received details—not about the house, other than a passing reference to "that little jewel," but mainly how to get to where we would meet, before driving on together to the property. This extra leg in our trip should have told us something, but we weren't in the thinking mood. House-lust had taken over from good-reasoning. With my darling wife so caught up in it too, I just kind of fell in behind her and hung on.

Driving from Wakefield, we stopped to meet Mrs. Nurney at her house, about a half-hour short of Lebanon, New Hampshire. We kind of wondered why she had us meet at her house and not at the property, but we didn't give that a great deal of thought. Going on these weekend house inspection trips kind of turned us into children focused on nothing really more than following the various Mrs. Nurney's yellow brick roads to whatever house was listed without much care as to where that road actually led.

Meeting the lady, I felt something tweaking my warning system. These negative thoughts, I am ashamed to say, were mainly a product of her odd looks – squat, one wandering-eye and her hair run-amok. She could easily have been Jonathan Winters in drag. She even babbled like Winters with her lips pooched out and rounded like she was blowing out a candle. Bobbye didn't seem to pick up on these oddities. Of course, she was of good, nonjudgmental Christian stock whereas I was more of the Back Bay unwashed.

Lady Nurney handled the driving and briefed us on how long she had been in real estate—four decades or more. She described how much she loved her job because she especially loved houses. And every twenty or so minutes, with a smile she would tell us, "We're getting closer to the little gem." Though she did say that a lot, the house seemed somehow to keep moving farther away.

Finally, her eyes widened and through her lips, now in a tight purse, she squeaked, "There, there she is!" Her right index finger stabbing past her steering wheel almost smashing a fingernail against the front window.

The house and its garage behind, almost out of sight, sat high above the road on a hillside terrace. The view was dramatic with the Connecticut River winding below, Vermont across the river, and everything wrapped in pine, oak, maple, and birch. There was no question of how high on the pastoral beauty charts it all registered, but still, there was something out of kilter about it all. I noticed Bobbye kind of cocking her head up, down, then left and right from the back seat too.

We turned up the long winding driveway, sheep pastures left and right, and yet our eyes kept telling us there was a perspective problem. And the closer we got to the front of the house, the more alarming it all became.

Up close and personal, as folks are apt to say, there was no escaping the reality of Mrs. Nurney's "little gem." It was little, all right, tiny for sure. Mrs. Nurney finally stammered out her confession.

"The family that built it, who live there now, are little people, so the proportions fit them, but are somewhat…reduced for regular sized people."

"You've brought us all this way to see a dwarf's house?" I sputtered.

"That word, dwarf, is too pejorative. I prefer small," she announced, her head nodding to emphasize my verbal error, while completely ignoring her absurd deception.

"Well, why don't we go in and look around," Bobbye said, harnessing my rising temperature. "Let's see if it's as small inside as it seems from out here."

Obviously my dear wife made sense and lady Nurney bought it too, so we all exited the car and strode up the walk onto the porch. Mrs. Nurney pushed the doorbell. We heard big people chimes sound from inside, only a stanza into them before the door swung open.

When we stepped onto the stone porch under the balcony overhead, we knew we were in trouble. I'm not even six feet tall, but still, I had to duck my head stepping onto the porch and moving toward the front door. As a matter of fact, as I continued to the door, I had to keep my head down. And when the lady of the house opened it, my eyes had naturally gone to a level they were used to going to meet those of another person standing about at my eye-level. No such luck here though. There were no eyes at my eye-level, no head either, just space.

Then a voice from well below said, "Hello Mrs. Nurney. You have come with the people interested in our house?"

"Yes, Mrs. Cricket, this is Ken and Bobbye McAdams, from Wakefield. They want to move out this way and they saw your listing with us in the Farm Journal. May we come in and you show them around?"

"Our son is here from college for the weekend. He can do the honors." Mrs. Crickcet turned to her regular-sized-son John and said, "these are the McAdamses dear, could you take them around for me? I have pancake batter on the stove right now."

"Of course, Mom," the young man said, and turned to us, his hand extended to shake mine first.

And then another voice floated up saying, "I am John senior. If you have any questions after you look around, I'll be happy to answer them."

It was bizarre. I felt like I was in a Monty Python movie or something. Young John was probably six one or two. The interior ceilings of the house must have been two or three inches lower than that. I could feel my buzz-cut brushing the ceiling above my head. And John was so hunched over, the tops of his shoulders were rubbing everywhere he moved. But looking at Mr. and Mrs. Cricket, they had a good two feet clearance over their heads.

"Did you build the house yourself, Mr. Cricket," I asked, not intending to be a smart-ass. Just curious and begging the question, why didn't he have a regular-sized person signed onto the project?

"I certainly did. All by myself. I am very proud of it, and we have been very happy here, though now it is time to move on," he smiled, arms extended and eyes shining as he looked up at me and Bobbye. "We are moving to Florida. For the weather. And taxes. I'm thinking about building the house down there myself again."

"Why not just retire and leave the work to somebody else?" I asked.

"I work with my hands. Always have. I'm not about to change now," he said with a slight puff to his tiny chest.

No one seemed to pick up on the fact that we didn't actually take the offered tour of the Cricket manse. Bobbye and I both looked at our watches and mentioned we had a showing with another realtor within the hour and would have to dash off. But we thanked everyone for their hospitality and the chance to see their extraordinary house.

Mrs. Cricket said she was preparing pecan pancakes for us if we could stay just a little longer, but Bobbye jumped in thanking her, while explaining we had about forty miles to go to our next viewing, plus picking our car at Mrs. Nurney's, so we really had to dash off.

Everyone nodded, smiled as Big John Cricket Jr. went and opened the door for us. Then away we went, well assured we'd had an extraordinary realty experience, though quietly relieved to be released from this most unusual tour.

After that adventure, we never again set out from Wakefield without map coordinates, room dimensions including heights, and photos – pictures with something of recognizable size in them, so we could judge just what on earth we were being sold.

But our bad luck held. Even with every precaution possible, it became evident that there was a reason for small prices on some houses. They were either at the ends of the earth, termite ridden, unsound, had bad wells, were just plain ugly and awful, or all the above. We grew discouraged. How were we ever going to find our small castle? Those puffy farm realty books, the ridiculous newspaper ads, the whole parade of comical deceptions just weren't going to make it.

A few days later we passed an A-frame. The kind you bought for just a couple of thousand bucks that you built yourself. Connect tab "A" to tab "B." Glue along the dotted line. Why not?

Idiot-phase two was now underway. I never knew there were so many kinds of A-frame cottages. Roofs, for instance. We found there were gambrels, A-frame gambrels, hipped-roofed A-frames, decked, raised, to the ground purist A-frames. Like everything else, quantity led to confusion, which led to the land-of-muddle. This one costs X dollars, but that other one was more livable for X plus dollars; yet this model has such gorgeous windows on the slope side... What do you think? Puff, puff. Like buying a car—options, options, options.

Till some knowledgeable smart-aleck says, "But you wouldn't actually buy an A-frame would you?"

Aaaaaaaaaah!

"Terrible investment. Banks hate them. Novelty items. They have no lasting resale value. Undependable. Poor risk. You want something more conventional, that you can get out from under if you have to. Forget the A-frame."

So, we talked with a friend who was rebuilding a beat-up farmhouse. How about redoing a wreck someplace?

He said, "Forget it. I'd never do it again. I've been living in a dump for a couple of years now. When I wanted to put a new ceiling in the dining-room I had to pull down the old one first. I ran into rats, mice, squirrels and all their mess. Everything came down on me, in my hair, eyes, mouth, I felt I'd go nuts. And I could never get away from it."

He went on to say that to redo a place, you first had to tear it down then rebuild it later. "You're faced with a ghastly continuous mess. No man, you want to build from scratch. Prefab. I'd go prefab if I was starting fresh."

Eureka! A prefab. We could probably handle building one of those ourselves, Bobbye and me. But you talk about all the A-frame models, prefab types are legion. To say nothing of the salesman's escalation factor. By the time the sales staff got through with us, the one-holler had grown to a veritable Versailles. We couldn't afford anything remotely like what they were pushing us toward. Which only caused us embarrassment and shrugging, stammering, sweaty retreats. Ah hell. I just couldn't figure how an unsuccessful, otherwise unemployed indigent writer was going to afford building his own dream house. Of course, who but an unsuccessful, unemployed indigent writer would even consider that he could pull it off in the first place?

We paused, just sat on the whole thing for a while. Then Bobbye said, "Kenny, all our attention has been focused north and west of Boston. How about we look south of Boston. Why not give that a try?"

For a guy raised in the Hub, as Boston is known locally, such a question of what is south of it was near heresy. Basically, nothing is south of Boston after maybe Quincy. And the term, South Boston brings up thoughts of Whitey Bolger, basement burials, crooked cops and the Irish Mafia. Oh sure, Providence is down there, but so is New York City, Havana, Cuba, all kinds of places that have caused a hell of a lot of trouble over the years, to say nothing of the New York Yankees.

"Kenny darling," Bobbye persisted, "I wasn't raised on Pilgrim's Progress and J. P. Marquand, so I just know there has to be something south of Boston – things like states, cities, highways to and from those cities. All kinds of stuff."

I offered to check it out. But, being a woman with focus, Bobbye decided to see for herself. "If you want to look around with me, I'm going down and see for myself. You're invited to come along."

I signed on.

Overall, as we drove south, I was generally impressed with the relatively high level of civilization we encountered. We had been urged to pack enough good solid Boston food along with enough bottled water for our entire stay. "Don't drink the water," is still a word to the wise travelers everywhere.

I will confess that we found town after town down there, many of which looked much like Lexington, Concord, Bedford, even Salem. Some will insist we were getting no different treatment there than Congressmen touring Vietnam got, but I don't buy that. Sturbridge Village – Okay, sure. A Potemkin prop, but what can you say of Stonington, Connecticut or Bedford, New York... all are real-life classics. Which indicated there actually are legitimate villages and towns south of Boston.

Late that night after we got back to Wakefield and had had a chance to digest our drive, we found we agreed. It would be feasible to live down that way. We might be out of the way, sort of in-between two worlds, but all things considered, it was pretty good to okay. We'd be pulled toward Boston in its sense of history, the Red Sox, and the past in general; while still tugged toward New York by Broadway, the summer influx of tourists and artistic escapees and loads of sports. And then there was the-in between coastline with many big-buck yacht people, maybe even some who are publishers looking for a new unknown writer. They'd dock in harbors like Mystic Seaport or ritzy Newport with its ambiance of Gatsby, F. Scott and Zelda parading down main street. Hell, I could be all flash in my Edinburg suit, Bobbye on my arm all gorgeous in her personally couturière CoCo C. creation. And Yale was nearby which meant a happy goodbye to Harvard's weak-wristed influence. By George, maybe this mid-Connecticut coast could be a welcome place of transition for both our futures. And so, we decided; yes, we would give it a shot.

Bobbye sent an inquiry to the local newspaper, the New London Day, inquiring about possible land for sale. Then, just a day or two later, Bingo! It scored.

A landowner was breaking up his forty or more acres, selling two-acre lots to whomever was interested. He and his wife turned out to be a charming old couple. And she was from Scotland. She spoke with a marvelous highland accent. Which set our bells to ringing. Yes, two-acre wooded lots could be ours if the price worked out to be right. It all sounded perfect, so we drove on down and found smiles everywhere filling our hearts with anticipatory joy.

The price dickering over the land didn't last long. You might say we had become willing captives of the nostalgic karma of Scottish coincidence. Hadn't we first been charmed by the wee cottages near Inverness? Hadn't the whole idea of establishing our own little corner of life come from memories of bonnie Scotland? Well, wouldn't you know, when we got down to Stonington to look the land over, Florence Bausche, the wife of the landowner who had answered our ad, turned out to be from... Edinburgh!

Bobbye said she knew we were dead, straight away, for every time Florence Bausche spoke, she filled us with visions of cobbled medieval lanes, broad beautiful Princes Street, the green park in the grand valley dipping down from the boulevard to rise up again in praise to the craggy cliffs and battlements of Edinburgh Castle. Bobbye reached out and squeezed my arm. Oh, how Mrs. Bausche's accent threw a net about us, along with how drawn we were to the crescendo of their crackling fireplace, its old stone hearth gracing the charm of this living room, the whole house, for that matter, built by Carl himself, aided by Florence, just as Bobbye and I envisioned ourselves doing the same.

They were so charming, but also tough, gnarly, cocky and combative. Hard of hearing, old Carl half shouted at me with the warning, "Don't try to bargain down the price of the land. It's good. It's fair and if you try, the deal is off."

"Aye, Bobbye, Ken," said Florence, "'tis his waih. Buut Carl... Carl, ooh he goes on so because of his hearin'. He has such trrrouble wi'th'ut."

But he did come down on his price a bit, on his own. I hadn't, nor had Bobbye, dared say a word. And it became clear to the two of us that the two of them wanted us there. We felt very warm and wanted. It was a very good feeling.

The property was near New London toward Rhode Island. There were two colleges nearby, good schools, several theatre groups, New York radio, but Boston Red Sox baseball!

Our closest village, we will call Ledge Rock, was particularly charming. Don't misunderstand though, there were some horrors around there too. Entering from the east side of town, you passed a totally tacky run-down gas station. It was operated by a rotund oil-soaked, grease-spattered cigar-chewing character no one could rate charming. Nor was the volunteer fire house just down the road particularly noteworthy having been slapped together with mismatched concrete blocks and peeling white paint. Norman Rockwell would have given it all a pass without comment.

But a bit from these two sentinels guarding the Route One approaches from the south and east, were many beautiful homes. Some were Federalist period, others early 18th century colonial; all in sparkling white clapboard.

One of these with a great large front, brick walls on each side, sat across from the middle school. It was colonially complete with its Captain's lookout cupola on top and being high enough that the sea was just in sight. For the longest time we believed the "Ones" lived there, until, much to our embarrassment it was pointed out that the "J" had fallen off the mailbox and was buried under a long winter's snow and forgotten. Our mysterious and intriguing "Ones" had suddenly become the rather pedestrian "Jones."

As might be expected, the village center was dominated by the post office and general store. As a matter of fact, outside of a cluster of lovely antique homes, there was nothing else but the post office and general store. But what a great place was that general store. The exterior was hardly prepossessing. A heap of ancient chipped and paint-faded steps ran up between two large middling-ugly storefront windows. Then a scuffed and warped threshold led through two scarred, loose-fitting dull green doors into a dark interior dominated by what appeared to be only random clutter and jumble. Those who ran the store, however, and those who traded there regularly, would contest this. Both groups would protest that everything was exactly where they could find it.

Entering across from the tonics, lotions, and sundries Bobbye pointed out, behind them was a marginally functioning old-fashioned soda fountain. "Kenny, look at that," she breathed, her eyes going large and round. "It's just like the one we had in Old Hickory, Tennessee. If we sat a policeman on one stool and a little boy sitting with a dripping ice cream cone on the other, you'd have a cover picture of the Saturday Evening Post."

I couldn't add to that so I just slipped my arm around her waist and kind of felt the whole place giving the two of us a welcoming hug, which caused Bobbye to turn up to me and gently whisper, "We are caught."

Admittedly, these first presentations of the store were at least eye-catching, but then, a few steps past the fountain, our feet encountered the luxuriously comforting feel of sawdust on the floor while our noses were lulled and soothed by that warm heavy good smell of meat, produce and cheese. And oh, that cheese! Where was it? Then my eyes fell onto a great, eight-inch-thick cartwheel of rich yellow New England cheddar resting on a three-foot diameter wooden platter supported by an old nail keg. And that's where the general store really began.

Such meat. Ground beef that was actually ground sirloin. Red. All red and it tasted like steak. Slabs of sirloin for folks like the "Ones" who probably pointed to and had it lifted from the case in huge slabs to be cut to their required thickness on a huge chopping block behind, itself a chunk of a great oak felled during the storm of '39.

How charming were the deep sagging wooden shelves gracing each wall. The reach-in bins of beans, corn, cabbages, and carrots, to say nothing of the cracker-barrel, a real one. And a pickle-barrel too. The winter-demanding pot-bellied stove was all there, and criminally real, luring nostalgia-ridden romantics like Bobbye and me toward crashing financial doom. Stores like this, real stores like this that are run by flesh and blood, smiling or even scowling, young and old, men and women, should not be allowed to ever close. Who wants to shop in those cold hard chrome places with one's joint-cracking, and eyeball-drying freeze-dried air-conditioning cranking 24/7?

Ah yes, Bobbye and I were discovering that we were captives of anything with a breath of history, the slightest hint of antiquity's charm. All of which, with the general store thrown in, made our purchase of the Bauche's two acres inevitable.

Originally the area we were negotiating for was 3,500 acres of forest, but in colonial times, much of that had been cleared for common grazing land. The same as the lay of Boston Common in the middle of Massachusetts capitol city to the north.

Through those acres were tumbled-down stone walls, stone fences some called them, marking the community lands from each of the farmers' holdings. Every which way the walls wandered, some having better withstood winter's frosts, spring rains and neighborly encroachments to still stand with dignity; while others, on less firm ground perhaps, or built with less skilled hands, were strewn in disarray, constituting mere memories, faint outlines of lost ownership wandering through the trees.

Walking these tracks back into the increasingly quiet woods around us, disturbed only by a rabbit's dash or the rustle of a fleeing deer, our minds did their usual tricks, toying with thoughts of those who first had cleared this land, built the walls, organized the wilderness. Where were they now? What had become of them? How had their fields become forests again? "Could we," Bobbye asked, "could we somehow become a part of their past in our returning to the land, trying again to subdue and control it?" she spoke wistfully, her big brown eyes moving here to there, seemingly following the lead of each of their fascinating green flecks.

At first, I didn't say anything. Hell, it all was by no means equivalent to the Louisiana Purchase, but we still felt... I mean felt the fact of the land beneath our feet. It was eerie in its power, yet it made us aware of being so much more alive, real and in a sense uneasy that we were laying claim to a portion of God's very earth. How do you act when you actually own a part of the world every human being lives on? The implications seemed awesome.

And yet all of this, the Bausche's, the town, the trees, the animals, the history, these were not the full reason we bought this land in particular. There was still one other factor, one overriding consideration, and you can color it dark, almost black.

CHAPTER THREE
A New Place

His name was Isaiah Moody. He was a very dark African American who lived with his equally dark wife, Loraine. They had the converted little red schoolhouse under a gnarly old oak tree on the edge of what would be our property. It would be the only house within sight of our front door if we ever had a front door there at all.

And what a beautiful thing we felt this was. We had heard all the usual stuff through our growing up years that no white people would consider building next to Blacks. Though Bobbye was from the South and I the North, that had been the word since the days of molasses and rum.

Around Boston, I only remember African-Americans generally being on a lower social rung, except for the black Republican Senator Edward Brooke representing us all from Massachusetts. In my hometown of West Newton, they had their section to themselves, down the hill beyond the railroad tracks.

We were raised separately. It seemed there was little hope of coming closer to each other, even in a spiritual sense. Though we went to school together, played sports together, we were always apart since each day the sun went down, they went down.

Bobbye's southern experience was different, but with much the same results. There wasn't the same territorial separation. Blacks and whites lived on the same land. Their bodies were close. The eating, sleeping, and breathing was closer, so a deeper, more powerful division of the blood and the soul had to be worked out. Welcome Jim Crow.

Nevertheless, Bobbye and I felt, against our traditions, that maybe we could turn this table a bit; like in a bad dream, turn suddenly around on the pursuing demon that had been chasing us through the night, turn on it... only to wake and find there was no demon there at all.

"Kenney," Bobbye said with a growing smile, "Now that we're in the process of becoming landowners, and the Moody's will be our closest neighbors, I think we're putting our own shut-up on all those who say nobody would risk every cent they didn't have, to do what we are doing right now. In our small way, we were telling the world that we two families can make it work. So, raise the flag high and God bless America."

She almost had me in tears.

A day or two later with our stamped, sealed, recorded and every-which-way spang-dangled deed in hand, we naively believed we were now clear to find the makings of a house, along with the money that makes the makings to build that house happen. We were about to learn of the quagmire of red tape waiting ahead. That and the corruption too.

Our first decision in this process was to face facts. Sticking to those facts once faced was something else again.

Time was not unlimited. There would be only so many warm months to work in and winter always loomed over the horizon. We would have to get whatever we built "tight" as soon as possible. And too, it would be our only shelter even as we built it. Tents were not the greatest things to live in for more than a day or two. To say nothing of the fact that one guy and one gal, working alone together, could only handle so much. Twenty-foot 2 by 8 joists on forty-foot center girders are a bit much for the ladies to be tossing around. So, some prefabrication and some help would have to be included too. The next job, then, was to find an outfit that would give us the limited degree of prefabrication we wanted.

Surprisingly enough, in just a matter of days we did find something. Though it was only a simple ranch style box. We couldn't pretend it was much more than that, save for the covered porch across maybe a third of the front; but we pictured it wrapped in redwood clapboard with a classic 200-year-old brick chimney up one exterior side and a wall of the interior living room.

Our minds' eyes told us it would work and would blend sympathetically with the woods around us through the seasons. We were excited, moneywise too. For the moment anyway, it all looked good. Over the past year we had added to our savings with my teaching full time which meant we were banking all of one check each week. We had paid cash for the land. We had most of what we needed for the basic materials; surprisingly little when you were going to supply your own muscle, but still, we would need at least again as much as we had to see the whole thing through. This would be a trick.

It was the beginning of March, snow was still everywhere, with not many months till June when the materials would be delivered along with the end of the school year which would also mark the end of our incomes. That, of course, left us with the hard to answer question, how do you walk into a bank, soon to be unemployed, and convince some crusty old banker to give you thousands of dollars to build a house (by yourselves)? Tricky, but we felt it was not impossible. We were young, and full of energy.

In the first place, I knew New England peculiarities and frankly intended to enlist them on our behalf. Some will scoff. Most believe that banks are not emotional institutions and trade strictly on facts and balance sheets -- and deal only with cold hard realities. But I disagreed. We are talking Boston here, not Nashville or Old Hickory, Tennessee. I invited my darling to read some of the literature of the Bay State. Cleveland Amory's *Proper Bostonians* for instance. Amory opened the book with the story of how, early on, moving to Boston, the Hallowell's asked him to dinner. He accepted and then, before sitting down to the table, Mrs. Hallowell asked him if he might want to see their children say their prayers before settling down for the night. He wasn't exactly sure why he might wish to observe the little ones in such a union with the Lord, but, as a guest, he accepted, feeling it was the right thing to do. So, as the two little ones knelt beside their beds, steepled their hands, touching their fingers to their foreheads, they commenced their prayers with... 'Our Father who art in Heaven, Hallowell be thy name...'" Which really rattled Amory's cage. However, the more he thought about it, the more sense it made, in Boston terms, as in The Adams speak only to the Cabots and the Cabots speak only to God. So, in what he had just witnessed, he was only observing proper Boston education instilling in these little ones that God was actually no more than a member of the Hallowell family. Why not?

Then I backed that up with my own small adventure of the troubles I had trying to cash a cashier's check in a major Boston bank when I first arrived from my Marine Corps discharge. I went to a teller's window and slid the check under the grill to him. Despite the fact such a check can supposedly be cashed everywhere in the world because it was cut on the stock of, and backed by the Bank of America, I didn't expect a problem, but I didn't stop to think that I was in beloved Boston.

Being newly arrived there I had not had time to establish an account anywhere, so I popped into the first bank I came to. This all occurred before the age of credit cards. I was out to buy a wedding ring for dear Bobbye and of course I needed the money immediately. I couldn't wait for an account to be set up while the check cleared and all that business. Besides, I didn't intend to bank with these people anyway.

Though a cashier's check is supposed to be cash money, along with proper identification, Boston didn't believe it. "Bank of America?" the teller said with a question in his voice. "No bank around here by that name. San Francisco? Oh well, California. No, I'm sorry."

Of course, I got a bit heated and raised enough of a commotion that I got a higher-ranking sort to come out to talk with me. After twenty minutes of getting nowhere with him, I mentioned that I, Kenneth G. McAdams, with my parents living on McAdams Road in Framingham village, Massachusetts, even born here, and just discharged from defending our country in the Pacific, why was I not credentialed enough to cash this one totally valid cashier's check in this bank?

Well, suddenly everything changed. There was an instant thaw. I had suddenly become someone—one of the McAdam's of McAdam's Road. Well of course. The check was cashed without further inconvenience. And I knew damned well, that if my name had been just plain Adams, that would have been enough in the very beginning of the whole affair.

So, I say that many of the New England banks of that period trafficked in puffery and built their foundations on the crumbling sands of snobbery. Lord knows that my McAdams Road thing was sheer coincidence. And if you know the street in question it's really nothing to get excited about. But where the reputation of the Bank of America had failed in staid Boston, a silly coincidence of a street name had succeeded.

With this in mind, Bobbye and I made careful preparations before selecting the proper institution to improperly try to wrest those thousands of dollars from.

Appearances, of course, were paramount. This meant two things to us immediately. First, my only good suit, purchased in Edinburgh, Scotland, was naturally very, very British. Secondly, Bobbye was enormously capable with thread and needle to copy Chanel's work as if her given name was CoCo. Her work was very well done. In fact, quite convincingly authentically so.

From there we piled anything gold we could find on her. The big heavy wedding ring I'd made, no diamond in it, too tacky-rich looking for that. Her golden charm bracelet, watch, another ring, a pin – every snitch of gold we could find anywhere. And she looked smashing. Then, with my pipe, suit, tweed hat, I looked as if I was somebody, at least one who could legitimately stand by her side. We were armed and ready.

The next step was to select the proper bank. It was obvious that just any old establishment around Ledge Rock would not do. We needed the kind that was immediately capable of recognizing us as people of substance. Which quickly ruled out the bland, factory-like glass-fronted, rear drive-through-teller type units. The right people, in those days, hardly worked in such places. No, those glass-fronted establishments were dominated by pipe-rack-suit-types who thrived on pompadour hairstyling and white socks.

No, we were looking for something indeed entirely different, when... *voila*, up popped a huge granite, ivy-and-moss-covered fortress straight ahead.

"This is it!" Bobbye breathed.

"It has to be," I threw in. "That granite means old New England in general, New Hampshire and in particular – the Old Man in the Mountain and Calvin Coolidge conservatism. The ivy spoke of a softened regard for tradition, at least a fledgling sense of the historic aesthetic. And the moss – a certain propensity toward ass-boundedness. Remember, it is the rolling stone that gathers none of that stuff.

So, we felt we had the nut in hand. The next trick was to crack it. We had to get to a man fairly high up. The lower ranks in any ivy-covered organization are inherently bureaucratic and might even speak with a lisp. Keep in mind, decisions and bureaucracies are not synonymous.

Without a thought, we reached out to take each other's hand.

The inside of the bank furthered our assurance. It was a small Grand Central Station with heavy steel cages surrounding and separating every cashier's counter. Fabulous. Like the monkey house in a zoo. One wondered if each teller's leg was chained to the floor. Only old Yankees here, I sensed from the historic realization that they truly had burned witches in Salem.

Bobbye and I made it to an island writing desk in the center of things to get our bearings. We had to find a door with a name on it, a desk plaque with a name, anything with some bank officer's name. Where?

Then a floor-walker type approached. Damn. No name tag on the front of his suit jacket. Also, we were in the center of the huge high foyer area and the little desk blocks with names on them were too distant to read. However, the direction this fellow was coming from seemed to be the way of the executive offices. No cages. Squeezing dear darling's hand for more assurance, we marched straight at the man, hoping to come up with something en route.

Well, just barely in time, I saw over his shoulder a door with something like -- Mr. E. Me..w..th..vi..pr..d..t on it. We were still too far to make it out completely, so now being close to the floor man, I shoved my hand out, giving my name, and half spun him around and looked past his shoulder and made out -- Merriweather -- on the far door.

"We are here to see Mr. Merriweather."

"Why yes, of course, Mr..."

"McAdams," I offered.

"You have an appointment to see Mr. Merriweather?" he asked.

"Oh, my goodness no," I smiled, "we are from Boston."

He looked at me, then at Bobbye, who smiled in return. Then he stole a glance over the two of us as his eyes came back to mine. Still at somewhat of a loss he said, "From Boston. Yes, of course, Boston. Could you wait just a moment while I see if Mr. Merriweather is free."

"Certainly. Lovely bank you have here," I announced doing a well-balanced pirouette.

"Why thank you, yes. Thank you," he beamed. "I'll only be a minute."

And that is how we got into the Vice President of Finance's office, and how we left his office a short time later with a commitment for somewhere around $14,000. Not bad at the time, 1963, especially for two who were unemployed like us.

The interview had been great fun. We'd stumbled onto exactly the right man. Merriweather had a great sense of humor and probably saw through our rather thin disguises. But he had the imagination and the authority to help.

His first question for us after we entered his dark, oaken office was, "What are your assets?"

After a brief pause, as Bobbye and I exchanged disarming smiles and mainly to get his attention focused on the two of us, we both said in unison, "You're looking at them."

And he instantly knew we were nothing more than a Chanel-like beauty on the arm of a tailor-made Scottish three-piece suit. In honor of our chutzpah he let out a grand guffaw, slapped his desktop and asked, "How much do you need?"

There is no question he liked us and was intrigued with our idea of independent living. I'll wager those granite walls were sometimes tight for him, too, and he saw in us a vicarious escape. Whatever, he was friendly to our cause. In time he grew to be a friend to our home as well.

After the bank and before heading to the town hall with our blueprints, deed, survey, and all that was needed for the building permit, we drove to our land for a look and a chilly March basket lunch.

There was still a lot of snow about, but it made the tumbled stonewall at the back of the property, up the hill, more visible. The barren trees, rather than forbidding, seemed to invite us further into the forest because of the open views they now allowed. So, like two happy children we trudged hand-in-hand, up the traces of what was now the almost forgotten farm road.

The snowy winter woods were so quiet. It was as if we were wandering deeper into the silent white sheets of an afternoon nap. So quiet. So lovely.

"There's a doe…" Bobbye whispered.

"And her fawn," I added.

"And the white rabbit hopping up by the wall. Look over here at the beautiful little grove of pines," Bobbye added.

That grove… silent. Lovely. It could be our special precious place. Our secret refuge away from all the push and shove at the other end of our craggy lane, beyond the old farm road almost gone now. Soon to be only ours… ours alone.

CHAPTER FOUR
Like Being Kids Again

We felt like kids again. But not for long. Mr. Merriweather had advised that between us and the money lay the formality of a building permit. It was a scant hour or two later that we discovered between us and the permit stood, or "lurked" might be the better word, one James Harvey Madlock, a real son-of-bitch.

The fact the town hall itself was on kind of at a dead-end backroad, nearly an inaccessible walk from the town itself, should have been our first clue as to the confusion in high places existent there. Most municipal buildings are normally somewhere around the center of things, but in this case a highway had been lured in to effectively clip off and isolate this small piece of the body politic.

Our second clue to the ambiguity long entrenched there should have been the hall's intriguingly eclectic architecture. It had a neoclassical–Greco/Roman colonial New England Puritan brick front façade, with kind of a sagging honky-tonk concrete block construction down the side toward the scruffy police station tacked on to the back end. (We knew it was the police station back there because of the seemingly fork-painted, Palermo-blue neon sign shivering on and off in the bright sunlight reading – "POL CE," (the "I" missing, perhaps for economic reasons). Yes, the whole conglomeration was a classic in the American Legion school of failed architecture.

And it was a damned difficult building to get around in, too. There was a huge heap of what was supposed to be front steps leading majestically up to the seemingly never-used upper doors. Bobbye later found a side cellar entrance to be the one everyone did use.

Inside, up the slick steel-edged fire stairs to the main floor, one found the interior laid out much as you'd suppose a London double-decker bus barn would be. The whole center area was an open space, two stories high, with still more stairs up the sides to the various offices. No wonder business in the place was carried on in the basement.

Looking into several dusty and otherwise empty offices, I began to wonder if everyone had simply gone home – forever. At the top of the stairs and turning the corner we ran into a dusty elderly lady who advised us that the Building Commissioner's office was way back down below, where we had first begun our trek.

Bumping back down those stairs again, we still found ourselves again out of luck at the first door we went through. Wandering into the empty outer office, I found a note on an

CHAPTER FOUR: LIKE BEING KIDS AGAIN • 55

inner door advising that he was out "Inspectin'" and would be back between 2:00 and 2:30 PM. I had 1:50 on my watch. I decided it made sense for the two of us to stay inside. Outside there was a growing chill as the shadows lengthened.

Looking back on it, I am struck with how naive the two of us were as we waited patiently for this assumed public servant to return and lend us a hand in getting our small dream house built. We knew there were frauds in the world; that there was hate and violence, chiseling and war; but we only knew these things in a detached abstract fashion. We had been raised by good people who had guarded us from much of the world's sting. We were trusting and faithful regarding others, and of course prone to surprise when dealt dirty.

The fact Madlock arrived around 2:30 seemed logical enough, almost efficient considering the note on the door. However, we weren't ready for the scent of booze and mint Life-Savers trailing him as he breezed into his inner office; nor were we ready for the sounds of the screwing-off and screwing-on of a bottle cap, followed by the chorus of large water bottle bubbling from the same direction.

Negative premonitions were growing. The fifteen minutes more he kept us waiting didn't do anything for our anxieties either. Perhaps I was being hasty. The affairs of state take time. The wheels of justice grind slowly.

Suddenly a radio blasted the quiet with: **"THIS RED SOX SPRING TRAINING GAME IS BROUGHT TO YOU"**... then the volume eased downward toward a more acceptable level... "by the Atlantic Refining Company and your neighborhood Atlantic dealer who say, 'Look for the red ball sign;' and by the makers of Narragansett Larger Ale and Beer. Hi neighbor, have a brew, have a Gansett lager ale or beer."

"You wished to see me?" he asked, as the "e" of his "see" kind of bumped into that of the "me." His eyes quickly went from me to Bobbye. And did he ever check her out. Up, down, and all around. It was as if I no longer existed and my dear Bobbye had become the VAGA GIRL of his dreams.

"Mr. Madlock?" I asked. He glanced at me for only an instant as his eyes danced back to Bobbye... a process which had him clearly and aggressively reviewing her physical attributes. I almost wanted to lay hands on this thoroughly questionable "Public Servant."

But his attention suddenly spun toward the transistor radio propped inside the empty "out" basket on his desk. It then occurred to me that he might even have lost cognizance that I was also present. So much for baseball and my beautiful wife.

Then the volume was run up again, as I put out my hand to shake his and I tried to speak over the radio, I said, "My name is Ken, Ken McAdams and..." His hand froze in mine as the radio suddenly blasted with "... **IT'S WELL HIT! FLOOD IS GOING BACK, BACK, WAY BACK... LEAPS... AND BRINGS IT IN.**"

Madlock's glazed eyes returned sadly from Florida long enough for me to add, "And this is my wife Bobbye... McAdams."

He gave a momentary wet squint my way then focused totally on my girl Bobbye, or as I had taken to calling her during this ordeal "dear Rob ." He looked at her again and his chalk-pale face managed a quick jet of color.

"Ah yes, Bobbye, you say. Of course, my dear. Please have a chair. Some water perhaps. And maybe a little something to perk it up? I do hate to imbibe alone. Perhaps a small nip for you?" he questioned, pulling a pint bottle of Jim Beam bourbon out of the bottom left drawer of his desk.

CHAPTER FOUR: LIKE BEING KIDS AGAIN • 57

Bobbye gave her head a quick negative shake, but Madlock was so totally engaged with her just being there, much as if I had never walked in with her or was now pulling over another chair to sit beside her, he seemed mesmerized.

He plunked down on a kind of municipal issue wooden unit, after having stiff-legged it back around behind his desk. He smiled in our general direction as he put three small paper cups on the top left side of his desk and put a shot in each without a drop falling short. His hands seemed to have stopped shaking once they became involved with dealing whiskey. Only the extra-long nasal hairs, long enough to braid I thought, only they continued to quiver. Interesting.

Of course, I was feeling a bit uncomfortable as Bobbye must have felt too. How could a derelict like this be in charge of the process and documentation for our housebuilding?

Though Madlock seemed only to have ears for Grapefruit League baseball, he couldn't keep his eyes off Bobbye. I couldn't stop studying him studying her either. He made me nervous because of that for sure, but then there was the even greater issue that his shaking hands held the keys to our futures, our home-built kingdom. Sadly, Mr. Madlock didn't cut an admirable figure.

With a shake of his head, eyes still locked on my wife, Rob, he eased more comfortably back in his chair and said, "Now what can I do for you?" Of course, his eyes were still not on me, making me want to shout, "Hey, I'm over here, pal," but I reduced that to, "Mr. Madlock we have recently purchased some land in the area... here are the papers on that; deed, seal, all necessary things and now we need a building permit from you... your office. Mr. Merriweather of Granite Trust advised us of this."

"Yes, I understand," he said, dragging his attention back to me and away from Bobbye. "Ah hum, the documents," he mumbled looking down on the small stack I'd plopped in front of him on his desk. "But where are the rest of the papers?" he asked with what struck me as a touch of wide-eyed drama.

"The rest? What do you mean by the rest? That's it. There isn't anything more than what you have there, sir."

What the hell else did he want? My driver's license, draft card... a Red Sox score card maybe.

Pulling his slouched-up-self to a reasonably straight perch, puffing at me with one of those super-official, very important, politically polite and a most condescending tone he said, "Without the additional necessary, most necessary forms, sir, we will not be able to even consider your application."

Suddenly I felt like I was entering a time-warp or dream state, one of the nightmare variety with me trapped under cascading shot glasses, beer cans and tumbling boxes of loose Cracker Jacks.

"What forms? Papers. I don't understand. I gave you the bill of sale, the deed with the town's seal on it, recording stamp, and the title search survey. Even the house plans are there... specifications, materials, the full breakdown. What else do you need? What's missing?" I'd asked, my volume rising noticeably.

"Mr. McAdams, there is no need for anxiety. This is quite a simple procedure," he puffed, then sipped from the nearest paper cup. "All we need in addition is your street and sewer plan, the overall survey of the development and a bond certifying that the septic requirements will be met throughout your development area which would come in at a price probably around $2000, perhaps $2500. It is that simple."

"What development?" is all I could get out through my clenched teeth.

"Well, sir, I see we are not getting anywhere here, and I am a very busy man," he said and emphasized the same with another pull on and finish of his first cup. Reaching for the second, originally designated for my consumption, he pulled that one closer and continued saying, "In short, you have purchased one parcel of land from Mr. Bausche who owns the overall development parcels, on which he lives and on which he rents the old schoolhouse as living accommodation for Mr. Moody. So, you, Mr. Bausche and Mr. Moody constitute a development. The law requires of a development, before any more than two dwellings can go up on that overall parcel, that a complete plan be presented addressing the items I just mentioned. No such presentation, no building permit. It's as simple as that." Sip. "I am sorry, but the law is the law." Sip, sip.

I wanted to cry... or scream... or just break something. Maybe Madlock's whiskey bottle over his head for starters.

"But what has all this to do with us?" I asked, sneaking a semi-panicked glance at Bobbye. "We simply bought a couple of acres to build our home on. We aren't developers. Bausche, Moody, they aren't developers either. Our land is our land. Bausche's is his. Both are separate, and Moody is only renting the old schoolhouse. We're just discussing two parcels here, not three. What are you talking about?"

"Sir, your land under these conditions is not your land, unless these requirements are met. Such a sale to you is illegal. Such a transaction for building purposes is not recordable. I am sorry, but that is the law, and I am a very busy man."

"But Mr. Madlock..." He holds up his hand, halting me. The ball game again.

Then Madlock lowered his hand with a shake of his head.

I was finding it difficult negotiating under these circumstances. And I was getting irritated.

"Look," I growled, "we've met all the requirements anyone told us about, and the law office that researched this thing apparently doesn't agree with your interpretation. Nor do I think the town or borough or whoever the hell it is who puts the seal on these things does either. Look there! What's that but the seal and the tax stamps, the whole works. Now what the hell are you throwing on top of this?"

"Sir," he puffed, his head tilting back and his nostril hairs reaching in my direction like tentacles, "we cannot allow such language here." Sip. "And I am very busy." Another sip, "I have explained things to you and that is it. My office controls all this. I control everything." Sip, "So that's it. You must leave. Both of you."

"But... but," I stumbled in frustration, "look here. Look at that signature on the approval page. Isn't that your signature? Right there—'J.H.Madlock.'"

"I have no comment."

"No comment?" I questioned, my teeth starting to grind. "What do you mean? Clearly it came across your desk in the first place and was approved. Everybody approved it. And now you're backtracking and saying it's no good."

"Correct," he said, as he poured another short shot. "This office controls. You do not. So, good day."

Madlock got up, grabbed his coat and hat, then walked out of his office leaving us with one empty cup on his desk and about eighteen or more ballplayers still on the blaring radio.

"Son of a bitch," I mumbled. Then, looking at Rob again I asked, "What do we do now?"

She put her hand in mine, gave a small squeeze and with a half-smile said, "Maybe Mr. Merriweather at the bank can help. I don't see there's anything else we can do, here."

"I guess," I sighed, shaking my head. "Maybe he can tell us how things actually work around this Cloud Cuckooland."

Bobbye smiled and gave my hand a pat as she got to her feet. With my head down, I followed.

We caught Ed Merriweather before he left the bank in Ledge Rock. Standing admittedly a bit nervously hand in hand in front of his desk, after declining the offered seats, we did a duet run through of what all had hit us at town hall, everything but the final Red Sox score which we had missed.

"So," I concluded, "I think this Madlock character is either insane or pushing hard for a bribe. I'm serious. He kept saying his office controlled the whole process, despite the fact his office had already signed off on our purchasing the land."

"Frankly Ken, Bobbye," Merriweather nodded, "we have had concerns about Madlock in the past. Don't quote me, you realize how tender a bank's position is in any community, but you might be right. He's not a local product. He's kind of a political refugee from Hartford. We have suspected he's looked for… gratuities, let's call them, in the past. It's public record that he was called before a grand jury in Hartford over this sort of thing while he was in the governor's office. But most interesting was that the buzz around the state house was that he'd been designated to take the fall on some wheeling and dealing there in place of the governor. Apparently, he was given this commissioner's thing as a payback for taking the hit. So, in that sense, he's already paid his dues, and he might feel he can get away with anything he wants down here now that he's been kicked out of Hartford. But remember, you didn't hear any of that from me."

Both Bobbye and I smiled and nodded at Ed Merriweather's wink.

"So," Bobbye asked with a tiny lady-like wrinkle to her brow, "can we enlarge our loan to cover gratuities for corrupt local politicians?"

"There's probably not enough money in all the banks nationwide to cover those," he scowled as he shook his head. "Sadly so."

"But Ed," I said, "we have got to do something. We've signed contracts and paid upfront for the better part of a house, lumber, nails, doors, windows--the works; all to be delivered in the very near future to the land this clown says we can't build on."

"Yes, it is a fix," he agreed.

"And that is exactly what Madlock wants to make it," Bobbye threw in. "A fix begging a payoff to him to get it unfixed."

"So, what can we do?" I questioned.

"In just a day or two, Wednesday--next there's a town meeting..." Ed said tapping a thumbnail against a front tooth.

"Can you do something creative there, Ken?" he asked.

Having been somewhat of an ad-hoc politician in my student days, I knew how well an unexpected attack could make things happen.

"I think I can show up at the meeting and lay Madlock's whole scam out in front of the folks there. I've got nothing to lose, whereas he has lots to lose... if he really thinks about it."

"I'll talk with our lawyers to make sure you'll be on firm ground waving your hand up in the meeting like that." Then, after pausing a moment, Ed added, "Don't get all bent out of shape over this. We'll work through it together."

Ed was such a gentleman. Bobbye and I appreciated his warmth and encouraging demeanor. I hoped we passed that on to him with our smiling goodbyes. Anyway, we promised to call him later that week to find out where things stood from his legal shop's point of view.

Our drive back to Boston was miserable. Bumper-to-bumper traffic. Worse than ever because we had to negotiate around

CHAPTER FOUR: LIKE BEING KIDS AGAIN

Providence, the capital city of an entire state populated with incredibly bad drivers... says everyone from Massachusetts. Add to that, sheets of rain falling to create puddles in the awaiting cavernous potholes. All that, plus our feelings of defeat-by-townhall. We and our dear, wet, border collie, MacIntosh made quite a troup... discouraged, tired, bedraggled, and wet, bumping along in our little VW bug. But then again, we were young with nothing but life's adventures ahead.

Jammed at another stop light, I looked over at Bobbye and winked. She smiled, and I felt a rush of early-marriage love course through my veins.

"Hey, Rob," I said. "I love you girl. No matter what."

Her smile broadened, and she added, "And I wouldn't have it any other way."

To which MacIntosh added a lick to Bobbye's cheek.

CHAPTER FIVE
Tenting Under the Stars

My Monday call to Ed Merriweather was not very encouraging. "Ken," he said, as I clicked the phone on to speaker so Rob could hear him too.

"Ed, I just wanted you to know Bobbye is on with me. We're on speaker."

"Oh good. Hi Bobbye. Hope all is well with you."

"You have more control over that than we do right now," she said with a bit of an edge. "What have you for us today?"

Before he could respond I threw in, "Ed, I figure there must be other ways dealing with this Madlock character. No son of a gun like him could have made it to his stage of life without accumulating an army of skeletons."

"Well, outside of what our lawyers researched on the whole development issue, they tell me Madlock does have some grounds. It works this way. The law has it that if a parcel is divided three or more ways, then it officially becomes a development. Since Bausche sold you one piece, while he holds the largest section of forty some acres himself and rents a piece to the Moody's, then the interpretation the town, i.e., Madlock has taken is that these three families would constitute a development. Clearly your title search and Bausche's lawyer assumed that the rental of the schoolhouse by Moody didn't qualify as a second parcel. It is on Bauche's overall piece, owned exclusively by him. Which all seems to give the nod to your position, except for the fact Madlock controls how the town reads it."

"Crap," I whispered as Bobbye rolled her eyes. She and I had made our commitments to this whole project by giving notice ending our teaching jobs, signing contracts for the land and the building materials, to say nothing of my book deal going under and the manuscript getting lost in the mail. We even put out the last of our own cash to get things going and committed our futures to Ed Merriweather's bank with the mortgage. If Madlock held firm, we were dead. No jobs, no money, undevelopable land, zip, zero, nada. What the hell?

"So, you don't think we have a winning legal position?" I asked in almost a whisper.

"Yes and no. There is room for either interpretation, but to go against Madlock in the courts might take years. And cost a lot of money. What do the two of you think?" Ed asked.

Bobbye did another eye-roll as I hissed air through my teeth.

"My goodness," Bobbye said, "there must be another way, Ed. This whole thing is so needless, so senseless. Why on earth would Madlock even want to interpret the thing this way when he doesn't have to?"

"How can I answer that?" Ed asked, lowering his voice a hair, "I would not put a shady consideration beyond the man. Like I said, we've had trouble with him before."

"Shady. What's that supposed to mean?" Bobbye asked.

"No comment," Ed said.

"I'll comment," I threw in with some heat, "I think that son-of-gun is looking for... bottom line, a bribe. He's nothing but a sleazy operator. Boozes in his office, for cripes' sake. Jim Beam's his bottom-drawer advisor. Not to mention the rumor he got thrown out of Hartford, was grand-juried for some kind of illegal crap, too. I think we can go after this clown publicly. Head on. Make him nervous about somebody coming at him in front of the world like that."

Bobbye cocked her head questioningly. I went on with, "I'm ready to go to the next town meeting and challenge him in front of everybody there. He'll be on the spot with a lot to lose. We're already in the tank as it is now, so there's nothing else for us to lose. What do you guys think?"

"If you're laying out the truth, I have no trouble with that. But otherwise leave me and the bank out of it. I'll at least come to watch the show on my own. It should be fun," Ed added.

"Me too, Kenny," Bobbye volunteered. "But I'll be in the back, by the door with my gat, ready to get to our getaway car movin' fast."

"Thank you for your support, Bonnie," I threw in dryly, then added, "Believe me, I'm going to be ready for this sucker and I don't expect him to be ready for me."

Before we closed out the call, Merriweather asked, "Do you want me to have a chat with him making the point that you and Bobbye aren't alone in this, but have institutional types interested in what's going on? From the point of view that you two have taken a loan from us which can only be executed through the issuance of proper permits. He should get the picture."

I looked to Bobbye for her input, but she only shrugged, so I said to Ed, "Let's not. I think it will be more effective if I just show up and hit him with it in front of everybody without his knowing you, the bank or any other big hitters are on our side. But thanks anyway. We'll talk after the town meeting."

Bobbye and I decided to take the coming weekend off, not stick around town but head south. This would get us away from the group of talented high school students who loved to crowd into our apartment and discuss "big issues." It was heartwarming for us to be designated "go-to" teachers who offered them an open door, but that kind of cut us out of our own together-time sometimes. This weekend it would have, for sure, since we figured to motor down to Ledge Rock with a pup tent, a Coleman lantern and butane stove to heat up the Dinty Moore stew we brought, along with blanket rolls, an axe, a bow saw, food, and our beloved border collie, MacIntosh along too. We would camp out in our wooded two acres, cut some trees, and lay out how we wanted to arrange the driveway approach to our house-to-be. Do all that while saying to hell with Madlock.

How exciting it was to putt-putt off from the tight little tollhouse-cookie-world of Wakefield, Massachusetts to pursue our great adventure of settling, pioneer-style, in the far away forest-world that we would eventually become a part of Connecticut. Okay, so it was in the Nutmeg State of all places, not Montana or the Rockies, but what the hell, woods are woods and we'd be camping out in them anyway.

On Friday, after school closed, we set off for southern Connecticut. The drive was pretty much uneventful except that we were discovering how the farther we got from Boston's sophisticated environs, the more roughshod the folks along the way seemed to be. Not wanting to sound like a Bay State snob, I still had to make the point which was made in spades when we pulled into a gas station not far from our destination. We were near the state line but still in Rhode Island, when we were blind-sided by a blast from one of the truly unwashed locals. As I was finishing gassing our beetle, and as Bobbye was crossing the paved area from the lady's room, a beefy tattooed type with a ham-sized arm hanging out of his driver's side window shouted to an attendant at the next pump, "Hey," he bellowed, "you there... at the pump!" So loud was this guy's shout that the attendant jerked his head up, as did I, and we both quickly picked out the unshaven face behind the voice that had startled us.

"Yes sir," the attendant called back.

"You got a clean xxxxxx here?" His word began with "SH" and ended in "ER."

Bobbye stopped short from her potty-trip, eyes wide with an almost fearful look on her beautiful face. Since she was the most recent occupant of one of the restrooms, old Bad-Mouth was demanding a rating of the same. How was she to respond?

Fortunately, as I said, the station was on the Rhode Island side of the line and the unkempt gentleman with the big arms was driving a long yellow Cadillac with, thank goodness, New Jersey plates. No, the slob was not a local after all. So, this was only a "one-off," hopefully never to be repeated, at least when my dear sweet wife was tiptoeing across the tarmac.

Oh, how good that Dinty Moore stew we'd heated up tasted later once we'd gotten the tent up, dog MacIntosh fed and our blanket roll spread, as the raw forest night started to wrap its arms around us. Nature can be so invigorating even when you're half-freezing to death. We were treated to the haunting sound of an owl announcing to the wilds there that it was taking flight. We expected we might even see it, high above the trees, silhouetted with the haloed moon as its backdrop. The thin dashing evening clouds were passing frowns on the face of that night. Everything felt so real, so fantastically alive. Under such a spell it was easy to forget about rejections, lost manuscripts, history classes, and negative characters like Madlock.

However, that first weekend in the tent, Macintosh turned out to be a problem. Even before sunrise, he'd gotten up ahead of us, crawled out from his burrow under the edge of our blankets, yawned, smacked his mouth a few times, then went through his morning stretch — front paws down, rump up, back legs extended straight out one after the other till he stood up again, sniffed a few times, then cocked a leg and aiming his shot straight at the tent pole and behind it, my head.

"Jeeesus!" I shrieked, bolting up and lunging out to swat MacIntosh's butt away. "Gawd damn!" I bellowed, though my shouts were getting muffled as my charge brought the covers off Bobbye, pulling her up, the tent down, and me all over our yelping dog.

What a mess. And poor Rob. To have suddenly been awoken in the dark, in a rolling, squirming, cursing, snarling tangle of blankets, lanyards, tent poles and a husband (me) flopping over her while I was slapping at our howling dog!

Breakfast went better. The smell of bacon frying in an open pan, its mouth-watering aroma filling the woods, was wild. Even now, my spine tingles just thinking of such camp cooking on frosty mornings. It surpasses hot buttered popcorn at the movies, baseball franks, circus cotton candy; it's on a level with the thrill children know from the bell of a Good Humor truck late on a sticky summer afternoon. So good.

After we ate\ which was our first camp breakfast experience, we had to decide what trees to cut for the driveway up to what would someday be our house. But we still faced the issue of just where to put that house in the first place.

The remaining weekend of March and all of those through April would go to clearing where the house would go. And that would be no mean task. We were in a forest. It's an old cliché, I know, but it really is awfully hard to see how you want to arrange the forest for all those damned trees getting in the way.

The land lay like this -- turning off the state road which went by the front of the Bausche's house, you would jostle and bounce past their corn and vegetable field, by his pump house, then past the Moody's schoolhouse on the dirt lane we would share, which was once the road to the centuries old farm up over the next hill. So, past Isaiah Moody's, maybe another fifty yards, a total of about one hundred in from the state road, you'd be at our tent. This was the lowest corner of the rectangle of our two acres, and the closest to the road back to civilization.

On the other side of the lane the land fell away first to a small sand pit, then to a pond, both well hidden from our tent by trees and shrubs. Our side of the lane had its own slope, but uphill. It was gentle at first, then more pronounced, growing to a long and steep rise whose crest was mostly hidden in the heavy growth. A tumbled-down, centuries-old stonewall marked the top end of our land. Then the lane itself wandered a couple of miles beyond, growing ever more-faint till it petered out at a high-wire power line on the top of a large bald ridge. No houses, no paved roads, only fields and farms, cows, and sheep.

Here and there along the way, before the power lines, were a few off-shooting paths that must have serviced long forgotten pastures, and perhaps smaller farms. As it worked out, we never did get a chance to investigate those all the way to their origins.

Anyway, we found it very difficult to look at a stand of trees, which in themselves hide the subtler contours of the land, and decide that a driveway would go here, our house there, the garage next to it on this side, and let's not forget a pump house somewhere nearby if not in the house's basement itself.

At this stage of the game, I had a whole succession of stupid ideas. These didn't occur to me until Bobbye finally pointed out what to her was the obvious. Her reasoning was painfully realistic. And difficult for me to deal with. The first case in point occurred when she pointed out that the winters would be hard and since we would be fairly isolated, our driveway should have the gentlest slope possible as well as the most direct path to our door. That effectively shot down my doubled-backed "S" idea across a trestle complete with drawbridge and a mule-operated rope elevator. It was maddening how she would squash my innate, but in fact inane, creativity.

With our plan of attack laid out it was simply a matter of carrying-on and carrying-through, but... have you ever tried cutting dozens of good-sized trees with a flimsy wimpy bow saw?

That's right. And yes, that was my hammer-headed idea too. Think of all the money we were saving by not renting a power saw. They're so polluting and noisy, right? Though, in fact, not much noisier than my cursing.

Okay, it had taken those trees decades to grow. Somehow that implied that we owed them the respect of cutting them down in a timely and natural hand-and-sweat sort of way. Have you ever seen Mother Nature grow a bow saw? And what was the sense of spending decades cutting the danged trees anyway?

I don't know what the Moody's thought when they heard all the sawing, chopping, grunting, moaning, and cursing coming through the bushes up the hill from their old schoolhouse. Or how they reacted to the appearance of a tent with two young idealists and a hound dog sleeping in it up there; but I'll bet a shiver ran down their spines thinking about future property values.

Late that Saturday afternoon we met Isaiah and Loraine Moody for the first time. Of course, we wanted to say hello to our neighbors and assure them that we weren't total idiots. And that we had some simple needs they could probably help us with, too. Like water. We'd never thought much about water before. Just turned on a tap and there it was, right? But by the end of that first full tree-cutting day, we found out differently. Our thermoses had run out. So, we were filthy, thirsty, and hot despite the cold. We got a little feel for the pioneer and his water barrel strapped to the back of his wagon. How would our VW Beetle look with a water barrel roped on the roof? Water, we suddenly understood, would be our first big problem. And for now, a sink or tub to go with it.

Bedraggled, crusty with dirt, Rob and I stumbled through the bushes toward the Moody's back door. What killed me was that their old schoolhouse was exactly what we had been looking for to buy initially, but without success. It was that "Charming and picturesque converted little red schoolhouse," the ads talked about, but the realty ladies never showed us. It was tight and snug. Two average sized bedrooms, a small living room with a large fireplace at one end, and the kitchen at the other, farm style. Damn, it would have been just the ticket for us, but do you ever find what you're looking for until after you have bought something else?

I guess Isaiah had seen us coming and stepped out onto the porch to say hello, which gave me a slight tick of uneasiness. This was our initial face-to-face, so important to a lasting neighborly relationship.

My first impression was how dark he was. But I'll bet he was a little alarmed at how white I was. Scots Irish pale. The four of us must have been something to see staring uneasily at each other. Regular chessmen, one pair black, the other white.

"Hello," said Bobbye, from behind me, breaking the ice.

"Hello," returned Moody.

"This is my wife, Bobbye, and I'm Ken McAdams," I jabbered, waving my hand out in front of me for a shake. We were both awkward, perhaps subconsciously contemplating hidden microphones and cameras recording this monumental 1963 event. "White man moves in next door to black man. They shake hands. And the whole freaking world does NOT come to an end." Though I doubt the event would have been phrased that way unless it was maybe Arthur Godfrey broadcasting.

The Moody's had no children. They'd been so busy for years helping younger relatives come up from Mississippi for their final years of schooling in Connecticut that they probably hadn't had time for kids of their own.

Of course, all this didn't come out at our first meeting. Most of it we learned from the Bausche's. Nevertheless, from that first

CHAPTER FIVE: TENTING UNDER THE STARS

moment we knew we were terribly fortunate to be coming in next door to these two unbelievably hard-working, warm, and gracious people. In retrospect, for us, it was embarrassing. Our project looked so lame next to all they had taken on and accomplished. We felt a little deflated.

After Isaiah went off to his first job as chef in one of the leading seafood restaurants in Mystic, Loraine showed us their artisanal well outside spicket and offered us all the water we might need. The bathroom was thrown in on the deal, which we gratefully used for a few basics, returning us once again to the human race. When you need others for such simple things as water, to say nothing of a pot to pee in, it makes a believer of you.

We didn't stay much longer after our washup followed by a cup of coffee. Macintosh was still questionable in the new area, and we had our camp to straighten up for the approaching night. Besides, I'm a lousy guest. I like having them, but I don't like being one. Somehow, I feel I'm in the host's way. So, after our cup of coffee, we said goodnight to Loraine and trudged back through the bushes, to our fire, our stew, MacIntosh, night-time sounds, and a cold in-tent, night-snuggle. We felt good. In control. Like that hunky guy in the Marlboro ad, though neither of us smoked.

How little we knew at that stage as we blissfully settled into our blankets, savoring the new feeling of actually owning some land, wondering vaguely if we were required to fight to the death to protect it... feeling strong, feeling weak, and feeling so excitedly new. We sank into welcome sleep... two tired, but very happy people.

CHAPTER SIX
Garvey, His Board & We the People

The next morning, I went down to the lumber yard and used the payphone outside their equipment shed to call Chairman Garvey. "Yes, this is Mr. Garvey," He didn't sound all that happy acknowledging the fact. "Mr. McAdams? Nooo, I haven't spoken with Mr. Madlock. 'Thought he was out of town. I just got back myself." (Horseshit).

So, since he theoretically knew nothing of our problem, I went through the whole mess in detail. Madlock having let it go through in the first place; my title search; Bausche's lawyer's opinion, each input costing us around $100 a pop; the seal, the recording, all that baloney. And, of course, how the whole thing had gone down the drain with Madlock's application of catch 22.

I told him of the building materials schedule, the delivery date, our bank loan, our coming joblessness, even the tent, trees, and dog who, for an instant, I was tempted to call, "Checkers." I asked him to help us get a permit out of Madlock.

He said he would have to study the matter of course, but really couldn't see any option open to us but to accept Mr. Madlock's recommendations, as he and the board probably would in the end anyway.

At first, I'd tried being polite, but only got more crap for the effort. I had started the conversation out reasonably, but that only got me more bull for the effort. As my temperature rose, I came back at him firmly to let him know I wasn't some kind of trembling gobbler intimidated by the administrative chopping block he and Madlock seemed to be laying us down on.

"Look, Mr. Garvey, there's something damned strange going on here. You probably aren't aware of it, but there are people in this town who think, and who are quietly saying so too, that your commissioner might just be in the business of setting up these difficult situations for his own personal profit. I'll admit there hasn't been an exact money demand made to us yet, though I did hear a whisper saying that $2,500 might do the trick, but this whole thing is just too illogical not to have some ulterior motive. If something like this were the case, and if it came out in the open, I doubt that your good name would come through untouched. And honestly, I'm the wrong man to pick on. I get angry and noisy. And the way things stand now I'm the only injured party... the only one with nothing to lose. So, I'm telling you, I know the whole board will be together at the town meeting, tonight. I'll be there and the New London Day will be there too. I'll make sure of that. So, it will be your call. See you later," and I started to hang up, but Garvey beat me to it. Without a reply, he slammed down his receiver.

CHAPTER SIX: GARVEY, HIS BOARD & WE THE PEOPLE • 79

At noon I called Merriweather. "Ed, maybe I've got the bugger, or at least the road to him," I growled.

"How so, Ken?"

I ran through everything, emphasizing my call to the Zoning Board Chairman adding, "I figure publicity's the only hope against low-rent politicians like these clowns. Hell, I've got nothing to lose taking a shot at them. They're standing on my back anyway. Either this will get them off or they'll just jump down harder. But I don't give a damn. So… if you hear anything before the meeting, please call. And Ed, if people ask your opinion, let them know how serious I am. If it comes down to it, I'll make such a stink at least Madlock will be sent packing."

"I'm calling everyone I know around here to get them together for a show of strength. I'd like a title for what I have in mind, something like 'Citizens United,' but somebody else already has it. Anyway, I'm lining up a show for Garvey's board, and maybe even enough publicity with the New London Day being there that with the election coming up, the Governor might pay attention to something like this. If you could call friends and ask them to come to the town hall meeting, Bobbye and I would appreciate it. Nothing political, just ask them to meet new people coming into Ledge Rock. Just a more-the-merrier sort of thing. You don't have to mention any implied political position by coming. It's only to show some concerns new people moving in might have. Anyway, I have a lot of calls to make, so I've got to sign off. Bobbye and I hope to see you there later."

"Okay, Ken. I got the picture, but understand, I have to sit on the sidelines. Hear no evil, see no evil. Anyway, man, good luck. These characters need a few bumps. 'Be talking to you. And yes, I will call some friends. So long."

CHAPTER SEVEN
A Good Man

As time went by, I slowly learned who the real pros were for jobs like this. Ralph Babonas for sure was a top performer. For myself, I figured I would rank somewhere between Stan Laurel and Oliver Hardy.

We were not cutting the trees close to the ground anymore. It was easier on my back, which in the end proved to be smart! What a sensation it was for me to eventually learn, in this case, that the easy way to do something was in fact the smart way. It felt almost like cheating. A complete undermining of Calvinism and the grim Puritan ethic which has long dominated we dower New Englanders.

Naturally I didn't know any of this until Ralph Babonas stopped by. Like Moody and Carl, people had given him fears Bobbye and I might be headed off the deep end on how we were preparing to handle our whole situation.

After listening to him, Bobbye gave me a sideways glance and an approving nod to his suggestion, because she had said much the same thing a few days before. (Bah humbug) By then I didn't dare say anything about fuzzy dumb stupid ideas like hand-digging foundations and such. Pros win over clown armatures every time, and clearly Ralph was a pro. I asked him if he did foundation excavations?

"Right."

"Road extensions and drives?"

"Gravel?"

"Yes. Would you do ours?"

"Foundation hole?"

"Right. And road and drive?"

"You just keep cuttin' the trees with a good shank on them, then I'll come in with the machine – front-loader, back-hoe, and pop them up, roots and all."

"When?"

"You got your building permit?"

"Oh hell ... no, we haven't, not yet," I said, embarrassedly feeling like a total novice.

"Sounds like you've met Madlock, our building poobah," he smiled.

"Right," I said with a shake of my head.

"I've got a lot of work waitin' on Madlock's permits. He's a building-trade's depression all by himself. But I've heard from the grapevine that that might change soon, maybe even this evening," Ralph added, lighting his cigarette. "A lot of folks are fixin' to come tonight to see what all happens."

"Really? What have you heard about tonight?" I asked, my eyes checking Bobbye's for signs of any late-breaking news coming from the lady's room or from wherever such insider stuff emanates.

"Word is that a couple from Boston's going to call out Madlock and the whole board for being on the take. I'll save you a seat and bring some popcorn."

I wondered who could have told him what we were up to? A couple from Boston? It had to be that scrubby-faced assistant at the bank. He could have overheard us talking with Merriweather. And no one was more impressed with our being from Boston than that kid.

"That's us," I blurted out, then looking at Bobbye I amended it to, "We are the ones going after them and Madlock tonight."

Ralph's grin stretched ear-to-ear. He seemed to look us over in a whole new light. "I'll tell you what," Ralph said, "If you are able to get clearance to build here, and that 'if' is based on what you pull off tonight," then he paused to ask the dimensions of the foundation from Bobbye and after jotting those down and doing a mental closed-eye calculation, he said "I figure it would cost you…" and he came up with a figure only slightly more than half what we had figured ourselves. Wow!

Bobbye and I had done a lot of research on what each phase of the project should cost — stuff like the excavation itself, pouring the foundation, cutting and gravelling the drive, that sort of thing. We were, whether we fully realized it or not, becoming builders and doing as full time builders do, sub-contracting out the specialty jobs that weren't worth tackling on our own — because of the cost and only occasional use of the equipment needed to do it, or simply the economics of time. So, we had a ballpark figure of what to expect. We'd budgeted to that figure, plus a 10% cushion.

When Ralph finished figuring and his price turned out to be just that, about half of ours, we kind of shivered over its seeming too good to be true. Could we trust his numbers? Could we trust Ralph... whom we really didn't even know?

"Is this a price for the job, or an estimate?" Bobbye asked. Through bitter experience we both knew the difference between the two. One is tight, the other bottomless.

"Price."

"Firm?"

"Yup. As long as I get to watch The Couple from Boston tonight."

"Deal."

We three shook hands making me, at least, feel a little uneasy. We'd just made our first building contract and it was dependent on my attacking the one guy who literally controls permits for building on our very piece of land. What the hell were we doing? I sure hoped Bobbye knew. But she looked more committed to our plans than I was. Great to know that I was the only person completely doubting my own judgment. I'd gotten the same feeling when we originally bought the land. Adult responsibilities. All this was making me feel more like a child, a little boy. Bobbye threw me a wink. She clearly was the big girl present. But still, how could we own land of all things? It was like setting ourselves up as gods or something. And now we were shaking hands with adult type people and barking out big sounding words like, "Deal." Leading to clearing land. Building road-extensions, houses, even taking on city hall. This wasn't a game of Monopoly with toy money along with another roll of the dice. I didn't dare think too hard about that. Like the child I felt myself to be, I'd just have to close my eyes, hold my breath, and run on through all this like we did as kids driving past graveyards.

"So, Ralph," I said, finding that I, and Bobbye too, by the look on her face, were already trusting the hell out of this guy, and not having any real idea why. "Who do you recommend for the foundation, assuming we are able to build?"

"Joey Gildea, from Westerly. He's the best cement man around and he won't break your budget. 'Better talk to him soon though. He gets booked for the whole summer real fast. Tell him I told you about him. Hell," said Ralph kicking a stone with his cut-up boot, "I'll talk to him myself. That way he'll do the job for you for sure. Plus, he'll be mad if I don't tell him to be at the town hall tonight. No one hates Madlock more than Joey."

Which I learned was Ralph Babonas's style. He always went that little extra for you. We didn't have to go chasing after Gildea. And for a guy alone running his equipment solo, like Ralph was, every minute, every hour costs plenty. At that early stage I didn't fully understand this, but in time I learned how short a day really can be.

"I appreciate that, Ralph," I said. "I guess we'll need all the good help we can get. Thank you."

He didn't say anything, just walked away a bit and looked the job over some more, stopping only to chuckle a few times. Was he laughing with us, or at us? I guess what goes down tonight will have the answer.

Then, through the woods, across Moody's, came Carl Bausche. He didn't shout anything, just waved as he approached. Being as hard of hearing as he was, Carl sometimes missed what was said if he wasn't close enough to pick up the lips and body language.

Once there, he and Ralph immediately started firing crisp shots at each other. It took me back a little. I wasn't sure they were joking.

"Hello, Carl," Ralph opened in a loud voice for all the woods to hear, "You horny old millionaire. Still digging big holes to bury your money in?"

"You're the hole digger, Babonas," returned Bausche, with a slight curl to his lip and a hitch of his head my way, "You up here to run your digger into Ken and Bobbye's pocket ... for a change. It'd be good to get you out of mine."

"My equipment's not big enough to dent your pocket, Carl. And what are you going to do with it all anyway? You know, 'fella your age better start making up his mind."

"Your name's not on my list, Babonas. You got enough of it already for that gravel. Eight bucks a yard and it wasn't more than dug hardpan. Someday the law's going to get you, and I'm Just waitin' to testify. For that matter, maybe even tonight."

Carl looked at me with a smile. Wait, did he know about the meeting tonight too?

"What do you think these kids's odds are?" he asked Ralph. And they both started laughing and patting me on the back which made me ask myself, what have we gotten into?

"You wouldn't go near a courthouse, Bausche," Ralph threw in, adding, "afraid you'd never get out. They're waitin' for you down there. Remember, I contract to the Borough, so I hear what's said."

Carl puffed a bit and looked to be getting genuinely angry, so Bobbye popped in with, "Ralph says Mister Gildea from Westerly would be a good man for the foundation."

"He's a good man right enough," Carl muttered, "I guess Babonas isn't crooked all the time either."

Ralph just laughed and raised a joking fist in Carl's direction.

"He's going to do the work for you two?" Carl asked.

"As soon as we get the permit," Bobbye and I said in unison. "We hope to have it one way or another by noon tomorrow," she finished for the two of us. Then I ran the full song and dance about Madlock and how tonight would be the showdown. Both Ralph and Carl seemed to enjoy hearing that and came together as friends again, mutually allied against the vultures they saw circling town hall.

On that note of unity, Ralph took his leave. I promised to call him as soon as I could to set the date for digging our foundation, and we both told him we hoped to see him at the town hall tonight. Then Bobbye and I went with Carl back over to his place to call Gildea and make sure he and as many friends as he could come up with would be at town hall by 8 PM.

Later that afternoon we started over to Westerly on a mission I had not briefed my darling on. She'd seemed to be ready for a nap now anyway. We'd had a few good days -- topping trees and letting them stand stub-up for popping later and leaving us conscience free. Like Ralph had said, do what's necessary first, frills later. Such unspectacular homilies were to take on greater significance the more time we were out in the woods on our own.

Bobbye started dozing during our drive. The work had been exhausting. I couldn't escape thoughts of how we still could lose everything, including our futures if things didn't go well that night at the townhall.

We were just under the bridge into Westerly when out of the corner of my eye I caught sight of it... parked in front of a pocked and spattered, cruddy sort of gas station. I jammed on the brakes and swerved off to the side as Macintosh ended half up in the front with us in the Bug, jarring Bobbye awake. Our dear dog and my loving wife were not happy.

With the traffic behind us clear, I backed up and hooked a rapid hard left at the intersection we'd just passed. I roared, as best a VW Beetle can roar, up to the gas station about 50 yards behind us on the right. And there she was, a gorgeous black 1940 Ford pickup truck with a big "4 Sale" on her front window. Mission accomplished. My heart was beating like an astronaut's must have been as he was about to step onto the moon. Oh man, she was so beautiful I got all trembly. She was better than Ralph's too. Sure, it looked like some turkey had painted her with a fork and she needed rubber, but with the eye of the classicist, I knew she was right. I knew. That non-rusted body, the clean glass, her unbelievably complete grille. She was as solid as solid could be. No fender dents. Solid doors, even unmarked bumpers.

I nearly ran through the gas station's plate glass window I was so excited. Of course, Bobbye had seen me react to cars like this before and only shook her head then reminded me that we had minimal money and that might become even less down the road. That was as much logic as she could muster, and I seized my opportunity to check this out.

MacIntosh jumped over Bobbye and out her open window. I found myself running right along with him as he barked encouragement. Yes, a smart border-collie who clearly knew a buy when he saw one.

I got the keys from the attendant. The sucker started. Oh gawd. I thought I'd have a nervous breakdown. I drove up the street. Jammed on the brakes. It even stopped! Eeeyow. I revved the engine and popped the clutch, spun the tires, then slapped through the three forward gears. Reverse worked too. Man, it felt like I had found a regular, damned, Rolls Royce.

"How much? Umm. For your truck? How much?" I panted at the portly owner coming out of his office. He gave me a questioning look as he eased the door closed. Before he even got a nod to me, I huffed and puffed that I was really interested in the Ford out-front. "How much? How much you want for it. The truck. The '40 Ford with the for sale in the window. How much you want for it?"

"150."

"125."

"135."

"Sold. Can I give you a check for $25 to hold it a day or two, then the balance when I pick up some plates?"

"Yeah."

"Great," I mumbled as I scribbled in our very thin bankbook. "Here's the check."

"Yeah."

"Thanks."

"Yeah."

"See you in a day or two, and, ah, thanks again. By the way, can my wife and I use your bathroom for a cleanup?

"Yeah."

Getting back into the car, tight as a drum with excitement, I woke up Rob and announced "I got it, Rob. $135. Money and paperwork to follow." She gave me a tiny smile as I added, "And we can use their bathroom for a cleanup."

She nodded and went back to sleep. I cleaned up in the facilities.

I think we both had a pretty good feeling on the road back to Ledge Rock considering my quick-time truck deal at the service station. At least at this stage of our adventure I did feel sort of confident we could keep pulling-off timely deals like that on into the future. I think Bobbye was reacting the same way especially since we had good people like Carl, Florence, the Moody's and Ralph helping.

And their joining in with us like this, it was as if they too were saying and feeling, yes, it could be done, we were the couple who could do it. We were not crazy. We needed that. In all this we were not unlike a pair of kids just venturing for the first time into the grownup world of challenge, victory, or defeat. Think of it, we were voluntarily shutting off the salaries we'd had, no longer employed by anybody. No health care, medical, any of it. We had both worked hard in the past and saved what we could. Since our wedding, we'd lived frugally, and we had no outside help coming in from anybody other than my Marine Reserve flying. Back when we thought the first book would be picked up, we sold my sports car, and took the plunge into Europe, seeing 5 or 6,000 miles of it. But we saw that as an investment, and on $5 a day we couldn't have gotten hurt too much. Now we were taking another plunge, stepping outside the norm, more in the frontier tradition like it was for our people moving west a hundred-fifty or more years ago. Bobbye and I were kind of like the prospectors heading to the Klondike. We were rolling the dice against the established order of things, putting our grubstake on the line for a way of living free and apart from the debilitating entanglements and dependencies of the usual corporate struggle. It was exciting. We were excited.

CHAPTER EIGHT
Cranking Up

The department of Motor Vehicles now topped our immediate list of struggles ahead for a day or two. So, after purchasing the pickup and completing the fast-time paper shuffle, we cleared the way that very morning for us to drive back to the nearest DMV in Connecticut. When we got to the gas station where the pickup was waiting, I got out of our bug and walked over to the pickup, and all I could think was what a beauty she was. Bobbye and MacIntosh followed over and they parked the VW in the front lot there. It was chilly but MacIntosh seemed content to snuggle down behind the wheel in the driver's seat as Rob slid out. We got in line. The whole affair turned out to be the usual sweaty struggle.

When I asked how to proceed with the required registration forms, I got a jumble of state jargon I didn't fully understand, but nodded as if I did, and strode ahead. I have had much experience with these processes, from Hawaii to Berlin, Germany and I must admit, Connecticut's registry was right up there with all those creating frustration and eating up nail-biting time.

Anyway, that struggle was completed, I paid the fellow at the cashier's desk the remainder of the $155 required and then sped onto to the Inspection Center. Believe it or not, there was no line there of any size. Honest. Nevertheless, as things go when dealing with governments everywhere, there was still one seemingly bizarre situation ahead.

In our pickup, (now known as Good Old Gal), we waited for some of the less classy vehicles ahead. Some showed signs of overheating and other problems - a hydraulic leak here, a radiator let-go there and even a clutch failure back behind us. Also, in front of us the fellow's engine appeared to quit totally, kind of like a fed-up mule would act. That was that. The poor man was beside himself. Apparently, his temporary registration ran out that day and to consider playing the windows game again seemed to be just too much for him. So, I gave him a wave, indicating we'd give him a push along the line as necessary. He was relieved, nodded, and smiled thanks. So, Old Gal and I showed our stuff by bumping him along, finally sliding him into the final inspection bay.

Those state boys really gave his car a real going over, everything but the engine, I might add. They jacked him up. They checked the front end. They looked over his new exhaust system. They checked his brakes all around and signed off on his tires all around too. Happily, he had plenty of battery, so his horn and wipers and lights and blinkers were championship. Finally, he got a friendly smile and a hearty well done from the chief inspector. They then waved us in, and the old gal gave a final assist, moving the fellow's successfully inspected car, pushing it to where we managed to roll him down the slope to the parking spaces below. Then, as Old Gal was moved into the inspection bay, I took it on myself to ask the head man how it was that a guy's car passed inspection without an operative engine?

"Look, buddy," he said to me with kind of a sneer in his voice, "I just follow directions and none of them mention an engine that runs. The only thing about engines is noise, and you tell me, is there anything quieter than a dead engine?"

Touché.

Then it was our turn. I revved Old Gal sassily into position. Of course, she ran like a top ... but flunked! Kingpins. It was true. The front end needed work. I could do it myself, and I was grateful to find the problem. I had missed it in my original pre-purchase runaround inspection. So, this meant I would have to return within ten days with the work done. That was fair. I wasn't upset, but I will admit I did see some irony in the manual saying nothing about a safe motor vehicle being able to motor.

Bobbye was less impressed. The roll of her eyes told me she probably felt I'd bought us a broken-down truck and was about to roll the dice on our future at what might be coming up as a rigged town hall performance.

I tried to keep us moving forward. Bobbye followed in the Bug. Leaving the DMV, I must say I did notice a bit of a grab on left turns which confirmed the need for front-end kingpins. No big deal. I could replace them in an hour or so Saturday morning.

Ralph had arranged for us to meet the cement guy, Joey Gildea. Once the truck things were sorted out, we took a run over to Joey's to sit down with him, one-on-one. Negotiations time again.

When Joey stepped out of his house and shook my hand it was like he was meeting Ted Williams or something.

"So, you're the guy taking on that bum Madlock?" He threw that at me for openers which made me sense that I had better be on my game tonight at the meeting. I was either going to walk out of that confrontation the town hero, or the town zero and yes, people were going to talk.

I mumbled something about writing-down what I was planning to say, but Joey was having none of it. "If it comes to a fist fight, you've got a lot of people who'll be on your side." Bobbye tried to smile.

Joey turned out to be a beautiful man. He was no B.S. but talked a mile a minute. Could even out-talk me, but I didn't hold that against him. I listened. His material was terrific. Like how he had spent the past winter.

As mentioned earlier, he didn't do cement winters anymore. The weather was so bad it wasn't worth it. But he still did okay financially, playing cards and such. He had a block-long Cadillac Eldorado to prove it. So, he just kind of screwed around making deals during the off-season. Travelled a lot too, particularly in December and January. Caribbean mostly. With the wife, on planned trips. But not always. Like when he and some of the boys drove down to New York to see off his brother and his wife on a two-week Virgin Island cruise.

They had a hell of a send-off party, Joey said. So much fun, none of them could see any reason to end it. So, Joey and the boys kept right on popping corks and sailed happily into the sunset. The next day, they had the ship's radio operator telegraph Joey's wife, (the others were single so what the hell), to let the little lady know he'd be home late ... about two weeks late.

Her reply was a classic too.

"So, what?"

They both had good senses of humor. Like when Joey finally got home. One of the neighbors said Joey's wife said she was going to Florida. Miami maybe. A week or so later, Joey went down to have a look. Once they got together, they went over to San Juan, then had their own cruise together back up to New York. It was beautiful. Joey was beautiful. They both were beautiful.

So, after the stories, we got around to cement. He mentioned that Ralph Babonas had already talked to him about Bobbye and me. They both agreed that we'd need a good job, so Joey was going to do it "personal," as a favor to Ralph. No sweat. "Forget the price, it would be right. Don't worry nothin' about that. When Ralph's dug the hole, he'll let me know, then I'm the guy'll fill it up. You'll come down one day and there she'll be. Okay?"

I guessed.

"And by the way," he said.

"Yah?"

"Madlock's a bum, so you fix him good. Right on!" he shouted, causing me a hair's embarrassment as my eyes flipped back and forth to see if anybody else there had been around to hear him.

So, we had a deal. I didn't know the price, but what the hell? I felt I knew the man. Joey was beautiful. Royalty in cement. And I am one tough negotiator, right?

As we pulled away, Joey called out "See you tonight!" And he threw a couple of air-punches in his driveway. I looked in the rearview mirror and locked eyes with Bobbye. If ever there was a chance to doubt the choice she had made marrying me and putting all of our savings past, present and future into this land we might not be able to build on, it was now.

We still had a couple of hours to kill until the shootout with Madlock would begin. The home-from-work bustle was dying down. The pulsating small-town center of Westerly, Rhode Island was changing its coat and tie to jackets, the easier night-out shuffle of the gathering movie few queuing outside the bijou for the 7 o'clock.

As the to-and-fro of street crossings slowed to the dogged patience of an old couple arm-in-arm at the corner, with the horns stopped honking and the teens done backing-off from their burnouts down main street, I felt the emptiness all around the center of town at that moment. Then it hit me. I couldn't face Madlock in a mood like this. I'd be better off pitching a brick through a window and running like hell just to get my juices up. Madlock was a handful and couldn't be approached with hat in hand. I knew I'd have to come at him swinging to have a chance. So, Bobbye followed me over to Mystic to eat at Moody's place. Maybe a friendly face and some final words of encouragement would perk me up.

The driver's side window in my new/old pickup jammed halfway up, so even my dear old truck was giving me the cold shoulder. I hoped Bobbye, driving behind us, didn't notice. I was sinking and freezing. The truck's heater was hardly putting out. Oh man, what had I gotten myself into?

And wouldn't you know, it was Moody's night off. Damn. I had to have a stimulus to prep me for the Dog. Booze? No, that was his thing. I'd feel weak and dirty. Besides, to this day I've never felt of drinking-age entering a bar. Probably all those fake I.D. moments of high school and college coming back to haunt me.

We found a greasy spoon just over the Connecticut line and we ordered scallops. I somehow hate tartar sauce even though it tastes pretty good. Maybe it's because all you can taste is the sauce, and only feel the crunch and chew of whatever it's on. Same for ketchup on fries. An insult to a good potato. Salt man, that's all- Mr. Potato needs. But that night the shaker was damp, and I got near violent shaking the darned thing. So, I unscrewed the cap and that really screwed things up spewing sticky salt all over the place.

Ignoring my flailing around with my runaway saltshaker, Bobbye looked at me asking. "You ready?"

After all this, I somehow felt I was.

As I drove towards Ledge Rock with the window stuck, Bobbye following in the bug, I was getting colder and colder making me meaner and meaner. I was building up one miserable temper. I was getting it up on high burner but-good that night.

When we got to town hall, there were plenty of cars outside, a good crowd, and I saw one with a New London Day card on the down-turned visor. It looked like Merriweather was helping.

I wedged old gal in between a fat aged Buick with rusted holes down the sides of the hood, which were supposed to be the answer to most things chic in the fifties. On the other side was a '48 Hudson Hornet, one of the ugliest cars America managed to produce between the Chrysler *Airflow* and the klottsey-to-be *Edsel* Ford barge. I was a little anxious for old gal's honor between the likes of those two. Bobbye found a spot just down from the Hudson.

Coming together, hand in hand, we walked across the uneven gravel to the curb and the beginning of the tall stairway-to-nowhere. After that long climb up those stairs, we stood for a moment in front of a half open door and were told our meeting was back down in one of the cellar crypts; so down, down, we went where we had just come up a moment before. That kind of exercise tweaked me that it was a tad bizarre that in this town nothing seemed to go on for real above ground. Which probably fits.

As we moved again down the stairs, Bobbye took a moment to properly focus my attention. "Remember what the goal is," she said, eyeing me hard, those big brown, green-flecked beauties of hers zeroing in on me. "We have land we need to build on. We have limited money and now no jobs. Win this war, Kenny, not some crazy fistfight battle with Madlock that could get us into bigger trouble and kill our chances for real happiness here. Okay? Cross your heart, hope to die?"

"My goodness, darling, of course," I said kind of softly into her ear, "nothing like that ever entered my mind. Trust me, this Madlock character is as low rent as they come, and he presents himself to the world exactly as the dirtbag he is. Never fear, with you by my side, bright and gorgeous as you are, I will be the Officer and Gentleman the Marine Corps trained me to be. Semper fi, my love."

"I hope," she smiled, hipping me down the first row of chairs. Finding two metal folding ones together near the end, which we took and, sitting down, looked around the room.

There were a lot of anxious faces, some legal types going through paperwork, but also many others staring directly at me and Bobbye. Many of them had encouraging expressions, while others were showing question marks. Moody and Loraine smiled and nodded; Carl and Florence gave us little waves; a new friend, Henry Dryer, winked as did Merriweather. Ralph and his wife came through the big double doors in the rear of what had originally been a courtroom. They moved quickly to a couple of rows down from us with a cluster of folks who had come in with them. Just then another bunch pushed and shoved in kind of a praetorian guard surrounding Joey Gildea and his wife. Bobbye counted twenty of those, and still the numbers were climbing. Finally, the Babonases found seats, large smiles on their faces along with a huge bag of popcorn they were passing around. Oh boy. It looked like a party was already underway.

The sound of mighty rap, rap, raps snapped our heads around to the dais up front. The gavel was in the hand of a short-disheveled gentleman whom I assumed to be Chairman Garvey. He was wearing a very bright, off-centered bow tie that even my color-blindness identified as not going with his plaid sports jacket. His ensemble came together as "Used-car-lot-chic."

They were all up there on a raised platform, sitting at a long table, below a locally concocted – NO SMOKING sign barely distinguishable through the room's smoke and haze. The year was 1963. Regulations pertaining to tobacco usage in public places were somewhat different from today. Nevertheless, the Zoning Board of the Townhall Executive Committee, in all its glory, was shortly to be in session.

Along with Garvey and his board members, on the dais was also the town's expert technical and legal advisor, James Harvey Madlock himself, complete with paper cup ... but no transistor radio. (Would he have the chutzpah to bring that thing in when the night-games started?) I would never know. As far as I was concerned, this would be my first and last stand before this august body.

Once things began and minor items were dealt with, I found myself unprepared for the incredible boredom delivered under the auspices of Old Business, i.e., -- sidewalk cracks and bird feeder ordinances. Motions raised and seconded. Madlock's boozing out of boredom suddenly seemed to make sense. And nothing changed when it finally came to New Business either. At least that was the case until I jumped to my feet. I had never been more ready for a fight. So far, the whole affair had become death by a thousand paperclips. My people must be tiring as well. I had to get my butt into gear.

Then another audience member stood to present a grievance. Had they asked for them? Had I missed my turn to get to my feet or wave my hand or whatever the hell the process called for?

Before I knew it, this other guy stopped speaking. Bobbye stared at me. I looked behind me. Every person I had met in the town was now staring at me. All those people who had arrived earlier I'd hoped would rise to my defense were all staring at me. Shit... Everything suddenly slid into slow motion. Almost in a daze I finally stood and opened my mouth thinking, NOW, would be a good time to figure out what the hell I was going to say. So much time spent being angry and imagining showdowns without any actual thought as to what I was going to say during the event itself...

Now standing, and I believe looking as mean, hard and as tall as I could get. Yes, I was doing my theatrically threatening-best without even having gotten permission from the Chairman to rise or speak. I was in the middle of the aisle with both arms up and waving them high above my head as if I was going after a swarm of mosquitos or bats maybe.

After Garvey had finished banging his gavel again at the microphone, he looked at me in a way that indicated, with any luck, I was going to get to speak. However, Madlock saw this, figured out my plan, and tried one of his fish-eyed oily smiles with a head nod, hoping it would be enough to somehow shut me up. But I wasn't buying any of that. Though still in my partial fog, I just stood and sneered hard at him which seemed to make him look as pale as the belly of a catfish.

Madlock let his left-hand ease over and tug at Garvey's sleeve, getting his attention and getting his eyes to follow the nod of Madlock's head in my direction. Garvey tried to bluff it by asking the assembled if there was any additional old business to be brought up before he moved things into closed executive session for the remainder of the evening!

Damn, it seemed those two had half-ass clowns had worked on their performance to cut things short before the opening gavel had even come down.

I shot my hands up again and let out loud and clear, "Mr. Chairman, yes there is!"

The Marine Corp had taught me one thing if nothing else --how to make noise. In bootcamp with Master Sergeants in my face, finding every possible flaw in me and shouting it out for the entire squad to hear. Now it was my turn. "Mr. Chairman!" came out of my mouth again blowing away the fog that for a brief time had been resident there.

Everything stopped. Some of Ralph's popcorn emphasized the point as pieces of it fell onto the floor as my words roared out.

"I am here to talk about how things seem to get done in this town. My wife Bobbye and I are new here. We bought two acres from the Bausches up off Route One. We intend to add to Ledge Rock's tax base by building our own home on those two acres. The whole process has moved along as planned, expected and paid for until we went to Mr. Madlock's office asking for our building permit."

As I went on in detail about what was happening to us and how that could drive us out of this town, back up to Wakefield, near Boston. Then I added, "That is not what we want," and I went into my being a starving writer, but one quite capable of telling our story in articles as well as in book form, which we would hate to do because we already love this town and the many people here tonight who support us and who know of others who have also had needless problems getting their originally promised Building Permits from Mr. Madlock's office."

And with that naming of Madlock, I pointed my finger directly at the Mad Dog, who looked like he desperately wanted to dive under the long table up there or somehow just disappear.

For a moment I was silent, and then what happened next, and was unplanned, but was truly heartening. Ralph Babonas jumped to his feet and shouted, "Mr. Chairman. All that Ken McAdams has said is true and there are dozens of citizens here this evening who will stand up with him, to tell you they have had similar problems with that office too. So, citizens of Ledge Rock, those of you similarly affected, please stand up!"

And they did. By the tens and more they got to their feet, almost the entire gathering was, as one, up and waving their hands. It was overwhelming. And it totally broke up the meeting. No one at the long table could do anything but nod, first more like ducking, which then became head-nodding agreement. Still on their feet, they all marched over to Garvey at the rostrum continuing to nod their heads, having shaken Ralph's hand on the way, along with mine and Bobbye's, too. And most significantly, no one gave Madlock anything but their backsides.

As things settled down, the New London newspaper reporter came over to Bobbye and me and asked if he could get a few quotes for the next day's edition. We, of course, were delighted, but I have to say Bobbye took a hold of my arm and whispered in my ear, "Kenny, I'll handle this, you go outside with Madlock for our permit. Okay?"

After holding fast there with my darling's lips pressed to my ear, for once I did as she suggested, stepping back and away from her and then over to the near-forgotten Madlock, whose faced had drained of what little color it ever had as he nodded toward me in a sad-faced, bobble-headed fashion. Bobbye knew how I could run off at the mouth, so the last place she wanted me was on the loose with a media guy looking for a story.

Before I could utter a word, Madlock spoke up saying, "Mr. McAdams, I had tried to call you about your permit, but no one answered." (Perhaps because I didn't have a phone yet) "And this is something that we can discuss outside right now. No sense interrupting this meeting for something so trivial."

Which only brought the gavel back down behind us. Bang, bang, bang! And each impact seemed to hammer Madlock up, up, and out of his seat like the fits and jerks of a bumper jack ratcheting up an automobile's ass-end. I could see the blood drain out of Garvey's fingers as he gripped Madlock's arm and started pulling him away from me, and hopefully away from all the good folks now milling around them there.

"There will be a brief recess," Garvey announced, which kind of had folk wondering what was going on since there had been nothing happening between gavel bangs and now a recess anyway.

Madlock, pulling away from Garvey, was up and half-jogging across the stage toward the steps at the far end of the stage on which he nearly fell down, finally getting to where I was standing in the center aisle. He started tugging my arm saying, "Ah, yes, umm, Mr. McAdams, umm how good to see you tonight. Um, yes, won't you step outside for a moment?"

"No, Madlock, I'm staying right here and making a lot more noise until I get our damned building permit," I hissed, eyeing him hard and close.

Some of the folks around started to turn questioningly toward us. Fortunately, Bobbye was now talking with the reporter and was not there to shut me down if I followed my instinct to punch Madlock in the nose.

I will say that that clown seemed to pick up on the intensity of my attitude and nearly fell back again on the few stairs behind him. Finally, however, getting to my side and tugging my arm he blurted out, "Oh, oh, ah no need for any rough stuff Mr. McAdams. No, no need," his head banged off its neck-stops, left and right.

"I'm sorry to tell you, Mr. Madlock," I announced a decibel or two louder than his bleat, "my noise will continue until I have our rightful permit in my hand," which I waved straight in his face. "And don't forget the newspaper is here right now, tonight. As a matter of fact look over there," I nodded behind him and as he turned I said, "My wife is there talking with the New London reporter. I am sure she is telling him the full story of what you have put us through... which I'll bet will appear on the frontpage tomorrow."

"Ah, mmm, yes, I understand but please, come with me, outside," he mumbled, his green skin now sparkling with an added reptilian gloss. "We, ah, please, come out with me. Everything is, ah, has been umm, rectified. RECTIFIED, do you hear?" he emphasized leaning close to me, booze-breathing me big-time and trying to eye me out the door.

"Rectified?" I prodded.

"Rectified, yes, *Rectified!*" he returned, kind of huffing with spittle flying.

"If not, I'll be right back in here and raising all kinds of hell. Maybe I'll even talk to one of the radio networks about all this on top of the newspapers."

"Please, please no. I will make everything right for you; You will not be disappointed. Just come outside, into the parking lot.

By my car over there. The Buick," he indicated, pointing a bent index finger off into the darkness.

So, like the old country song goes, "It was on a Wednesday night, the moon was shining bright that they robbed the Danville train... " but in this case it wasn't the robbers Frank and Jessie James who pulled off this caper, it was Ken and Bobbye McAdams who were successful in finally winning the building permit from the incorrigible hands of Commissioner Madlock, assisted by Chairman Garvey. What a victory! What a glorious moment for us.

So, Madlock skulked back into his basement entry as our fans streamed out of the adjoining cellar door. Bobbye was waving our building permit, surrounded by a long list of our new and old Ledge Rock friends – the Moodys; Carl and Florence; Henry Dryer, Joey G., Mary Shandra, and her huge dog. We all shared hugs and handshakes and a sense of what was finally getting done for us and what might be ahead for us in Ledge Rock.

Moody invited everybody to his restaurant to open it for a libation in celebration. All readily agreed. Bobbye gave me a long kiss and then climbed into the bug. I put the key into Old Gal's ignition and took a moment to consider what we had pulled off. It felt good. It felt impossibly good. There was nothing that was going to stop us now. I turned the key and... nothing. Just the clicking of a dead battery. I got out of the truck and ran after Bobbye. Catching her and hopping into the passenger seat, a long line of cars behind us, she said, "Truck trouble?"

"Not tonight. Tonight, we celebrate!"

CHAPTER NINE
So, Where Is the Book?

I'd never believed in no news being good news. It leaves me stuck in the passive role. I'd rather try to control my own destiny. And the no news, when it came to the whereabouts of the manuscript of my Great American Novel, was hardly encouraging. That large, 800 typed pages (probably about 450 pages in book form) was lost. How could 800 sheets of paper neatly stacked in a heavy cardboard box, weighing many, many-pounds simply vanish? And to think how much time, how much grinding drudgery, with occasional moments of great joy, had gone into producing that lost package. It was all very depressing particularly because all this was long before computer-file storage and huge electronic memory banks existed. My only backup was a smudgy carbon copy on slippery onion skin.

Though Farrar & Straus had quite unexpectedly changed their minds on my book, (I won't go again into the whispered why's and where-fore's of that) but they were nice enough to send the original manuscript to a national First Novel contest on my behalf which then, somehow, led to the entire manuscript getting lost.

As I had said several times before, I talked to the Post Office again. No word. Nothing lying around. No further word from my benefactor, Marcus Aurelius Goodrich either. Of course, the book award contest's closing date was drawing near. It would be perhaps two more years before there'd be another such contest. Two years! Where would I be? What would I be doing in two years? I had to get into that contest!

I wrote to the publishers sponsoring the competition explaining my dilemma. I told them all I had of the book was a messy, smudged carbon copy that I promised to patch up if the original didn't appear in time. That was all I could do.

I hoped they would say yes. I hoped they'd just say not to worry since they planned to make me the winner anyway. Wouldn't that have been nice?

Back at Lynnfield High the end of the school year started gathering steam. At least I was feeling more comfortable as a teacher by then, but the homestretch toward exams was building its own load on my and Bobbye's shoulders. I was giving a lot of quizzes and essay assignments in an effort to precondition my kids for the kind of final they could expect from me. This meant a terrific load of work every evening. There were the usual preparations for the next day's classes, but now there were added quiz corrections and finally reading and evaluating 90 or more essays on top of everything else.

CHAPTER NINE: SO, WHERE IS THE BOOK? • 109

Bobbye and I had been used to going to bed around 10:00 PM. Those days were over. A lot of one-o'clock's and two-o'clock's in the morning were taking command. And I am an eight-hour guy. If I get less than that I usually end up with a cold. So, I got a cold. And all this was on top of working on my second novel.

With the weekend upon us, I figured to use Saturday morning to rebuild the front end of the truck prepping for its next inspection. Though a pre-WWII pickup, Old Gal was a Ford. With anything really old, if it's a Ford, parts-wise it's okay. Sears and others stocked everything. So, I just pulled up to the nearest auto supply place and picked up the kingpins, bushings, bearings, and tie-rod ends I needed. Beautiful. I figured a couple of hours should give me a tight front end and an inspection sign-off as soon as we could drive down to Ledge Rock again.

Actually, no. Somehow there is something about me and machinery being on different pages. I love machinery, but I'm not so sure it loves me in return. Or does it just tease and string me along? I'm not sure, and to think Bobbye and I were committing to build an entire house on our own.

Years before, in high school, I'd bought a 1932 Model B, V-8 Ford. It was a 5-window coupe, a model much sought after today. I paid $25 to an MIT freshman for it. He didn't know what a gem he was letting go. Of course, at age 15, I wasn't the sharpest wrench in the toolbox either and restoring this car became quite a lesson in all areas of mechanics and machinery for me. Could it have been a dark prelude to our house building to come?

The "Hot engine" I thought was under the hood was merely one without exhaust pipes or mufflers. Sounded great anyway.

Fortunately, the chassis was sound and the fenders okay, though the doors were rotted out, and there were holes in the floor. But I was only 15, too young to get a driver's license, with three older brothers all who had licenses and cars too. Bad. But I took that year until my 16th birthday to work on rebuilding the car.

First, I redid the interior. I did it all in Naugahyde -- the inside of the doors, the dash, and the overhead liner. I found some newer seats in a junkyard, along with a couple of better doors and placed all the above in their appropriate positions.

I let the exterior remain untouched. Once I had the mechanical and control items rebuilt, I'd prep the beauty, then let others do the painting.. Those decisions then moved me to focus on the engine. It was not hot. As a matter of fact, it was shot, and I discovered it was one of the first Ford V-8, which meant the main bearings and piston rod bearings were poured-babbitt, not inserts. Having no way to create such things for myself, I was dead in the water. I returned to the supply shop, Grant Ring and Bearing Co. in Cambridge, where I explained my problem, threw myself on their kindness and mercy, and gaining a newly rebuild V-8 flat head engine at an incredibly cheap price. Dear people. A friend from high school, Donny Christianson, drove that beauty at the Sanford, Maine National Drag championships and won the division title, besting a '57 Chevy doing it. Wow again.

But the front end work on my new/old pickup was still to be done. My two-hour estimate immediately went to hell and beyond. Banging out the old heat-swollen and rusted pins didn't come easily. As a matter of fact, it took closer to two days. I banged with a sledge, heated the seats with a torch, slammed and hammered every which way I could, all the while cramped under the front end until, finally, I had to detach both the danged fenders, giving me more room to bang away and finally pop the pins, freeing the wheel units to take the replacements.

All of which should have given me advanced word on how the Good Old Gal and I would get along together over the long haul. Nothing is more discouraging than having to go through so many steps to get something done that looked so easy. But isn't most of life that way? To accomplish B you must start at A. Where Old Gal's front end was our first complication on our emotional purchase, the most frightening reality was that until Bobbye and I got to the C's of our house building, we would have to struggle through the hard work defined as the A's and B's of car care.

Having to do that necessary pickup truck repair, we hadn't been able to make a move toward Ledge Rock over the weekend. We did call Ralph Babonas though, telling him he could roll out his digger. He was delighted to know that Madlock had really been squashed. He said Wednesday would now be his day for digging. I promised I would be there too.

When Wednesday rolled around, my last class was a study hall that Bobbye volunteered to cover. That got me on the road early that afternoon and when I pulled into the inspection area of the Connecticut Department of Motor Vehicles facility, Old Gal just breezed through the whole process like the queen she was. And the inspector even asked if I'd consider selling him the truck.

As I pulled up to our property, I saw Ralph's backhoe kind of hunkered down with what looked like one of its hydraulic stabilizer legs collapsed. Clearly it was out of action, but down in the growing excavation was a bulldozer Ralph must have brought in to make up for his broken hoe equipment. That was going to cost some bucks, but he said, "Ken, I gave you my price before. That's it. I'm supposed to know the country around here and how much of a job I can handle with my equipment. If I screw that up, like not figuring these huge boulders a foot or two below the surface, then that's my problem not yours. So, the bulldozer comes out of my pocket, not yours."

This was Ralph's second day on the job. He had anticipated finishing the whole excavation in just one day. And now his own machine needed fixing, i.e. time, parts, and money, since he was now having to pay for the dozer, the driver and the extra time. After he told me the costs were his, not mine, he laughed saying, "All this gives you an idea what a lousy businessman I am. But... my work is the best."

My mouth just hung open. I didn't know what to say. After dealing with the likes of Madlock, I felt I was being confronted by a saint. My eyes started to tear, and I covered that up by just reaching out and hugging the guy. It all made me think of the Michener movie, The Bridge at Toko-Ri, when Fredrick March, as the flotilla commander, watches his squadron ace escape from a crash-landing in the sea and asks himself, "Where do we get such men?" Well, that's what I asked myself about Ralph Babonas. I guess it was then that I knew Ralph was a friend I never wanted to lose.

That night, still by the excavation, my task was to direct Ralph's big flashlight onto the hydraulic fittings he was trying to braze back onto the backhoe's stabilizer. If he didn't get it done that night, it turned out, he'd default on his contract with the Borough. It would cost him an entire year's pay. But he was so cool about it. I would have been half nuts in his situation, and yet he just kept brazing, puffing on his cigarette drooping from the corner of his mouth, working along, and joking all the time. What a tough, good man.

CHAPTER NINE: SO, WHERE IS THE BOOK?

Having gotten back after midnight Thursday night, once the backhoe's leg was working again, Bobbye and I were up bright and early for Friday classes. That afternoon we loaded our stuff for the trip back down to Ledge Rock, then chatted with our border-collie, MacIntosh, advising him to remain on our front porch and guard the house until we got back after dark. There were no leash laws in those days.

As ever, MacIntosh nodded and blinked his understanding of his assignment, then off we went. We were headed into Boston to the knocked-down brick brownstones of Back Bay, where the huge Prudential Center would be going up. We'd heard that the construction foreman in charge of the demolition would let us, for a tip or two, have some of the old brick for our fireplace, hearth, interior living room wall and exterior chimney. To buy the thousands of bricks our project would require, carried a price we could not afford. At the demolition site in Brighton, word was that just a few bucks to the men would make it all possible.

Our idea for the exterior of our single-floor ranch house was redwood clapboard siding, set off by the two-thirds of the side wall with the brick chimney running up from ground level all the way through the roof's overhang, on up to and above the roof's peak.

Years before, during summers in high school and college, I had been a mason's assistant and had picked up some ability laying brick. I believed I could pull this off, as long as we found the right, weathered, old exterior stuff. And, as the half-assed Proper Bostonian I was, I could not conceive of looking around Ledge Rock for such brick. I had to find it in Boston to bring down with me for the job, bringing a part of the old sod with me to this new part of the world Bobbye and I would be living in.

So, we drove into Boston. We went over to the wasteland that had once been blocks of proud brownstones off Huntington Avenue, soon to start rebuilding and rising from that rubble to become the gleaming glistening Prudential Center, years down the road. Even then, during the height of the demolition, we discovered the area was not entirely empty and homeless. Driving our old truck up and down the borderless streets, piles of rubble everywhere, as we neared the end of one soon to be gone street, and saw two very old people sitting by the edge of the rubble. The woman was in a rocker, the man struggling for a feeble dignity in a straight-backed dining room chair. On the sidewalk between them was a round kitchen table with a red and white tablecloth over it. On that was some bread and two standing brown paper bags. The round base of the table had two chunks of plaster wedged under to keep it level. The old lady's rocker and old man's chair were drawn up to the table as best they could be. Behind, and beside them, stretched a small train of tattered possessions – boxes, a trunk, two lamps, parts of an iron bed, a worn easy chair and a footrest missing one leg.

These forgotten people and their few possessions were stage-front. The backdrop was the apocalyptic outline of the inside rear walls of their nearly demolished brownstone. There was only a remembrance of sidewalls. No roof, but it did have half of two floors; two half ceilings, the outline of where stairs had once been; a lonely toilet standing squat sentinel on its half of the second floor; and a first-floor icebox with its small upper doors and their sturdy hinges like eyes peering blindly off at the scene of "progress" everywhere around the sadly displaced couple... who it seemed now had nowhere to go or to live.

The lady was gray. Her hair, her kerchief, her face. The man was dust-covered, ghostly white – hair, face, his old-fashioned collarless shirt. The worn threadbare suit and torn coat he wore were black. He tried to sit erect, grasping for dignity by their gutter-side, ruined home, made black comedy. His eyes seemed to be looking beyond hers, but they both shared the same silence, tears running down their cheeks.

When we slowly rolled up by them, we saw that the tableau was complete. Between them, framed by their aged faces was the empty rear door frame where the back wall of their house had once been. And through its stark framing lay nothing but flattened rubble, dead city blocks long denied people, long left only to the wind, the rain and the rats.

Theirs must have been the last house to go. Perhaps they hadn't believed it would ever happen, that this day would never actually come. Now that it had, where would they go? Bobbye and I didn't know. We doubted they did either.

We pulled up beside them. Bobbye had her window down and reached for her purse. Rustling around in it with her left hand, she came up with what cash she had there.

"We've got to help these people," she said, not bothering to count the bills in her hand.

"I've got to hold some for the foreman. For the bricks. I don't have a lot," I said, feeling inadequate as hell, facing the fact that we were practically out of dollars ourselves and, on top of that, we had signed up for big bucks to build our own house in Ledge Rock.

"No matter," Bobbye said, her big brown eyes looking almost pleadingly at me, "what little we have is far more than these poor people have. Ken, we've got to help them."

She was right in more ways than she was paying attention to. Her commitment and plea prodded a thought I'd heard in church when they were raising money for the poor at Thanksgiving and

Christmas time. Somebody said, "If what you give doesn't hurt, you aren't really giving what you can."

Stopping, foot still on the brake, I pulled what I had out of my pocket, set aside two twenties, and then handed what was left to Bobbye. She smiled one of her super sweet smiles, adding a nod, then she turned to the sad couple, reached her hand with our bills in it and said only, "Please."

The old man's eyes opened wide, his brows popped up and the slightest smile nibbled the corners of his mouth. He reached out with both hands and took Bobbye's into his... and his tears didn't stop nor did his wife's as he opened his hands for her to see what was there.

Then, moving away and going slowly down what remained of the street, we saw bricks everywhere and loads of workmen crawling over them, many with brick hammers in hand chipping the mortar away. It was like newsreels of flattened Berlin at the end of the war.

Scanning around the area, I was looking for somebody acting boss-like. We needed a foreman-type who we could ask about working some kind of deal on the bricks. We needed several thousand, mortar attached or not, just whatever was available.

Loads of workmen were crawling over the piles of bricks like ants. But each pile of mortar-chippers seemed to be working in association with individual dump trucks. Each truck had company names painted on its doors... which gave me an idea.

"Bobbye, I worked summers for a construction company near here. I'm thinking I might be able to borrow one of their trucks on a weekend to pick up a mess of these bricks to run down to Ledge Rock."

"You think you really could?"

As she asked, I spotted a big Harley-biker looking guy who was striding around each group and talking briefly with one or two of the chippers. I could see what looked to be bills passing between him and the chippers as they shook hands. Yes, that was the boss-type I needed. I eased Old Gal over to the curb. Bobbye and I tumbled out and shuffled over to this guy for a chat.

"Hello, sir. Hey, you look like a Marine. Am I right?" I threw at him with a smile.

"Ya, why you ask?"

"I flew A-4's in the Pacific. Blacksheep squadron, VMA-214. Semper fi," I added with my handshake which he returned half-crushing my smaller hand.

"I was in 'Nam. Perimeter at Danang. VMF-232 was there then. I heard the Sheeps was due-in after we left. So, brother, call me Sarge and tell me what I can do for ya?"

"I need bricks and I'm Ken. This is my wife, Rob," I said, first glancing toward her but, when she smiled, I watched his attention to her become much closer. Thank you, Bobbye, beautiful lady.

"We are building a house down in Connecticut. I used to lay brick summers. I figure we'll need somewhere around three, maybe four thousand. Exterior. No interiors. I'll lay them for a wide fireplace, hearth, and exterior chimney. I figure to use a Heatilator fireplace unit, brick-faced blending in with how the whole living room wall is done, in what you can let me have here."

"Sounds like you know what you're doing," he nodded.

"Sometimes yes, other times no. But what kind of deal can I make for what you got?"

"You're talkin' three, four thousand?"

"Right."

"Your old pickup can't haul anything like that," Sarge said with a toss of his head in Old Gal's direction.

"I expect I can get a six-by dumper from the people I used to work for."

"What kind of help you got? My people are all contracted to the city."

"I'll have four young bucks plus myself. I could roll in next Friday afternoon. Around three-thirty. What do you think that will cost me?"

"This stuff all has to be hauled away. You want to come in to help, that's good. Saves the city a few bucks. That's what's going on with all these trucks around here," he said with a circular wave. "But I decide who gets what and when."

"How about I give you two twenties now to hold me a slot for Friday. Then I'll give you five more when I come in with my dump truck?"

"Sounds good," he said as he put his hand out for the two twenties and a shake. I braced myself for another hand-crushing, but he had mercy on me this time. And we had a deal. Then, with a wave of his other hand, one of his guys trotted over and the big guy moved to another petitioner.

Sarge's subaltern moved in taking his place. This guy was also big, very hairy and had a black Toscani cheroot in the corner of his mouth. Most of his attention seemed to be on Bobbye, until I reached out for his arm turning him more towards me.

"Hey wallio, whadayah think you do?" he barked, pulling his arm away and waving both hands like somebody walking down a hallway of cobwebs.

"Hey, hey, paesano, whadayoudo?" he repeated edging closer and getting a bit in my face.

Without Sarge there to keep us gently apart, I had to talk softly while carrying no stick at all. The future of our house project depended on putting all this together without any bumps in the road. I'd have to get the dump truck from my old construction company friends and lock-in entry here for the bricks. I'd need this guy.

"So, Sarge cleared me and my truck for Friday to pick up about 4,000 bricks. You'll be here? I'll have an envelope for Sarge and a couple of ten's for you. Okay?"

"Wha' do ya do? Construction?"

"No, I'm a schoolteacher. A few of my kids will be with me to help load."

"School teach, huh?" he said, "My son's a teach. He does the social studies up ta Lynn."

Bingo.

"Hey, that's something. Social studies. Me too, but I'm over in Lynnfield," I added with an Alfred E. Neuman grin.

"My boy's name is Dominique. Siciliani."

"You folks aren't from Newton, are you? I went to high school there with some Sicilianis."

"No, Lynn again, but I know the one's yuz mean. Football, ya?"

"That's it. Early fifties."

"The same. Cousins. So, what can I do for ya, Teach?"

"That's funny. My kids at the high school call me that. Teach. But, hey, call me Ken. And you are?"

"Dom, Dominique. Same as my boy."

"So, Sarge set it up that me and my boys will roll in with a six-by dumper that can carry maybe ten tons. That will be Friday afternoon. We'll load maybe 4,000 bricks. Old, with mortar still on them, or new, no problem. Whatever shape isn't important," I said.

"No sweat. I'll be right around heh Friday," Dom nodded. "If I'm not, ask over ta the shed there. They keep track a me. So, till then. Ciao."

CHAPTER TEN
On the road

For our next run, we changed our routing down to Ledge Rock. The long, bland stretch of Route 128 around Boston was bad enough, but the scrub pine, junkyard straight nothing expanse down Attleboro, Taunton way, and then the horror of Providence was just too much. Besides, neither old Gal nor the VW were exactly Ferraris, so why not travel scenically? We worked that out on old farm road routes that were great. It made us feel we were getting further and further from squashed suburbia than we really were. Plus, there was little traffic. It was what hardly exists anymore, a pleasant drive in the open country.

On my previous DMV registry run, I'd found a neat food stand along the way. Great French fries, real ones, not the mushy cardboard frozen variety, and great fried clams. Of course, I didn't know what a fried clam stand was doing in the middle of truck farming country. I probably should have given it more thought, but the food seemed good. I pointed it out to Rob as we rattled by heading south. We agreed to stop for a bite on the way back the next day.

Arriving at our future place, Bobbye was impressed when she saw the hole in the ground that would one day be filled with the foundation of our Cloudcuckooland castle. Though we had bought the land, paid for it with both a check and a checkup on the local politicos, even paid for all the parts and bits of wood, asphalt shingles and glass that would someday, someway be that house, compelling Bobbye to say, "Oh, Kenny, just standing on the edge of the excavation, seeing a real hole in the ground like this, with these high mounds of dirt all around the edges... it's the first tangible confirmation that we really are going to do this. In a way it is frightening. And since we're both a little foggy on how to actually build a house, I get the feeling we should apologize to the forest for the unholy mess we're making smack in its middle. It's as if we are becoming acne on the face of nature. Yes, I hoped that our hard work would turn it all into an enhancing beauty mark, but houses built are like books written -- somebody does them, but to do either, we're asking a lot."

I had to admit, oh man, it was a big hole. And it's all my fault. I started to get uncomfortable that someone might drive up and see it and report me for tampering with Mother Nature. We'd have to stand widely together in front of it to try to hide the damage done.

Then Babonas dropped by and looked with pride at his work.

"Some nice hole," he offered in the local dialect.

"Absolutely," I answered in turn.

Ralph seemed mildly amused by my small level of embarrassment.

Then Moody came over to stare into it, then Carl with Florence, too. Everybody remarked on the hole and how nice a job Ralph had done.

Then he broke some bad news. Gildea, who was supposed to be doing the foundation, was missing. Ralph hadn't been able to reach him all week, and now his wife wasn't home either. It was the end of April. The materials were going to be dumped here in mid-June. We had a seven-man crew lined up to help get the main structure going the day of delivery. Joey had to get the foundation in with at least a week to cure. Roughly two weeks total, which gave us only days to play around with. Oh lord. And this on top of my wandering manuscript with its June deadline making me feel as if June would mark the end of the world for us, or worse.

Florence somehow sensed my anxieties and suggested we join them at an auction. She told us that whenever she felt low, she went to auctions. They were medicinal, she said.

"Well," Bobbye smiled, "for us to feel better, we just cut a few more trees. And now we've got to lay out the final course of the drive with Ralph before we go anywhere. The auction can be our reward for getting that done."

"Sounds like a plan," I threw in and we started walking the layout of what someday would be our driveway.

Though this particular auction didn't turn out to be much, we did see the possibilities for getting an awful lot of things, cheap stuff we'd need once we were finally installed in what we built.

So, other than telephoning back to Watertown and lining up Taverna's truck they'd let me use to haul the bricks, we found ourselves pretty much at a standstill till school was out. This all made us feel blah and vaguely depressed. On the way home from our look at the foundation hole, a stop at the clam bar seemed a good idea for picking up our spirits. Well, you know how it goes. By the time we reached Walnut Street, Bobbye was vomiting all over the place. Since I'd shared the same clams and felt fine, I carefully explained to her that it was all in her mind. She heard me out... then threw up on my foot.

Monday morning, I was advised that my teaching job was to run out a week sooner than anticipated, but with no cut in pay. The assistant principal called me in to explain that the teacher I had been subbing for would be back early from Cambodia. It was suggested I prepare and administer the final exams in advance on the materials she had covered first semester, and on mine this last. Though there would still be a week or so till the end of regular classes before summer vacation. Everyone agreed that she could best use that situation to tell the classes of her far Eastern experiences. This way they'd finish the required year with me, free of any last-minute teacher change just before finals.

I was delighted. This was going to give me an extra week before Bobbye finished. Not only were there house odds-and-ends I could do in that time, but the second novel's manuscript was just about put together to run down to New York with it.

That night I got a letter off to John Farrar asking for an appointment. I carefully explained once again who I was – the author of the first book which Marcus Goodrich had presented to him; as well as my hope that he would take a look at this early production second manuscript. I tried to make clear my current difficulties and that he would be seeing only a first draft of that next novel. One which I had some hope for, and I hoped he would feel the same.

Tuesday, amazingly enough, some other good news came at last. The Post Office called. They believed book number one's manuscript of *Grand Deceptions*, smashed and battered, had finally limped into their hands. Imagine that for efficiency. A scant year and three or four months after first submitting the thing, I was finally getting it back, to submit to another publisher. The luck of the Irish, don't they say? With luck like that no wonder the Irish spent four or five hundred years under the English boot.

Frankly, at this point, I turned coward. With so many struggles edging toward their climax I didn't have the guts to reread the book, much less try to do anything about the inadequacies it might have. I just dashed to the Post Office, grabbed it up, rushed home, typed another cover page, repacked it, and blasted it back off to the First Novel Contest as recommended by John Farrar. If it had merit it would be recognized. If it didn't, at that late date, there wasn't a damned thing I could do about it. Certainly, this was a hell of a way to enter a competition that could define the course of my entire life, but I had no alternative. In the Post Office, before I shoved it over the counter to the character with the rubber stamp, I paused at the addressing table, put the package down in front of me, and mumbled a small prayer. Let God do with it what He would. I had worked hard writing it, that was all I could do, nothing more now.

I'd already paid a terrible price just trying to get it back to submit via Farrar & Straus. If hardship and misery were points in literary contests, I asked God to whisper mine into the ear of whoever would read it. And if nothing came of it competitively, I begged the good Lord to at least take a personal interest in getting the damned thing back to me quickly, safe and sound.

Then, with a swoosh I slid it across the brass countertop to the mail clerk. From my hand to his. What would happen to it this time? I turned away and half ran out the door. I had too much to do to worry anymore about that.

That evening I made my second call to Pete Taverna about using one of his trucks to haul our stash of bricks down to Connecticut. Pete was one of the Taverna Bros. Construction Co.'s second generation. The original Bros., Pete's father Patsy and his uncle Carmen, or *Carmenuche* as he was known on the job, had put together a light construction outfit that their four sons were carefully groomed to take over and run when the time came.

Dom, the oldest, was sent to Northeastern University for the engineering degree. Frank or Fronggi, who busted his ass double time was the second son, the mason. Pete, number three, a really sharp guy who looked a natural for a general manager. And finally, Paulie, the baby, the youngest tagged with the same tail-end slot as I had in my own lineup of brothers, had been the volatile, explosively frustrated youngster who had needed the flashy car, leather jacket, the D.A. for his own piece of recognition. Which made me think of my motorcycles and leathers too.

One of my own brothers, Randy and I worked for these two generations of Tavernas a few summers. Mixing mortar, carrying block, digging, and more digging then, would you believe, originally running a jackhammer, starting at age thirteen, which was more than half-way running me, but making me feel for all the world like the toughest, meanest young dude around.

My first full time job in life commenced under Taverna tutelage at, yes, the tender age of barely 14 years. I don't know if you see too many 14-year-olds running jackhammers nowadays, but if you do, you know you are looking at a kid full of pride and satisfaction. Those were tough, mean, cement-poisoning summers, but down the road they were coming in handy, beyond whatever money I was being paid. The most important payoff was these dozen years later, being able to go to Pete and ask to borrow one of their big dump trucks for an evening.

I had fed the bricks and mortar to Frankie for a couple of years and hopefully I'd absorbed enough to tackle that fireplace and chimney on my own. Watching Pete, I'd learned to build beauty into the work, and from Paul I'd learned that you had to be mad, pissed-off, enough to push yourself all the way to the end of a job once begun, to show the others, and perhaps yourself, that "the Kid" could do it all too.

But what was really a knife in the gut at that moment and what made me feel like an unbounded bastard for pushing so hard for that truck with good Pete, was his father's rapidly approaching death from cancer throughout the time I was bothering him for this kindness. Nevertheless, through it all, the great sorrow of his father on one side and hungry me on the other, Pete took care of me, the kid from years back. He fixed the truck deal and like Babonas, at his own expense, made our house in the woods come that much closer to realization. What a good man. How many of them are left?

Even though I would have six wheels under a four-yard box, I was still short of manpower. This is where my final solution to the classroom clowning of my 9-G lowest echelon "students" came in. These General Class lads could not believe it, could not believe that I, the *Teach* was real when I rolled them into a tough Watertown construction yard that Friday afternoon and piled them up into the box of a huge working dump-truck. For them my hotrod stories had been something, and bike stuff too, but now they were experiencing the steel and shining reality of clattering, bouncing, and banging down the highway to... they had no idea where. But they didn't care. I could see on their faces, their hard gut and muscle joy of riding this big truck to hell and back, if it came to that.

Oh man, did they ever revel in it all. Roaring down the streets of Cambridge toward Roxbury standing in the back, two sheets of steel away from me in the cab which tended to dilute my control and command. It was all pretty humorous anyway, no matter what the board of education might think. They were shouting at what they called "Harvard weenies" and "Radcliff broads." Ah hell, I wasn't a regular teacher anyway, just like I hadn't signed on to be a regular Marine. Regulars everywhere can become pretty dull.

So, much hooting and hollering later, we arrived at the Prudential site. It took a lot of lumbering up and down the devastated streets to find Dom Siciliani. When we did, and he had led us over to an out of the way brick heap, I slipped him five twenties which disappeared so quickly I wasn't sure I'd really given them to him. I guess I was playing the game right. I don't know. But he pointed to the pile of mortar-covered bricks and the caved-in basements nearby and said, "Anyting youz want around heh, from that pile theh to theh, it's okay. I gotta go." And off he went.

Like a coach, I grouped my lads around in a circle to make clear what we had to do. Throw the bricks into the truck. What kind of bricks? The cleanest with least chips, definitely whole. How many? About 3,500. I added that I didn't want any of the lads disappearing or we might never get back to Lynnfield together again, which would really screw up the ball game. I explained that we could probably flip the bricks from the closest pile directly up onto the truck, but as we moved farther away, we'd either have to fire-brigade-them, or individually carry bundles over to the truck.

As in my military days I asked if there were any questions? There were none, so I barked, "Let's get to work. Move out!"

This was answered in two ways. Four of the guys let out a gung-ho series of shouts, obscenities, and admonitions to "get the friggin' job done," while two of the others instantly disappeared. It figured. If I had directed everybody to make himself scarce, these two clowns would have remained defiantly immobile staring me down as the rest whooped off into the ruins. So, I decided not to worry about them for the moment and got to work.

The first problem encountered was the enormous enthusiasm the lads had for throwing the bricks directly into, or at, the truck. In the beginning they performed legitimately, keeping a fairly careful count of how many they had tossed, and I periodically added their numbers to my own tally. But then things began to deteriorate. They started racing each other, which led to sloppy tosses, which led to bricks falling short or banging against the side of the truck. I ran around like an artillery commander whose rounds were falling short, shouting, waving my arms, and kicking the troops in the butt.

The count mounted rapidly, but so did the depletion of the nearby pile. At first, we started to pick more carefully over some of the dirtier brick we'd first discarded. This kept us on the first pile for a while, but in time we were forced to the next. By then we had about 1200 bricks in the truck. It had only taken a half hour or so. Working from the farther piles, we finally ended up just stumbling over the rubble to and from the truck. The truck, however, seemed to prefer this to the other method. Fewer lumps and bumps.

It didn't take long for morale to start fading. Since the boys were all furious smokers back in the johns at school anyway, old Teach called a butt-break to try and ease the growing aches and pains. This brought the two wanderers back to join the others to watch while I went ahead hauling armful's as best I could. A dirty and awkward task.

Then one of my lead chaps, one of those who had wandered off shouted, "Hey Teach, you looked down into that cellar? Through the door there?" he said, waving a cigarette in the direction of one of the broken-hinged cellar doors he'd come out of.

Having equipped each of my troops with quarts of cool water, which I had drunk a lot of en-route myself, the idea of the dark cellar looked to be an excellent place for a young social studies teacher to cool off a bit. Naturally, standing waiting for my eyes to adjust to the dimness the same character's voice rumbled from the darkness deeper in the cellar, "Okay, buddy, whadaya think you're up to?"

Though it was the standard trans-American police salutation, the voice didn't have the gravelly pitch the Sarge had laid on me when we first talked brick-piles and dollars. Nevertheless, when caught stumbling around in a dark strange place, and as teacher-in-charge, so to speak, I was at some disadvantage. It could have been "Sarge" talking and preparing to clobber me for going where I should not have gone. I figured I had to at least come on with some degree of cool, so I managed to mumble what I thought was an appropriate reply, "Just looking for the pot at the end of the rainbow." Which earned me two long guffaws and one "Ain't-he-too much?"

And yes, it was this same lost legionnaire who had surfaced and tried to sound like a cop. So, I followed his invitation to come see what he'd found. Again, stumbling and tripping over the debris, pipes, and assorted trash strewn everywhere in the half-lit cellar, I followed.

Son-of-a-gun, my bully boy really had come through. With the extrasensory perception of a true break-and-entry type, he'd found an absolutely gorgeous cache of ancient bricks. At the far end of the basement, barely visible from a faint trickle of light through the half-blocked remains of a window, evenly stacked on straw, row after row, stood somewhere around 5 or 600 of the most beautiful old colonial bricks I have ever seen. Unbelievable. I was there for old bricks. I'd briefed these guys long before that I was going to work them for their school screwups, rather than just give them the usual dose of double detentions after school they usually earned. So, like putting out a contract to the Mafia, these guys got right down to it, coming up with a cellar full of long forgotten, absolutely authentic, 200-year-old collection of gorgeous hand-forged bricks.

We took some of these out into the light. They were longer, flatter, wider than the others we'd seen around. Very dense. Very heavy, with deep varying shades of finely fired clay. The sides bore the marks of the wooden molds they'd been pressed and formed in. And on many, the faint thumb and fingerprints of the workman who had lifted them from the molds to be fired were still there, heat-blasted into posterity. The more we looked, the more fascinated and excited I became.

Things of beauty -- their colors seemed to have been varied by the time or intensity of their exposure in the kiln. Some had material imperfections causing magnificent eruptions, lava like black on a face or side bulging warping the brick. Good Lord, they were beautiful. So heavy and slick smooth as if they hadn't been trod on or rained on or maybe even hand-polished for centuries. Holding a couple in my hands I felt like I was in touch with Paul Revere or the War of 1812 or bits and pieces of the Under-Ground Railway. Exciting as hell. And just stacked there on that dirt floor with each layer separated by the dried, half-to-dust straw of how many centuries? For sure now, our new little pioneer house would have history binding it, keeping a tiny part of old Boston still alive there in Ledge Rock. I felt like I'd end up on the cover of the National Historical Society Magazine or something.

Of course, having that damned high intensity of Puritan conscience always gnawing at the base of my skull, I trudged around till I found good Dom to ask if I could load any and all the bricks we had found in the cellars by our piles too? He answered with the traditional—"Who gives a shit?"

I thanked him warmly, handing him an additional ten spot which caused a smile, a quick flip into his shirt pocket and his, "You must be nuts," comment.

What the hell? Then I strode back to the guys, and we hand-carried those original continental babies to a place of honor, stacking them carefully in the front part of the dump box. Beautiful.

The rest of the loading was anticlimactic, just there-they-were and up-they-went. In an additional hour we were done.

If the lads had been older, I would have bought them all a round or two of beers someplace, not that they hadn't had their share on their own at times, but I didn't feel the school board would have smiled on such liberalism. So, we dropped by one of those great old wooden diners and loaded up on burgers, fries, and cokes. They enjoyed it. I did too, to say nothing of how grateful I was for their sleuthing. They truly were proud as hell and went on to volunteer for me the best places to steal lumber, who fenced the power equipment I might need, and along as usual such general-purpose advice on the best way to strip a car. I said thanks but no thanks, feeling liable enough for the day as it was. I did, however, pay them four hours each at an exorbitant rate for their time.

We got back to Taverna's yard around 6:00 or 6:30. Bobbye met us there then ran the lads back to Lynnfield. As she pulled away with the boys all aboard, I called out to them as they started from Taverna's, "Goodbye lads, study hard over the weekend. I'll see you Monday, bright and early."

They answered with affectionate raspberries, marginally rude gestures, and a regular wave or two.

Then, after climbing up into the cab of the big truck, I roared away to play tough-night-riding teamster on down to Connecticut. I had to get there, dump the load, and get the truck back in time for Pete's boys to use it that next morning. Man, I felt good in the chilly spring night air, hitting the highway alongside all the roaring big rigs heading south. Goddamn.

There's something about the night highway. It's the pro's road. The big semi's flashing their lights to the rig behind that the road is clear ahead. The dimming to the opposite-bounds and the nod given their successor's trailer pulling clear ahead. The convoys, the hell-for-leather competition. Thirteen or more gears forward with double-stage superchargers. Watch the RPM's man, keep your eye checking the manifold pressure; you're sitting right on top of it all baby. And the names; like the airlines, or manufacturers at Le Mans -- TransAmerican, Peterbuilt, Freightliner, KW, MACK ... Names in the night we have all seen and are somehow warmed by. It was like seeing old friends.

CHAPTER ELEVEN

Running the big six-wheeler from Tavernas' yard in Watertown down to our site in Ledge Rock was no easy task, but a warm and welcome challenge. Once out of the Boston metropolitan area, onto the highways and byways heading south, it was the same old story of how the night highway always has its share of idiots. The never-dim-lights types behind you burning a hole in the back of your skull is one of the usual offenders. Or those approaching who blast their high beams into your eyes as if lowering theirs would mean castration or something even worse. Clowns like that ruined the secondary night roads, so unlike the pros who showed flashing back and forth codes of mutual assistance, all of which gave me a feeling of hope for the Republic ... those perfect moments of strangers in the night respecting and helping each other out.

So, there I was, feeling hardly more than a kid myself, but now one with six enormous wheels under and a precious payload embraced by the roaring iron and steel around it. It was like I was riding with the pros -- Bogart, Cagney, Garfield, Clark or Robert Mitchem. As the big guys did, going like hell, feeling on top of the world following signs saying -- Truck Route Left; All Commercial Traffic Right; No Vehicles Over 5 Tons. I couldn't wait to roll into a truck stop, swing out of the cab, slam the door, and sailor-up the steps into a grand old diner.

Oh, how I loved diners, the real ones you get in New England. Not the fat fake long corrugated latter-day chrome things of Middle America; nor the sad honky-tonks next-to-the-gas pumps of the southland with their open-faced glass-fronted shacks that are big down there. But the real ones. The old skinny railroad car jobs with the black tar roofs and brindle red wooden sides. The sliding doors fore and aft, with maybe another opening added at the middle. These were the real thing, so I kept holding off for the one of these beauties I knew of down toward Westerly, just coming out of Rhode Island. Holding off for it, letting a hell of a lot of near classics slip by till at last, up ahead, I saw the big high sign set back on the edge of all that empty dirt in front for the big rigs to wheel-in and easily park. I held off, held off, getting ready to turn in at the sign ahead. But, oh no! The high sign read, "Soon to reopen under new management."

I was practically in tears. The one time in my life I was big-timing it in my own truck late at night, getting ready for a black coffee and maybe a burger... only to find the place was out of business. I almost wanted to turn around and go home again.

Then, further along was a new big truck stop! This place had a huge rotating roadside sign telling of bunkrooms, showers and "Good Eats 24/7."

I had to park far away from the nearest door. Nobody was near enough to hear my door slam, but I was still all swagger up to the end entry. It was a slider with a screen door in front of that, confusing my opening issue. But I felt like a real trucker striding across the lot and at the door quickly figuring out how to slide it with my right hand then bump the regular door inside open with my left trucker's shoulder. I was getting it together.

The place smelled like fries and coffee with the hint of doughnuts. Too early for those I thought. As I walked in, the faces that turned up toward me had smiles and nods. It was a real truck stop. I felt warm and oddly enough, welcomed. Coming across the parking area in the chill air and now into the warmth and light inside, it gave me that sensation of coming home.

Though I was not from there, this small event turned it all around in my heart. Coming out of the dark and into the warm light, it was as if I was symbolically leaving the past to set out with my darling into our future. I felt a sudden charge of excitement speed through me, head to toe.

After two cups of strong black and a grilled ham and cheese, I swaggered back out to my big six-wheeler. Turning out of the lot, I was still off the highway on the narrower state road. Somehow the diner's owners had lucked out big-time keeping his location at the intersection of the Interstate and the state roads, accessible by both. I don't know who owned the place, but he must have owned a good chunk of the statehouse to win a setup like this. (Shame on me. Why must I always think the worst of our public officials?) Of course, Madlock is one reason, and then there's oil, gas, coal, and timber, and ... whatever people need, and the government can allow for campaign contributions received.

Now, making the turnoff from the main road and having rolled on for a dozen or so miles on the narrow stater without another car ahead or behind, I began to feel more of that delicious back-road loneliness the out-country can give. No streetlights, no traffic, scarcely a house breaking the tree-lined roadside; and those that did were dark, locked and looking lonely. It's a marvelous feeling, chilly, damp ... but suddenly a frightening little thought occurred to me. I had forgotten the jumble of instructions Pete Taverna had given about how to work the truck's dumping mechanism. I hadn't wanted to look less than reliable fumbling around with it when he was speaking, so I did my stupid usual of looking salty as hell like I was born in a dump truck or something. Smart-ass. Now I was turning off the pavement, onto our mini-dirt two-track past Moody's lights, further into the woods, darkness reaching out to lock me in silence. Suddenly, I felt almost frightened, alone, my headlights, like my own big eyes searching for the edge of the abyss where I suspected the world ended and would send me and the truck tumbling into space, bricks and all. I went past what was our roughed-out entry, further down the grown-over ruts with the trees clustering its privacy. We had thought of it as our secret place of solitude. It ran to another spot deeper in the pines which Bobbye and I had found very peaceful, quiet and now, with the nighttime, behind the wheel of this huge truck full of bricks, a place I didn't feel right violating with so much motor and wheel crushing noise.

I stopped just short of its entry, then backed around some to get the six-by reversed to start up the rough twist of what one day would be our driveway now only a rutted two-track leading to where the house was planned to be.

But then, as I started moving backwards, I heard a horribly loud... CRACK! I jammed on the brakes. Was that a gunshot? I set the parking brake, which I noticed was devilishly close to the dump lever, giving me another horror that if I pulled it and not the parking brake lever I'd end up dumping thousands of bricks all over the place even blocking my way out. Which would probably summon Madlock to write me up for rural contamination, huge fine to follow. My God, what had I nearly done?

Another gunshot! Shit, two more pistol sounding rounds went off. I'm not kidding. Crack! Pause. Another report! Then still two more! And the next sounded really close. Good Lord, had Hoffa's boys gotten word that I, a non-union guy, was driving a big f-ing truck? I didn't know what the hell was going on here but instinctively, having been a Marine, I rolled out of the cab and flattened myself on the ground next to the truck ... as it turned out I landed right under the gas tank. Idiot.

Bang again! Why hadn't I joined the Sierra Club when they sent their application? Or no, I had the sudden thought this might be some kind of terrorist thing, or a Black Panther operation organized against white honkey me? And did this imply Isaiah Moody was a Black Panther militant himself?

Bang!

How many shots had been fired? Damn it. I couldn't remember. What kind of a hero would I make with such poor math skills?

Bang again!

So, I decided to call whoever's bluff.

"Hi," I shouted toward the flashlight beam about 50 yards away. Perhaps "Hi" wasn't as aggressive an opener as John Wayne or General Patton might have used, but it had kind of popped out before I could give it more thought and muscle. Besides, it was my first gunfight and I didn't even have a gun. I figured I'd cool it some, showing a willingness to negotiate. Talk softly and carry a big pocket watch or something like that. Then the flashlight beam hit me in the eyes, putting a new light on the matter. Back to conciliation.

"Hey, man," a voice came at me from the blackness behind the light. It didn't sound very Waspish or even country either.

"Hi," I fired back, standing my ground.

No answer, just the light getting closer, suspended seemingly by itself in the darkness, as leaves rustled, and sticks snapped. Whatever it was, came closer.

Don't shoot till you see the whites of their eyes, raced through my head. But I had two problems. No gun, one; and the other was this guy's teeth. Big white beauties I could see, but nothing on the eyes.

"Hi," I cautioned for the third time, and drew the line there.

"Did I scare you, man?" the teeth questioned, a dark head, neck, shoulders and all the rest of the stuff slowly growing around them like something out of a science fiction film.

"Oh, ah, no," I returned with a jaunty croak. So far, the only supportive evidence I had of my coolness were my dry undershorts. Head, face, everything else was drenched in sweat.

"You Ken?"

I didn't know how to answer. Admittedly I wanted to be as agreeable as I could be under the circumstances, but my military training kept repeating to me to only give name, rank and serial number.

"Uh," A compromise answer. I'd held short of a full "Yes." Well hell, I'd only been a peacetime Marine anyway.

"I'm Jay Smith."

I wasn't sure how to play that. Did the "Jay" mean "Jay" or just the letter J? Like J. Edgar of the FBI. He sure had the smile. Or "J" for John, big with Indians and such?

"My wife and I are visiting the Moodys. We're up from the city," he said, holding out his hand.

"Oh, hi," I said, taking his offered hand in a manly grip, applying good pressure so he'd know he wasn't dealing with a wimp. Nor was his pressure bad either, I had to admit. But what really hurt was that his hand was one hell of a lot bigger than mine.

" I'm with the Bureau, down in the city and we come up from time to time to visit. You're the fellah building the house here, right?"

"That's it. Hey, I don't want to sound too nosey, but what's the deal with the gun? I mean you might scare the hell out of somebody some dark night out in the woods here. Like some poor guy driving a dump truck backwards into a tree. Unarmed types can kind of come apart under fire," I said trying to sound both funny and cool.

"Oh yah, well, I'm sorry. I was just trying out this new piece. The woods and all, I didn't think I'd bother anybody. Sorry."

I'll confess the word "piece" made me think of much quieter things he might have tried out in the woods which wouldn't have shaken me so much.

"Can I give you a hand?" he offered.

"Yes, come to think of it," I returned, though secretly thinking that I'd rather have the gun, his hand had already proved intimidating enough. "I could use your light to guide me up the way here?"

"Sure thing."

"Good. I want to haul this load of bricks up near the excavation there, then dump it," I said as I started into the cab.

Then, with Jay's help, I motored the big sucker right to the prescribed spot and started trying to figure out how the dump system worked. Once Jay was up beside me in the cab, we both pushed and pulled and finally got the dump working. He actually knew more about it than I did, but he was cool enough not to rub my nose in it.

After the bricks were settled near to the excavation, I followed him over to Moody's for a cup. Loraine was there. Isaiah was still at work on his second job. And I met Jay's wife. Wow, what a gorgeous woman she was. A regular Dianne Carol, but with more curves.

They gave me a peep in on their sleeping little girl who surely took after her mom. And we had a few laughs about gun-sounds in the night. Jay turned out to be an okay guy, and I hoped to see more of him. I was anxious to get some insights into the black man's feelings and attitudes working under the very white and intransigent J. Edgar Hoover. That would have been too much for the moment, so I said goodbye with thanks for their help, the conversation, and the coffee.

Random thoughts were running through my sleepy mind, managing to keep me well awake on my big-rig drive back to Watertown, Mass. where I rolled it in on schedule for Pete Traverna to have ready for work that next morning. I called Bobbye from his office and she ran back over to pick me up and get us back to Lynnfield ready to keep our hit-parade of events clicking along in fine style with the next day free to fix Old Gal's front end.

CHAPTER TWELVE
Pulling it all Together

The cement man cometh! Hallelujah, amen. Babonas had passed the word to us. Yes, the Caribbean wanderer was back in town, his wife was back from her own jaunt and now all was reconciled. "You know, these things have a way of coming together," Ralph said. "Especially as work season approaches."

As happy as Joey was, however, he was still, as he would phrase it, "*Some behind*" on his lineup of good weather jobs. Since Ralph Babonas had pushed us in at the head of the line, before Joey's-ocean-jaunts, our job was still sitting pretty. Two weeks would do us. One for building the forms then pouring the mix. The second week for curing and back-filling. Great.

I left these matters to the construction gods praying for sunshine. Of course, it rained steadily all that second week, but Joey had the tarps on top to protect the new cement while it cured.

Our two weeks up Boston way were super-busy anyway, so Bobbye and I slid the house situation onto the backburner. Not only was I putting the final exams for my kids together, but that was also the week of the school "Stay Out" protests. This was a product of the year's political unrest growing from the separate and damn-well unequal schooling that had been making it to the press. It truly was segregation. Being young and liberally oriented in those days, I thought I'd take a couple of days down in Boston itself to see what the rumpus was about. Since I had several "Problems of Democracy" classes, the principal gave me a few days to research the situation.

Rob and I had been going to church in the Roxbury part of town where we were the only white faces in the sea of black. We believed that would be good for us to get the feel of being on the other side. As prim and solid is downtown Boston, places like Roxbury, Jamaica Plain, Dorchester were the pits -- rundown, torn up, and falling apart all over the place. So, knowing of the ancient beat-up schools around there, I was somewhat surprised to hear some old guard politicians praising what they claimed to be the absolute equality of schools throughout the entire Hub.

After talking with kids in Roxbury, and also in Dorchester, I learned of a totally different situation. The Dorchester kids, for instance, had no books! No history books, no English books, no math books, none of any variety to take home. Classwork for several classes was done mostly on mimeographed copies of old book pages, but even those sheets couldn't be released to the kids to take home for homework because there was only one set per classroom.

CHAPTER ELEVEN • 145

So, it was clear to me that without books for homework, the kids in that system had no chance of learning a hell of a lot. For the most part, I wasn't dealing with flaming black Panther militants or redneck thugs, just kids. And one little girl's predicament really hit me. She told me she wanted to go to college but didn't think she could. Sure, she got all A's, but not really A's. I asked her what she meant?

"Like Spanish," she said. "I got A in Spanish, but we ain't got no teacher. She quit the first day last fall. So, what goes on is the teacher next door comes in and says, 'Sit down and be quiet.' Then she goes back to her class. So, I'm quiet. I get the A. Those that ain't quiet flunk. But mistah, I don't know no Spanish. How can I go to college like that?"

Then she walked toward the sooty window, a gangly, skinny, sad little 13-year-old. She stared through the grayness for a moment, then turned back toward me with the wet lines of tears running down her dark cheeks and said. "I just don't think I know nothin'."

So, I went right back up to Lynnfield and started sniffing around some more. I told Bobbye what had happened and what I had heard and seen, and how very depressing, maddening it all was. A day later I told the other teachers what I had discovered. I went to the kids in my classes too. One day I took a whole period to give them a peek into the in-town inner-city situation.

Since our suburb of Lynnfield was fairly well to do, what I was telling them about the inner city was all new to them. And the more we kicked it around, the clearer it was to my students that with a worthless school system like I'd discovered, that the kids were stuck in, they would never be able to pass SAT's, earn scholarships, even get into a junior college. So, after they "graduated" from such schools, they would be lucky to even get fast-food jobs. And when times were tough, no jobs would be open to them at all. Which could lead to crime, jail, hate and quite possibly death.

My kids were terrific at picking up on these broader implications of what the product finally is of inadequate school systems. Oddly enough, however, when I put all this into a letter to the editor of the local paper, I got whacked by a whole legion of naysayers calling me a Pinko, a Commie and a worthless Hate-America-Firster. And I didn't do much better on a local radio show. To a large extent the best I got was apathy and cynicism. Which made me look at myself a little more carefully. Despite all this bad I'd discovered, other than writing the piece for the newspaper and going on the radio to make a few speeches in discussion groups, I wasn't committing myself to a hell of lot to straighten it all out either. As a matter of fact, I was taking my dear wife Bobbye, with our dog MacIntosh, and getting to hell and gone out of town. What kind of fighting spirit was I showing in running off to the woodsy bucolic Norman Rockwell world near the Connecticut shore? All of which gave me a strong sense of personal hypocrisy.

Of course, our reality in all this was that we had committed ourselves to the land there. Building our house there, with the total reversal of my writing fortunes, our moving was our investment in our future. Down in Ledge Rock it would be me, Bobbye, Moody and Loraine, just us together on that little integrated dirt road. As long as Moody and I didn't end up shooting each other we would know such experiments could actually work. Then we would tell the world. Besides, looking back, hadn't I made up my mind getting out of the Marine Corps and marrying Bobbye that I'd be damned if I'd have a regular life? There was no way my future would be one of mucking around on commuter trains, fighting traffic, blowing my brains out for some half-assed corporation that would only list me as expendable. I'd never wanted to hang by my fingertips for the rest of my life at the mercy of some paranoid corporate prick a rung above me. So, I listened to that more adventurous voice which told me to pull the loose ends together at school; whack out the final manuscript pages of book #2; make sure of the cement work as well as the final lumber arrangements and through all this keep close to Mr. Merriweather and his gorgeous bank. All that while saying nothing about learning more and more each day of what it meant to be a decent husband to a lovely lady, Bobbye my wife.

My only major qualm of conscience came on Memorial Day watching the parade through the town. At the head of the procession, carrying the flag was the town's truly unknown soldier. Not a real soldier, just a young black kid. I don't know where the hell they found him or rented him or whatever, but the very white little town actually had a black face in its parade. Maybe it made everybody feel better or something. With it, like "Hey everybody, look at us! Wow, we got one too! No rednecks here."

Somebody told me the kid carrying that flag was the same every year. Package deal I guess -- like a rented tuxedo. Was our moving in and building next to Isaiah and Loraine something similar? I don't think so.

My final exams ground to a halt. I corrected them, and glory be... the kids who had gotten A's for the regular teacher got A's from me, and so on down the line. I hoped this meant I had done good as a teacher now that I had been one. But I'll say, an awful lot of those kids came back after the last day to say goodbye. Yes, my bright stars came along with a clam head or two, and even a couple of my beloved thugs. Later, some even kept in touch with us for a year or so after, more with Bobbye than with me really; but it was all a heart-warming reward when you're new at something, and unsure as to how you had done. Outside of cafeteria study halls, potty-passes, education credits, along with a touch of second-class citizenship, it's a job I wouldn't turn down if the wolf someday came to the door ... again.

Good dear Rob still had her classes to finish. I had that extra week to play with, so into the magic VW I went, fat second manuscript under my arm and off to the big city for my second go-round with Mister Farrar of Farrar and Straus. Though I had been lifted to heights of great joy through the mail by this man, and subsequently deposited smartly on my rump by his partner too, I had never met John Farrar face to face. I was, of course, looking forward to it and had every sign of a successful mission going for me.

I'd made an appointment for 10 AM at his office in Union Square, New York City. Though I had been to the Big Apple many times before, mostly in college, I really didn't know a damned thing about Manhattan. So, in true Boston fashion, I donned my three-piece Scottish go-to-the-bank suit, finest pumps, my pipe, and all the other necessary gear for a proper literary image and checked my watch. Calculating that it would take about 4 hours from Boston to New York I got up at 5 AM, was in the car at 5:30, and simply drove straight to M. Farrar's office, parked in an empty place directly in/front at 9:55; rode the elevator to his upstairs retreat, and sat in a chair opposite him as the clock struck 10. Simple. And quite Bostonianly done. About 240 miles, 60 mph average, 25 minutes for traffic and parking, five more for doors and stairs, etc., no problem at all. Could I ever pull off such a feat again? 'Doubt it. Now that I have some familiarity with New York, its traffic, the clogged glutted highways and bridges, and

CHAPTER TWELVE: PULLING IT ALL TOGETHER • 149

the impossibility of ever finding a street parking place, I could spend the rest of my life trying to duplicate that feat and never come closer than plus or minus twenty-four hours. But there I was. Sammy Simpleton, shoving my manuscript across the desk to this renowned gentleman; chatting about how nice it would be if he liked it, so he could also handle the first. (For which he said with a nod he still had enthusiasm). He went on to say he would arrange an agent, the same gentleman he would select for the first reading.

Mr. Farrar went on to show me some lovely Renaissance art, Giotto I believe, then he gave me a copy of Carlos Fuentes' latest book, "The Death of Artemio Cruz." The meeting was moving forward encouragingly. There seemed to be an empathy between us. We shook hands. He promised to get word to me soon--as opposed to the last go around of many, many months. And so, my second manuscript went into his hands and who knew where it would go from there.

I reached Lynnfield in time to pick up Bobbye and we dined quietly in the kitchen before a movie that night. Another ho-hum day. Maybe I should have been an astronaut specializing in moonwalks or moon-landings.

So now both books were out. The first was entered in the "First Novel" Contest, the second to Farrar's care and feeding. It was a marvelous feeling having two horses running like that. I was filled with the excitement of the possible -- the anticipation of a smashing success. What a delicious gentle ache it caused through my middle. It is one of those best times in life – the before moments. The thrill of hoping, mentally savoring, spending in advance all the joys such success could bring. If it isn't the greatest part of success, it has to at least be the foundation on which later happiness would build.

Of course, there are dangers. The most obvious of these being that I could endlessly bury myself in the dreams of success, yet never actually gain it. That was the sort of non-writing writer Hemingway called out.

But at that moment these weren't my problems. I was a guy in one sense near an end, in another, at a new beginning. Other than my Marine Reserve flying I was returning to an income approaching zero. Bobbye and I were ending a stage of economic productivity, kind of like retiring. But how many retire at twenty-five?

In another sense we were also at a beginning. Writing. The books were finally out there and maybe even to be optioned. They had passed through our hands anyway, and were pending in publishers' offices like bets down, fortune's wheel spinning. Bobbye had cut the employment umbilical too. Her teaching days were over. No longer would she be the provider of dollars and cents for us both. She too would be focusing on our house on Blueberry Hill, helping to build our nest there and in time, setting about to fill the place with tiny pitter-patters and howls in the night. This would be her beginning as a mother as opposed to her original role as the girl roommate and provider for a struggling writer. From here on we had our house to build which would be the only roof over our heads. And books to sell, our only marketable stuff on the shelf. We would either make it, or we would not. It might be very easy, the books both being accepted to the jangle of cash registers, splatters of favorable ink, to say nothing of the ruckus of banging and sawing noises from workmen we could then afford to bring in. Or it would be damned hard. The books going down various drains, our meager resources dissipating, our thumbs growing fat from misdirected hammer blows, failure and disaster looming over our heads like rain clouds over a house with no roof. But at that

CHAPTER TWELVE: PULLING IT ALL TOGETHER • 151

stage, we weren't bent out of shape worrying about which way it would go. We were young, healthy, still excited by fallen President Jack's call to a New Frontier, and eager to have a go at it ourselves via our own version of a century's old pioneering experience. And so, we were on the way to pitching a tent in the forest of our future homestead and building our own damn dreamhouse ourselves. "Look out world, here we come," we could have shouted and let the Devil take the hindmost.

It rained all that week and much of the next, threatening a possible disaster. Finally, though, it slackened enough to allow Gildea to get the foundation in. But it was close. The pour wouldn't have a full week to cure, but Joey said not to sweat it. He knew because as he said, "I build good."

We wouldn't have known the difference anyway, so we tried not to worry.

Back in Wakefield, our dog MacIntosh knew something was up. Dogs are sensitive creatures. Mac was infinitely so. He was almost human. When Bobbye and I, for instance, were watching television one night, he crawled up on the couch, wedged in between us, turned and ended up sitting perfectly erect, human-like, his front paws dangling down like a child's at a table. And the looks he'd get on his face. Of sympathy, anger, of questioning all were the usual of dogdom; but the most comical of the lot was the look he got when he'd been out whoring. He'd never been "fixed." So old Tosh had a lot of his carousing mutt father still in him. From time to time he would disappear for two, maybe three days at a time which were really something to cope with worrying about where and how he was.

At first, we'd assumed he'd been hurt, maybe even laying near death in some lonely god awful place. So, I'd had to go all around the neighborhood embarrassedly shouting his name at the top of my lungs. I felt sheepish and ridiculous when doors or windows would open, curtains pulled aside people peering and pointing at me. All very depressing. But then, when I'd finally find Tosh huddled in the freezing slush and snow, half-starved, shivering, but first in line pressed against some hot-lady-dog's back door; he'd look mournfully over his shoulder at me, though not budging to come away, then he'd give me the silliest look a dog could muster. Time and again as we repeated this scene through the seasons, he looked like he wanted to bark the message to me... that it's my father's horny old genes that have gotten the best of me. It's the family curse.

So, I'd move gingerly through the crowd of scruffy-furred gentlemen-callers, take Tosh by the ear and lead him sadly away. The others, all together, would get up and move their queue one spot forward filling that opened slot. Then, again, the cold and the snowy vigil would continue into the night.

Having been through this before with horny-dog Macintosh, knowing his well-trotted love routes as well as the various seasons of his lady friends, we were somehow bonded together. I'd write all day. He would ... how can I put it with any delicacy? Then, after the fact, I'd go to retrieve him, drag him home. The poor mutt would be reeling like a drunken sailor, horny beyond imagination. But through it all our mutual understanding only grew. Of course, we never could talk these things out on a man-to-dog basis, but we got to know each other well enough over time to share many of the same emotions and hang-ups.

As Bobbye and I started to put away, wrap, and pack our things over a period of a week or two, old Tosh sensed that we were going somewhere. He started to mope, even growling at people

CHAPTER TWELVE: PULLING IT ALL TOGETHER

a time or two which was totally unlike him. It took us a while to realize what was bothering him. He seemed nervous sensing that we were not only leaving Wakefield, but maybe leaving him behind too. When I was hard on him for his occasional growling, it only made things worse. That got us worrying that he might be getting sick or heading into an early senility due to his long sexual excesses. I thought this might be a lesson and a warning to us all.

Finally, when the day for goodbyes to our neighbors came, when our absurd old pickup was loaded to proper Okie standards, the VW revving behind it, we opened the door wide and called, "Macintosh. MacIntosh, come on boy. Let's go."

He had been morosely stretched out next to the side of the house on the walkway to the back, his head on his paws, his tail limp behind him. He'd been that way for days like he truly believed we were going to leave without him.

But when we called, "Here Tosh. Come on boy," first his glassy sad eyes had trouble rousing themselves to even look our way. Then, when he finally saw me in the truck waving and encouraging him, the film slowly cleared. And his eyes brightened. And sparkled. Up came his head. Pop-up went the ears. His tail began to furiously sweep the walk. Then he was on his feet. And in a bound or two he was on top of us both, nuzzling, licking, chomping on my arm, slobbering, scratching, jumping all over the both of us, first Bobbye then me in the tiny cab of our shivering old truck before Bobbye took over the bug to follow. What a moment, for man and beast alike. It was only then that we understood what the problem with him had been. And it made us very sad and very happy too. What a good old dog MacIntosh was. How much he must have loved us and how much we loved him. We were all so happy then. And as we set off down the dreary gray street we had known for the past two years of struggling happiness, we felt for the first time truly married, husband and wife for sure, with companion funny-dog, off on our first real adventure as a family. A house, a house, we were off to build our own house!

We did our tent thing again, but with the balmy June weather it was hardly the same. No snow, no shivering, no Macintosh fighting tooth and nail for the warmest creases under the blankets. And I guess it was also too early for mosquitos. It was a pleasant night full of mystery. We were by ourselves, severed from the organized, structured life we had always been a part of. Any organization or structure in our lives from here on would now be of our own doing. We were through the babysitting stage. High school, college, the military, a regular job; all of these elements of our lives which had defined the boundaries of our living were now gone. Each hour of each day would chart our course down the road of our futures. Yes, all shiveringly exciting.

There in our wilderness retreat we were part of those thousands of wooded acres, the dusk breezes rustling, the new foliage, insect noises, animal sounds; Bobbye and I felt ourselves warmly newborn, free. It was a strange feeling that first night. To think that the next morning would be defined by the sun rather than an alarm clock. And that breakfast would be for strength, the real strength and energy needed to put shelter over our heads not riding in a bus, car, or train, through the mad crush of morning traffic to a cold, impersonal office where I would be required to sit like some kind of gnome all day, laboring over an insignificant part of an enormous whole. Where would a life like that lead?

CHAPTER TWELVE: PULLING IT ALL TOGETHER

Wouldn't it be a life of each day's smog separated from the next day's same, only by the setting then later rising sun? Not for us.

That first day, I decided to walk down the lane to the main road and put in place and mount the new mailbox, then wait there for the flatbed truck bringing all the stuff with which to build our house. I figured to stand there until I saw the truck appear with a half dozen builder-looking guys following in, I'd been told, a blue Pontiac. They would be looking for me, of course, though they had never seen me before. Nor had they ever been to this part of Connecticut either. They were from up in Massachusetts, about two hours northeast from where I'd be with our newly mounted mailbox.

CHAPTER THIRTEEN
By the Side of the Road

Thinking about it, the whole drill seemed too much to ask of folks to drive that distance, following directions given over a telephone, and actually, find an unknown guy (me) standing by my spiffy new mailbox out there in next-to-nowhere-land.

By the way, let me ask ---have you ever stood by a mailbox beside the road early in the morning when you think your truck is just rounding the bend down that road? And as you believe that, you might feel yourself go through a stage of trying not to feel like the village idiot rooted there on the soft shoulder grinning inanely at the passing traffic. Then you start to wonder if a few of the passersby might begin to wonder if you need a lift or perhaps you might be some kind of misfit, or even a child-molester? And as soon as that pops into your head it's hard as hell not to think of yourself as exactly that.

Then a guy did pull over and leaned across his front seat to ask if I needed a ride. I said no, I was just waiting for a truck to come by. He gave me a funny look like he might have thought I was saying his car wasn't good enough or, on the other hand, that I had a thing for truck drivers.

And yet, guilt like that can be infectious. It grows. As people drove by and stared at me, some slowing, some speeding up, all seeming to look hard at me as if I had to be guilty of something.

It occurred to me, however, having a background in aviation, I might look like a skyjacker.

When would the truck and the boys finally come? I felt like I might be edging toward a crack up. It even occurred to me that some in the passing cars might be thinking of my standing by the side of the road as a simple invitation, a shameless angling to be picked up by a New York hairstylist driving the old road to Boston. Oh heavens, the challenging self-generated insights into one's own psyche that can be drawn from simply standing by the side of a road.

Then I saw it. The truck! Yeah! The truck and the guys in the car behind it. I'm free. I'm not a wacko after all.

As the big flatbed boiled dusting-up and over our little lane and onto the car following it, I felt we were finally getting the game underway. There was excitement in the air. Hissing brakes, rough shouting voices, car doors slamming, all with strong male laughter, the back-and-forth that guys exchange before getting down to a job to work.

Then out of the Pontiac driver's seat came quite a spiffy comic book character indeed ---Tall, bearded, the guy had an almost Christ-like air. Heroic characters always seem to be tall. I am not. Damn irritating. But though this guy had on the usual contractor's outfit, the khaki shirt and trousers, the high-laced leather boots,

CHAPTER THIRTEEN: BY THE SIDE OF THE ROAD • 159

his heroism was mostly defined by his Aussi infantryman's hat. The kind with one side brim pinned up. I don't know why the hell he had that rig on, but I grudgingly had to confess he looked great. And he was a handsome stud too. Kind of a larger than life Tyrone Power. And he knew it but was still graceful about it. I liked him.

"You're Mr. McAdams," he announced. (I was tempted to counter with, "No, shit." But I restrained myself.)

"I'm Bob Powers," he said, holding out one large, roughened hand. Powers, wouldn't you know it? Why couldn't I be Ken Steel, or Tommy Tough, or something like a guy in high school, Champ Fischer? Or best of all, the Ivy League sprinter in the early 'Fifties -- Scott Paradise? Terrific names. Sports have always been number-one in the world of names. Roman Gabriel for instance or Harlan Svarey, Charlie ChooChoo Justice, Mudcat Grant... so many of them.

I guess the bottom line was that I was already intimidated by this guy. I didn't know if he sensed it, or if I showed it in any way, but nothing on my part could have topped Bobbye's response upon meeting him. She threw up! Which sure would cut any man down to size. Even a tall hunk like Powers with his Aussi hat.

Frankly, I was kind of proud of Rob. My first reaction was a quiet, "That-a-girl." But when she let go again and the lads were kind of hopping around out of the line of fire, I figured Rob wasn't just hamming it up, but was actually sick.

"You okay, Rob?"

Barrrf!

I don't know, I felt kind of helpless. It might be that when people throw-up they're so busy doing it it's hard to break in. And it sure K.Os conversation.

I walked Rob over to the Bausche's and asked good Florence, "Bobbye seems to be sick." I asked if she could arrange a nap for her, since I was needed to unload our big flatbed. Florence was great, wrapped a blanket around Bobbye and helped her to their guest room.

Everybody figured we'd made the right call, so back to the truck and unloading I went.

I showed Powers all that I could about how I figured his big rig could get up the turn in the drive to the foundation, and where it would be best to stack the materials. Frankly I was sort of winging it, assuming what I figured to be proper builder's poses; one hand on a hip, the other pointing this way and that, occasionally drawing inane diagrams in the dirt.

Powers was respectful enough, but after about 10 minutes of my long-winded crap, he offered his own summary.

"No good. The rig'll never make your turn up there," he said.

"You better believe it," some young worker-character added, grinning idiotically behind him.

"Why not?" I asked.

"Too steep, first off, but the turn's the big problem. The rig is too long to hack it. And the trees hem it in. Makes it too narrow."

I pondered for a moment, then some big shirtless kid shouted, "Well, boys, let's get out the axes and start whacking down those trees."

It was like I'd been hit by lightning. Cut trees! Over my dead body. I'd selected and cut all those that were going to get cut. We'd chosen the forest, to live in the forest. No idiot army of college boys was going to flatten our forest.

"Hold on there, kid," I shouted, "don't dare touch one of those damned trees. They're Chestnuts and oaks. They're going to stand as is." I was torqued.

"Then we aren't going to touch the job," Powers fired back, as the tall kid, ax in hand, looked from one of us to the other. "And that kid, Mr. McAdams, is my son."

CHAPTER THIRTEEN: BY THE SIDE OF THE ROAD

I wasn't built too badly, had thrown a few punches in my time, but Powers was a head taller and his son had an ax in hand, plus six helpers. Duke Wayne, of course, would have liked the odds, Frank Sinatra would already be swinging, but I felt I needed these guys and couldn't afford to bust them all up. So, I gave them a break. I explained my feelings about trees and birdies and chipmunks, the whole Mother West Wind thing. I tried not to lean on them too hard.

Powers quieted down, but still he didn't see how he was going to get the materials up to the foundation. I was beginning to get a hollow-shitty feeling mid-gut. Was this the final drain for the house to go down? We'd handled the bank loan despite our joblessness, even battled and beaten city hall and Madlock. The truck registration had been a chore, but we'd come through that okay. Ralph's backhoe had come apart on the job, and for that matter the whole foundation thing had been a scare with Gildea's disappearance and then the heavy rains. All along with the book's problems but, damn it, even they were straightening itself out to some degree. Damn it, we just couldn't accept that it all would come to nothing over a scant 200 feet of rough road.

Powers agreed to wait for the rig to try a trial run. It might make it. But it didn't. Great. The G.D. trucking outfit had carefully selected the baldest set of tires they could find for this particular operation. Hats off to all such meatheads.

So, together we pushed that big bastard, seven sets of hands pushing, Powers at the wheel. First, we pushed, then pulled. Nothing worked. We had to come up with something else. The last option was for the trucker to take the whole load back to Philly and charge me, or dump it on the ground right there, and also charge me. But, damn it, there had to be another way.

CHAPTER FOURTEEN
Don't Mess with A Union

"Bob," I tossed at Powers, "what if we unloaded small loads from the Big-rig, put them into the pickup, me and maybe the rig driver could do that, while you're feeding stuff onto your people."

"Drivers drive," announced the driver. "Nothin' more, nothin' less. Talk to my union down in Philly, if you got beef."

Which was the end of my brief partnership with the truck driver.

"Short of costing you a lot more money, Mr. McAdams," Powers said, shaking his head, "I don't see that we can do the job." All of which gave me the eeriest, iciest chill down my spine. Had Madlock eaten a magic apple and turned himself into Bob Powers to defeat us at last? Maybe it was the word money that made me think it. It sure was the word money that gave me my next thought.

"Damn it, Bob, your company signed a contract with us to get this house onto our lot and send you guys in for two days to help put up the rough shell. Well, half of one day is shot, and now you're talking about charging me more to get even the basic job done in the first place. Hell, if you people didn't want to come down and check the site first to see if it could be done without shuttling, then it's your problem physically and financially, not mine."

"Look, don't get rough with me, or out I go," he said, heating up. "This isn't my company you're talking about. You signed with the prefab outfit. I merely contract to them. Sure, they're all fucked up. I don't argue that. But for me to bust my ass unloading, reloading, then unloading all that material again, man, that's going to cost somebody. Otherwise, you can shove the whole job."

He paused a minute then said, "Look, I see how you're stuck. If your contract reads like you say, then you have no-sweat. We'll go ahead and shuttle, and I'll attach my extra bill to them, not you. If they try to hand it on to you, fight it or pay it, whichever way you want to go. They're dumb bastards, anyway. Everyone's taking them, so it looks to me like they deserve it. I'll bet they fold pretty quick, anyway, so you might as well get your house up. Better than losing everything, huh?"

"It's a deal. I'll work the trucks with one of your guys. We'll feed you and keep ahead. Okay?"

"Okay by me, but it'll be a ball-breaker."

"You better believe it," came that odd Mr. Smiles again. Who was this guy anyway?

And it *was* a ball-breaker, all right. Sheets of plywood, endless 2 x 4!s, windows, joists, trusses, shingles never-ending. I soon learned how little of a prefab we had. I had envisioned whole complete sections of the house being lifted by a huge crane into place. No way. As it turned out, only two elements of the house were in any way prefabricated other than the usual doors and windows. These were the basic wall sections with their window and door cutouts, and the triangular supporting roof trusses forming the interior ceiling joists and the roof stringers. That was it. And the other large sections were middle walls, free of outside clapboarding and interior plaster board. To all intents and purposes our house would be an on-site construction. Since the crew would now only be around for a day and a half, Bobbye and I would be the sole builders from that point on. Being faced with the reality of this, of nail barrels, lumber and the like, the enormity of the project began to have real meaning. I was tempted to ask, "How the hell do you build a house," but thought better of it. I knew the answer would be pretty complicated, which would only be a further embarrassment. Suddenly I felt awkward-to-the-max, obvious, and small. Maybe Bobbye'd had the answer by taking one look at the whole deal and throwing-up. I envied her morning stomach.

When break-time came, I moseyed over to the Bausche's to check on my girl. It seemed she was feeling better and had at least held down some broth. She took a pass on fried clams, however. Thank goodness for Carl and Florence. I have no idea what we would have done without their help. Isaiah and Loraine were both at work all day. We surely would have been stuck without the Bausches.

"You better believe it," came the voice of Mr. Smiles, seemingly having read my mind. (Which didn't say much for my mind.)

Having gotten back up on the rig, I started handing packs of shingles down to him and I asked, in the process, "You going to college?"

"You better believe it."

This guy was a classic.

"Where?" I grunted, handing down another bundle.

"I'm a War-eagle."

"No shit? But what the hell's a War-eagle?"

"Auburn man," he gurgled. "I'm from Boston, but I go down Dixie to Auburn. You better believe it." He grinned and hunkered around like some kind of half-naked ape.

"Play ball?"

"You better believe it."

Unreal. But the clown suffered no embarrassment from such repetitions. Over and over, and over again he'd crank out his, You Better Believe It's with his crazy Boston-deep-south mélange that sounded more like zoo-jabber than any organized human talk. If only I could get him to a medical school somewhere to open his nut, I'll bet they'd only find one circuit with all lines from every part of his body, anal-sphincter, the works, probably main-lined through that one tiny circuit. No matter what came at him nor whatever he performed, the contacts would snap shut and the lower front part of his head would bark, "You better believe it." I couldn't take it anymore and shifted to another part of the truck.

There is nothing like a strong militant, highly organized union to break one's back. Of course, if it weren't for pigheaded owners and insensitive bureaucratic "Let them eat cake" managements, we mightn't have had such unions in the first place; but whatever brought it about, I'll say in this case it was painful to be sweating like a champ, really humping like all the guys were, while that trucker sat on his ass smoking a cigar, sipping his coffee and from time to time dozing off after telling us, "Drivers drive. Nothin' but drive. You got a problem with that, talk to my union down Philly."

Hell, if he'd just gone off somewhere else, it would have been one thing, but he persisted in staying right there and periodically letting me know that he was actually a terrific guy. It was his union, you see, that wouldn't let him touch anything but the steering wheel of his truck. Which, I might add, unnerved me a bit over the thought that he might have to do potty at some point during the day. Then which one of us might be assigned to tidy him up?

So, on and on we went. Off the back of the rig with the stuff, up onto the smaller pickup, then truck it to the top where the rest of Bob's crew was furiously making a subfloor with it, spanning longwise and fat-wise on top of the glorious foundation Joey the Cement King had so recently laid. Pray to God it didn't crumble.

First, they fabricated a full-length central support girder out of three 2 x 10's nailed together in staggered fashion. I'd had Joey put footings for lalli-columns down the center line of the basement floor. Babonas had suggested this to me, or I wouldn't have known of it. We tried to align the girder butt-joints over each of the post positions for basic strength. Then we laid the 2 x 6's flat along the top edge of the foundation for sills, bolted to the cement. From there it was just a matter of laying the 2x8 joists across from the foundation sills to the central girder, both sides toward the center then nailing these together over and into the girder. Next we boxed around the outside butts with full length 2 x 8's. On top of all that went the plywood sheets, and voila we had a subfloor. Fantastic.

But it was still a long way from a house. Actually, with the mounds of excavated dirt and rocks, with the deep moat-like ditch full circle around that, the small cellar window cuts, and the flat subfloor on top, it looked military. Like a pillbox, or an armored helipad, if there was such a thing. But hell, it did look like something anyway. Which was a step forward. Thinking about it, after all the baloney we'd gone through, we were half crazy with delight having been a part of building even one small pillbox. And, the more I stared at it, walking over this way to see it from one angle, then from another, stumbling back over the runty little bushes, (which we finally found were gorgeous blueberry makers), I clumsily ricocheted off trees for the long fade which made me feel myself to be more and more like General George S. Patton commanding.

I felt like I was setting up a defensive position, one which would be the anchor or pivot point around which my armor would sweep in a double-pincher containing, then crushing Rommel (Madlock)'s frontal thrust. Ah, Rommel ... the master of armored war — but whose books I had read, and whose very writings I would turn back on the likes of him. (Madlock)

For a brief moment, I thought of directing my company chaplain, Major Y. B. Believit, to produce a prayer, an admonition to the Supreme Being, Commander of all men, to make sure and firm this pillbox we have made could live on. Then, it occurred to me how that prayer would be framed..."Dear Lord... You better believe it..."

"Huh, what?" I was back from the wars. "Yes. I mean you are right. It is going up just fine, isn't it?"

"You better ... "

"Oh hell, forget it." And I walked away, back to the trailer to heft another load onto the pickup, but I had discovered something about myself. I had discovered that I was still approximately eleven-years-old. When I was actually that age, I'd make something, a plane out of balsa, or a tank or ship out of clay, whatever; then I'd hold it in my hand, or put it down on the linoleum playroom floor, the battlefield of my boyhood dreams, and ponder it for hours on end. I'd crouch down by it; scoot back across the room from it; stand up over it; look at it from every conceivable angle, all the time making battle scene noises half to myself, worthy of any movie soundtrack. Booora! Baarrrooooom! Krrrrblarah! You know the stuff. So, there I was now. Age what? 26, going on 27? I don't know. Probably off the linoleum of my childhood, but still much the young boy doing the same damned things. Why not? This, the house, was my first man-sized toy and I was going to enjoy it. I couldn't bear to waste all those balsa wood gluing and clay modeling years. Yes, this was my moment. Bulldozers, backhoes, six-byes, a squad of men, hammers and nails like small arms fire; it was all there and I, as Hop Harrigan attached to the Seabees during this critical moment in the Okinawa campaign, was damned if I'd chuck it all on such an absurd concept as adulthood and maturity. "Screw you," my heart sang as I heaved lumber from truck to truck despite the withering Nippon fire.

To this day I haven't changed. Building something, anything, I keep stepping back, studying it from a million angles, savoring it, living it to a thousand tunes; building it onto God knows how many different fantasy-completions before wearily trudging it back to its less fascinating reality.

I think Bob Powers came up with the same evaluation of old YBBI, the smiling Youbetterbelieveit character who had apparently decided that he was not only a philosopher, but a carpenter of some merit as well. He'd deserted the truck-stuff tossing, to take hammer in hand, a bag of nails on his belt, and good intentions to help tack the middle wall sections in place. As it turned out, he needn't have bothered to lug so many nails with him, I think one, two tops, would have been enough. He just could not hit the damned things right. Of course, he hit his thumb okay. And fingers, wrist, forearm, elbow, forehead, the sides of his head; he flailed mightily like a man possessed. The only safe place within ten feet of the guy was, however, on the head of the nail. It seemed to me that flies, some gnats, whatever, clustering on that nail head were as safe as safe could be. The other guys, Bob, his boy and two carpenters edged away as the din went on. Crashing, banging, the actual splitting and splintering of wood, along with our lovely 2 X 4's disintegrating all around that never-to-be-driven nail. Bob finally started yelling at him, though without much success. I thought it might come down to drawing straws for a one-man suicide rush, or maybe Bob would risk the whole crew, figuring somebody would finally be able to throttle the sucker.

Bob's yelling at him, using one of his other nicknames—*Dumbsonofabitch*, didn't make it either. Too much concentration and racket. Something had to be done with this maniac before he destroyed the whole damned house. He was running amuck. His eyes, though always somewhat glazed, were now opaque; mouth lathered, nose running a gentle trickle. Yet, to the end, that nail sat serene, an island-haven in a storm-swept sea.

Finally, just as one was accepting the need for Divine intervention on the behalf of the nail, YBBI let go one mighty barely glancing near-miss that, at Herculean velocity, actually nipped the upper edge of the nail's head. The beating of wings of all the startled insects was deafeningly granted; but the gunshot zing of that projectile put the whole party flat to the ground. Ricochets. It nearly played the National Anthem hitting everything around so fast and often. Clearly, YBBI had to be subdued.

Rising to a man the crew rushed him, hitting high, low, in the middle; enveloping him in a human wave, as a battered thumb and forefinger held his second nail, and the bloody hammer twitched and quivered over his head desperate for one more whack. Who knows, they might have saved his life.

Handsome Bob finally put the mighty War Eagle back on the truck, which YBBI accepted without shame, cheerfully oblivious to his own failure.

Later on, when the din and roar of the day had subsided, the crew piled into their vehicles to drive all the way back to Hanover, Massachusetts. (Boston people have a hell of a time spending a night away from the bean and the cod. In this case they elected a full four-hour round trip rather than a night in a nearby motel.)

I walked over to the Bausche's to retrieve dear Rob. She was okay. A little weak, but she seemed to have purged her system all right and was ready to go back to the site. She was anxious to see how much had been done. Florence and Carl joined us in the short trek through the bushes, and passing the Moody's, Loraine and Isaiah joined us too.

Though the day had begun much like December 7th at Pearl Harbor, after work finally had started in earnest, we'd made a good deal of headway. Seeing the progress made, Bobbye was delightfully surprised. Her stomach and the truck problems had occurred in unison, so she was a little startled to see the foundation covered over, and four roofless sides up with props tacked to hold them vertically and in place. I think all our eyes stole a look up to the sky checking for rain. It was the evening thunderstorm season, but we could see that by this time tomorrow we'd have a roof up to protect it all. I did say a little prayer—Oh Lord, just a day, please. Just one more day without rain.

The Moodys had us for dinner. It was Isaiah's night off again. Though to many, mostly we Yankees I guess, fried chicken would not seem the most stomach soothing food. For dear Bobbye, being from Tennessee, it seemed to work like an elixir. The more of that crisp crunchy batter that went digging and scraping down to her dear tummy, the better she seemed to feel. Well hell, in some parts of the world, the best thing after a tough day is raw monkey brains. I guess it's just a matter of perspective.

While Loraine and Bobbye clattered about washing, drying and putting the dishes away, Isaiah and I had a chance to talk. It proved productive.

Though we both, I think, still felt awkward toward each other. For my part I didn't know if I was appearing to him as the standard starry-eyed white liberal asshole or not. All I was trying to do was be normal. Which is damned hard sometimes when you think about it too much.

I thought Isaiah wasn't all that at ease either. Bobbye and Loraine didn't seem to have such problems. But then, I believe women have more built-in common ground than men. And too, men are natural competitors. No matter how much commonality they might eventually share, they still will start off eying each other, feeling and testing.

For once I didn't do a hell of a lot of talking. From bits and pieces Carl had mentioned, Moody had had an interesting life and I hoped to hear more of it firsthand. And I did. Here's how it went.

CHAPTER FIFTEEN
It Should not be So

Isaiah had come out of Mississippi and that wasn't simply a physical movement. He had come out of Mississippi the state, Mississippi the way of life, and Mississippi the state of mind. He'd done it by working his ass off, two full time jobs since God knew when; and he'd done it to save his ass in the long run because he didn't seem to feel he was the type of guy who could spend his life as "boy" when he knew, and proved in the army, that he was a hell of a man.

Isaiah had served with distinction in combat in Europe during the Second World War. As a matter of fact, he was highly decorated, and in his own quiet way was pleased and proud of his record. He had fought hard for his country, risked his life several times, well above and beyond the call of duty.

When he got back to his hometown in 1945, he had his mustering out pay, his uniform, and a chest full of ribbons. He had a big smile on his face too, and the walk of a man proud he'd done his duty for his country, risked it all and was back safe and sound.

There were a lot of other men walking around the same way too—but they were white.

At that time a new suit of clothes in a small southern town was hard to come by. Civilian production hadn't started to make a dent on big city needs, much less those of the small out of the way places either. So, for a new man phasing back in from the military to the civilian world wasn't all that easy. Particularly if you'd gone to war young and done most of your growing up there. But what the hell, Isaiah knew he looked damn good in his uniform anyway.

That was until one day he ran into the chief of police who said hello and welcome back and all that, but who also gave him a word of advice. He explained that Isaiah might have been off to many new places, faraway places but that now he was back home. And that he had better start getting used to being home again. Which led to the Chief to say that a lot of the folks had been watching him strut around in his U.S. Army uniform with all the decorations on it; and they just plain didn't like a black boy wearing that uniform. So, and the Chief explained that this was for his own good, he didn't want to see him out in public in the uniform again.

Isaiah tried to explain that he had no other clothes, and the Chief listened politely, but made it clear that Isaiah would not step out of his house in uniform again. That was it. No more, no less.

He never did. But he had to sit inside his mother's house for a week wearing only some old slacks and a tee shirt, while his mother went everywhere looking for a suit. Happily, she finally did find one. However, it wasn't exactly what he had in mind, but at least it was something he could get out of the house in. It had big wide colorful stripes. And it was too small. And it made him look like a circus clown, where before he had looked like something else, a man of substance, a hero. But at least he could go out of the house now, and that was the whole idea wasn't it?

Isaiah's first step out his mother's front door had him bump into the Police Chief straight away. But the Chief was all smiles. He'd got a good laugh out of Isaiah's clown suit. Funniest damn thing he'd ever seen on anybody, he chuckled to himself slapping Isaiah on the back. But what did you expect, he smiled as he told Isaiah that his crazy outfit was "Just fine." And he added that the young combat veteran was "A good boy." After another pat on the back, he walked away shaking his head and continuing to chuckle to himself.

Isaiah moved to Connecticut. Then he used his mustering out pay along with the money his two jobs brought in to bring up to Connecticut his young nieces so they could go through the good high school there. Some guy.

We talked back and forth about it all. I told him of the church we had gone to in Brookline, Massachusetts and how even it unconsciously ended up segregated with up-scale elite college people. And how we moved out of that church to become the only whites in the all-black Roxbury congregation. We talked of the schools around Boston too. The rising stay-out scene, and how the real issue wasn't busing or neighborhoods exactly, but how invariably the only really long-term high-quality education existed where white faces were. That was mainly where the money got spent. Blacks weren't stupid. Without a lot of white faces in their classrooms, the budgets would either never get up to par, or they'd stay there only till the heat was off.

We batted a lot of this around, and in so doing began to get the feel of each other. And though we were hardly from the same backgrounds, and I sure as hell had many more advantages handed to me than Moody, we began to feel real mutual respect. Not the churchy B.S. kind. It was clear to me and, to Bobbye, that no man on this earth worked harder than Isaiah, and in turn I think he might have felt that Bobbye and I stood for a new generation on our side of the fence too. I mean that night we started getting past the black and white of it all, like any two new couples would, just getting used to being neighbors and friends.

On the way back up to our tent home, our military pillbox, by the light of our kerosene lantern, it seemed to have become more of a frontier stockade. But as I felt a High Noon swagger coming on, like we were a couple from maybe two-hundred years earlier homesteading in the rough country a long way west of there. As a matter of fact, the area around us in Ledge Rock had actually been Indian country back then. Mohawks, or was it the last of the Mohicans?

"Look out for that hole, Kenny," Bobbye shouted, grabbing my arm and stabilizing my wander.

"Um, yah," I mumbled.

"See," she said, pointing down in front of what was nearly my next step, "that hole you were set to trip into, that's where the cellar stairs will start down. Oh Kenny, isn't this exciting?" Bobbye said, hugging against my arm. "Our own house. I guess I sound like an old movie, but I'm so excited. And so happy. I love you," she said.

As she said that, it actually did feel like we were starring in an old movie. So, we did a moonlight fade, holding a long deep kiss, standing in the middle of our roofless four walls; the trees and stars leaning in for a smiling glimpse, owls, crickets, all those scampering things happy to have us joining them there, in those woods, soon to be where our home would be.

CHAPTER SIXTEEN
The Day Later

The next morning motor noises were coming up our dirt road announcing that Bob's truck and the Pontiac half full of sleepy workmen was bumping its way toward us again. Once they parked at the bottom of our controversial future driveway, Bobbye and I, along with dog MacIntosh, walked down to greet them.

"Hey Bob, how's it going today, man?" I asked cheerily. "Where's the rest of the gang? Looks like you're missing two or three."

"Hi Ken, Bobbye. Good morning dog," he returned, roughing Macintosh's ears with his large fists. "I figured to lose some. Always happens when the first day is a rough one for a crew. I guess we scared a couple off. It's a shame. I usually try to bring newbies on slowly, but yesterday there wasn't any other way. Today will be a chore, so, you're right, we're two short and even running behind timewise. I'd figured to get here a hell of a lot earlier, but traffic was horrible."

"Understood, but I'll help and Bobbye can chip in too. The two of us can cover your shorts," I said. "How about coffee for everybody? Got a big pot going."

"That'd taste real fine. Thanks," Bob said with a smile.

"You better believe it," mumbled a voice from behind him, the last warm body falling out of the Pontiac's back left door. Shit, the War Eagle has landed again.

"Hey Bob," I said, "I see your head carpenter stuck with you anyway. But I hope you didn't let him have a hammer and any nails."

Everybody got a laugh out of that while the Eagle kind of kicked at the dirt, turning a mite pink.

This day went a hell of a lot better than the day before, right from the start. The big trailer truck was gone and only a small load of material was left at the bottom to be hauled up. This set everybody free to pitch onto the house's basic design, which was only one floor anyway, so I didn't think we'd suffered much by the absentees. Since the wall sections were already up and bolted together, next it was a simple matter of setting the doubling plates all around the top of the wall sections, locking the sides to each other. Then we would lay the pre-constructed rafter-joists across these with their notched steel plates at the apexes for the ridge board. These all formed the skeleton of the roof, as well as constituted the support joists of the interior ceilings and attic floor.

While one bunch of us was doing this, dear Rob, now back in good health, was lugging up water and passing coffee around and then lemonade to counter the day's mounting temp. Bob and

CHAPTER SIXTEEN: THE DAY LATER • 179

his number one were putting in the interior studding more or less conforming to the blueprints, which would define the rooms and interior walls. It was amazing how fast all this was moving now. By noon we were laying the plywood sheets on the roof. Shortly, as far as the roof went, it would only be a matter of rolling and nailing black waterproof felt, then shingling over that.

Inside, when Handsome Bob had the studs done, the whole gang went ahead to work with Bobbye and me plugging in the window units, while leaving all the interior doors stacked for us to hang later.

Having been slowed the day before by stevedoring the things up the hill, to say nothing of the flatbed load's late arrival in the first place, we all ate lunch on the run. There was hope in sight and that kept us hustling. Bob didn't want another added day. Nor did I, figuring we'd really have a fight on our hands with the house people over who paid for the extra time. We'd be close to having the shell like we wanted it in place anyway, so I was planning to tell him we'd take it from there no matter what. Of course, we were not about to let Bob know that... yet.

The only hitch came when YBBI ran out of idiot tasks. There just weren't any more lifting-pulling, shoving, heavy breathing-in and heavy breathing-out type jobs left for the happy Neanderthal. He could have leaned against a wall or a tree as a brace maybe, but super-liberal-bleeding-heart-idiot compassionate me cried out, "Give the kid a chance."

You recall YBBI's first bout with a nail? That was a fat flathead nail. At eye level. You'd figure he might have driven it through one board into another. But he'd blown it. Probably, by the Devil's own design, the only thing left for YBBI to attempt next was to nail plywood sheets up under the overhangs. I was doing the facing boards there myself, so what the hell, I'd be close enough to keep an eye on him.

It was a near slaughter. He had been hell-on-wheels whacking away at nails right in front of his nose; but, God All-mighty, you should have seen him trying to drive nails in over his head. Yes, over his head was right – plywood plates to be mounted up under the roof overhangs. I guess he just wasn't hooked up right for that. Like sometimes with the telephone company his brain seemed to be nothing but a panel full of busy circuits. Head tipped back, tongue flailing the air for balance, like a squirrel uses its tail, his hammer hand indiscriminately was bashing away, left and right. YBBI was again butchering our house. Chipping, chunking, scarring, gouging every piece of plywood he could lay his wild hammer on. Oh, what he was doing to the underside edge of the front porch.

Bobbye, however, now feeling one-hundred percent, simply walked over to YBBI's stool and told him she would yank it out from under him and send him flat down onto his butt, if he didn't get his act together. She wasn't taking any bull and she might have saved his life talking sternly to the wild-eyed war eagle. Bravo, girl!

Now my military pillbox had become more of a frontier stockade by the dimming sunlight. Bobbye would persist in shooting it all to hell with chatter about the kitchen going here and the bath there, and the living-room couch up against this or that phantom wall and so forth. Frankly I found it a hell of a lot more intriguing sizing up the approaches our elevation would cover if the cattle people tried to run us off. Though the Indian threat to the rear was real, I gauged, dangerously so unless we opened some clear space between the stockade and the tree line. (More random thoughts.)

CHAPTER SIXTEEN: THE DAY LATER

But the roofing went super well. Bob's son and the others were shingling champs. They really knew what they were doing plastering the stuff down like gangbusters. Nevertheless, I decided we had to get away from it all for a bit, so Bobbye and I took the VW down to fetch a case of cold beer for the troops. The day was nearing twilight. The job was getting done. Even YBBI had been neutralized and now the shadows were growing long. Most of the crew was loading their equipment back into the car. Bob's son was burning a pile of rubbish. Only a few nails were being driven here and there.

A half hour later we were all gathered at the foot of the hill looking back up at the basic shell of what would eventually be our home. Everybody but Bobbye and Bob's boy had a beer in hand. When Bob said no to his son having one, the boy snuck a wink my way, letting me know that his seventeen years probably weren't all that innocent. The kid was cool, keeping his eyes wide and his mouth shut. So, we toasted the house, the crew, myself, herself, Bob, the hill, the boys who couldn't hack it, our success, and hopes for having nothing but good luck ahead.

Old YBBI turned out better at beer drinking than carpentry. I expected him to crash the beer can against his forehead at some point, but he came through okay. I guess his elbow did work bringing things up toward his head better than down and away from it toward a nail. He was a warm soul though. We wished him well in his summer job, happily two states away from us.

Then they were gone. The last image of the caravan we saw was the rear right wheel of the flatbed turning up onto the state highway and starting off toward Massachusetts. It looked kind of like a grasshopper's back leg working faster and faster to get going because of the long dark pee splatter it bore from Macintosh's farewell salute. In a sense, you might say, they had left pissed off.

Bobbye and I had a can of Chef Boyardee over our Coleman, and a bottle of the Black Cat wine we'd first tasted at a great old stone inn in the Black Forest back when. It sounds awful, but back in our woods, very tired and very much living an adventure and loving it all, especially each other, we were two thrilled young folks... taking on the world.

We did a flashlight balancing act across the pair of 2 X 8's spanning the excavation ditch around the foundation. We brought the kerosene lantern, our two air mattresses and bug-spray inside, i.e.. under the new roof and inside the basic walls. All the tools and stuff we had stashed under tarps for the night, while we were under our own roof at last. And almost as if God wanted our night to have orchestration... the wonderful sound of rain began. Oh, how corny it was, but how absolutely new, cleansing, rehabilitating, cuddly-warm and wonderful it was too. That sound. In an empty shell like we were finally in, the splatting on the roof was like a joyous war outside and above. Then a wondrous roar set in. And we felt so good, so new, so brave, so much in love. Yes, so young, and deeply in love.

As fate would have it, dear Rob's air-mattress broke that night. Who was around to care? Certainly not the wind, nor the rain. We were alone, on our own, "in" our house on the hill with blueberry bushes all around... at last.

In the morning everything was muck. We unloaded the VW and the pickup, hauling the bits and pieces of furniture and the rest of the stuff inside, back up and under our new roof. We turned what would be the last bedroom on the front side into a temporary warehouse for this stuff. There it would sit in isolation until the rest of the house was done. Oh, and about the furniture. We had the treasure trove that dear Rob had won on The Prices is Right in NYC, just before the wedding. Bobbye got selected to be on the show when the director asked who wanted to be a contestant and beautiful Bobbye raised her hand and announced she was "Bobbye Lou Menefee from Tennessee," which won her a slot. And decorated our new house.

The rain made it clear that mud was not only nasty gook, but slippery dangerous gook too. We'd have to get more gravel down on the drive. But, perhaps most important of all we needed a way to wash the mess off. We had seen this coming those first tree cutting days back in March. The water system would have to now be our first consideration, along with the electric power to make it go.

Carl knew of a fellow, Ken Medley, who worked the night shift at the power company, who free-lanced days. He agreed to help, connecting the temporary service a few days later.

Though that weekend coming was my Reserve drill time, even this was going to fall into place. I'd take Old Gal, the pickup, to Weymouth, stay at the folks' place Sunday night, then drive over to a friend's plumbing supply store on Monday for the plumbing fixtures. His shop was where else but in… Watertown.

Hot damn, things were beginning to click. And even this early, some of our fears about how the hell to build a house were starting to ease. We were already seeing that simple necessity in logical order defined each job to be done. We needed water, we needed power. Then, with water pumping in, we'd have to accommodate wastewater flushing out. After the electrical was strung, insulation could go in. Then walls. Ceilings. Floors, cabinets, fireplace, chimney, a heating system, once the exterior was tight. What the hell? The whole thing laid itself out so sensibly. Just like a big Jigsaw puzzle, each piece depending on the ones before, interlocking with parallels to become the base for those to follow. Lincoln Logs, Lego's weren't much different. Nothing to it. Nothing but doing it.

Admittedly we still could have panicked. We had the big picture, but each of the individual bits and pieces were pretty frightening. How do you plumb a house? Put in the electrical? Lay floors?

Thank God for Sears Roebuck catalogues. Monkey Ward's too. Sears had manuals actually telling you how to do everything. Really. Plumbing, the works. And so, by that nightfall, first with a kerosene lantern, then with one bald bulb, we poured over our how-to-do books.

Bobbye read about knocked down kitchen cabinets. They didn't look so hard to assemble. She sent for them. Kind of like getting a Green Hornet whistle ring off a cereal box or something. Exciting too, waiting for the postman to arrive with half your kitchen on his back. "Keep the dog inside, folks."

Later that chilly Monday afternoon I chugged up the drive with a truck full of an electric stove, water heater, toilets, bathtub, a ceramic sink, faucets and fixtures, copper pipe, joints, T's, cleanouts, yes, and even the stainless-steel kitchen sink. And a check. My quarterly Reserve duty, which meant grits for a month anyway. I felt like a regular partridge in a pear tree.

Which I nearly became. The truck's hydraulic brake line burst somewhere between Webster, Mass, and Putnam, Conn. Going downhill, of course. Isn't that when you apply brakes? 'Like to have set me free. Out of control, accelerating, thinking of all that junk behind me waiting to cut the cab and me in half when we hit. Trying to gear down, pulling on the useless parking brake, and finally grinding the right front wheel against the curb creating huge smoke. (All the time secretly feeling like Robert Mitchem in one of those rum-running movies.)

Old Gal had demanded that I always carry my toolbox along, and happily I was able to squeeze off the busted line, which got us home short of only one brake. After a few thrills like that it was satisfying to patch things together and make it back in one piece. I felt mildly heroic.

In a few days we had the temporary electric hooked up. We got one bulb and a few plug outlets for $125 plus Medley's labor. The $125 was for a whole damned new telephone pole of all things. Hadn't figured on that. The distance of the line running from the old pole by Moody's to our place was too long by itself. Like the house sales tax, we were beginning to get the feel of those unexpected extras. And it was only to get worse.

Though I had had to grovel under the truck to fix the brake that next morning, I had gotten back relatively clean and tidy. Since Rob hadn't had the benefit of the air station showers, she noticed. Her days of chipping old mortar off the brick pile were beginning to tell on her. Rather than invade Moody's every day for washing relief, we were forced to figure our own bathing system. Accordingly, we'd invented the Long Board Solution. Using a lobster boiler and a turkey pan, we'd heat a mess of water over the Coleman. We'd combine this with cold water in an old three- or-four-gallon diaper pail I'd found at the dump. Then we'd strip bare. First Bobbye would lather, (which could be a distraction), then she'd move out onto the boards spanning the excavation ditch from the surrounding dirt mounds to the back door. I would follow with the big pail. When Bobbye was ready for a rinse, I'd dump my pail on her. Then it would be my turn. After I was all lathered up, she would dump the pail of water on me. We went through this routine in the evenings after figuring we were by ourselves way out there in the woods anyway. We never paid attention to anything but going from buck-naked dirty to buck-naked clean. This routine went on every day until one afternoon our dance was suddenly interrupted by the Moody's yelling, "Ken, Bobbye! Look out, folks comin!"

And so, they were. A guy from the Marine Reserves and his wife. But good Lord, how long had we been doing our naked dance for the Moody's to observe? It gave us a creepy feeling. (I hesitate to think how Isaiah must have sweated future property values, even for renters, going down with the likes of us balls-ass naked white folks having moved in next door.)

Suddenly more than a week had gone by, and it didn't seem that we had that much to show for it. We did, however, have some tangible things. Although Merriweather had been out to check the shell and had released another $4,000, it was money already spent. The truckload I'd brought in that week was another big chunk of it too. Then I'd backordered an oil burner that would end up costing us over $570. Money just flew away. I mentioned this to Ed. He said we could have the rest of the loan when the place was livable. "Hell," I said, "we're living in it now." But he explained that "fit for human habitation" was more explicit than that. Which hurt.

One of the senior officers at Weymouth turned out to be an artesian well-driller and he was on his way out too, yet after the terrific flurry of the first few days of seeing the whole basic structure booming up, this lull was frustrating. We didn't know then that this was more the rule than the exception of how things in truth went.

Ralph Babonas stopped by and with the well man in-route, I thought we might get some sage advice on just where to drill for the water well.

"Well, Ken, let's see what we've got," he said, sitting on one of the huge rocks by the excavation sipping some of Rob's good coffee. "How deep is Carl's out there near the highway?"

"Forty some feet, the one he and Moody share. Then he has the shallow well in the basement."

"Yep. And the place next door's the same, as I recall. Around forty, fifty feet. Then there's Mary Sandra's —met her yet, by the way?" Ralph asked, a new thought apparently coming to mind.

"No. Something special?

CHAPTER SEVENTEEN
Skunk in Glass

"Ralph turned on his boulder perch, "Bobbye, come out for a minute. Want to tell you about one of your neighbors."

Rob had been by the back door, so then she balance-walked across the board bridge to where we were sitting.

"You two met Mary the night we knocked Madlock down at the townhall," he began. "I don't recall if she had her huge dog Teddy with her. If she did, you'd remember. Teddy is the biggest damned thing you ever saw. Half collie, half St. Bernard, third half horse. It travels with a little bit of a black and white mutt, funniest darned pair. But anyway, Mary's a spinster nurse, lives with her mother over there, straight across your dirt road, past the pond. She just loves animals.

Besides Teddy and the little one, she has a half dozen cats, a couple of live-in ducks, along with a raccoon that's got the run of the place too.

"Well," he sipped his coffee, lit another half crushed cigarette, "about a week ago I was down to the village store there, when Mary walked in. The moment she's inside, we all started smelling skunk. Then the closer she moved to the back where I was cutting myself some cheese, the stronger the skunk stink got. Finally, everybody kind of stopped, ending up looking at Mary. Before anybody could say anything, she says, 'Yes, it's me, folks,' and she tells us her story.

"Other mornin'," she says, she looked out her kitchen window to see a skunk wrestling around on the grass with its head hung up in a peanut butter Jar. It had gone in licking but couldn't get back out again when it finished. Naturally Mary felt terrible for the poor skunk, so she went out to help.

"She said she knew it would be tricky but figured to take a hoe and try from a distance to maybe hold the jar against the ground firm so the skunk could pop itself out. 'Course she didn't want to get sprayed, so figured to come from the front. Which she did. And got the hoe on to the jar all right, but the little critter was more afraid of her than the jar, so it whoops its old tail up over its back and lets Mary have it right in the face.

"She didn't seem to know a skunk can fire in any direction it can point its tail. But still she felt worst of all about seeing that poor thing running off into the woods with its head still in the jar. Asked us to look for it. Sure Mary. Then she said it had been a week of ketchup baths and tomato rinses, but she just couldn't get the smell off. 'Couldn't argue that none. I left then and didn't bother anymore with the cheese."

We got a good chuckle. Could just picture her and the skunk face to face through the bottom of a peanut butter jar. Poor dear lady.

CHAPTER SEVENTEEN: SKUNK IN GLASS • 191

Then Ralph got back to the wells again.

"So, Mary's got about the same depth too. Everything on the downside of the hill seems forty-fifty feet. While up-side, Henry Dryer living up over the top of the hill, he runs maybe a hundred.

"Now, if you laid that all out on a map, I believe it would indicate the closer you got to the pond down there, the shallower are the wells. The farther from it, the deeper. So, reason would say to drill as close as you can to the pond. Right?"

"Great," I said, happy to have the problem solved so easily. "When Colonel Duffard comes this afternoon, I'll tell him that."

Macintosh came over and Ralph started patting him and scuffing his neck. Babonas nodded, winked away a curl of smoke running up into his right eye, adding, "But then again, you never know where water is. Sometimes the top of a hill's the best. 'Lota farms on hilltops."

"Oh," I said feeling less than assured. "Well, then, ah, where do you think?"

"Up to you, Ken," he said. "There's the logical way to look at it, but then again that doesn't promise anything. But I've never seen water run uphill. Who knows? Underground it's all a matter of ledges and how the layers run and where they're busted. Logic says they're busted at the pond, but you can't be sure. So," he said, getting up and heading back towards his pickup, "it's all up to what you think. Carl tells me he knows a fella who' does divining for $25 … if you believe in that stuff. $25 is a few feet of pipe, too. Yup, 25 bucks is 25 bucks. So… Thank you, Bobbye, for the coffee. I'll drop back soon. And MacIntosh, help him with his problem," Ralph said, smiling and giving Tosh a last scratch.

"Thanks Ralph. You're sure a beauty alright. Bite him, Tosh."

Ralph laughed.

"Oh, hey, how about gravelling the drive when you can?" I called as he got into his truck and started down the hill. I gave him a middle-finger salute, but he only waved and then was gone. I guess he'd bring the gravel, I didn't know for sure.

When Colonel Duffard from the Reserves arrived, it sounded something like this.

"Well Ken, where do you want her?"

"Oh, it seemed to me down here in this lower corner. It's nearest to the pond down there. I figure, well, you know, water tends to run downhill." Actually, I didn't feel too sure of that.

"Surface water," he replied deadpan.

"What do you mean?" I didn't dare ask if subsurface water ran uphill, though if he said it did, I might have believed it. I think that I get intimidated by experts.

"That pond is a low point filled by the surface run off of the higher ground around it. Might not have anything to do with what's underneath. Then again it might."

"What is underneath?" I asked, looking for something definitive.

"No idea," he mumbled contentedly, lighting his pipe.

Come on. Why must folksy experts hedge so? I Just wanted somebody to say-"Drill

there. That's where the water is." No. I'd have settled for Just, "Drill there."

"Well, I don't follow," I said with some frustration, "if there's a pond down that way, why isn't it logical to drill near it?"

"Because there is a hill in this direction," he announced cryptically as hell, pointing behind him.

"Up is down and down is up, you mean," I said testily.

"You might say."

"Oh, shit, Colonel, come on. I give up. I don't know what you're talking about."

"Simple."

"Yeah. This hill you're on could be an upheaval with the grain of its strata running in the opposite direction from the pond. The pond could be on another section all together. This would make maybe the top of the hill the best spot, or someplace down the other slope. It's all a matter of the substrata, not surface drainage."

"That's just fine. I don't own the top of the hill and I don't own the other side of the hill, so what do we do? Where do we drill?"

"I'd say that there's no figuring it out for sure one way or the other, so stick it right up next to the house."

"But that's twenty-five feet higher at least than we are here at this spot," my finger jabbing at the ground vaguely hoping to produce a geyser. "And twenty-five feet can be money."

"True."

"And damn it, the pond is down this way."

"True."

"And I'll bet it would be easier for you to get your rig in for drilling here, rather than up by the house."

"No question."

"Well, damn it, let's put it right here," and I dug an "X" with my heel.

"You're the boss," he said grinning.

"Balls," I said, and we both chuckled. He said he'd have his equipment in either the next day or the day after. And as he got into his car, he nodded up the hill towards Bobbye, "That little girl of yours sure works hard on those bricks. Looks like you got yourself a good one."

"Sure did," I smiled. "She's a Tennessee girl. A true hard worker. The best."

He gave me a nod and a smile as he drove off.

That night while snuggled together on our single remaining air mattress, Bobbye asked, "Kenny, what do you suppose is happening with the books?"

Ouch. I wished she hadn't. I didn't want to think about the books, nor be jerked back to thoughts of being a writer who wasn't writing. The moment I'd finished the first novel and had it in-route to Marcus, I'd felt somehow awkward, empty, disjointed maybe. Visible, vulnerable, I don't know exactly what to call it nor how to describe it. I just hadn't felt I could explain myself or justify myself as a so-called writer if I wasn't physically writing every day. Particularly when I was living off my wife.

Bobbye's question brought back those feelings. But brought back as well the gnawing anxiety that I had let those very pressures rush me into the second book, before it was firm in my mind. God, I felt awful about showing up at Farrar's office with only a first draft. How could you expect to sell yourself on promises? Yet he had been so enthusiastic about the possibilities that, if he liked it, how interested he might be coming back on the first again. And he had spoken of getting an agent. Damn, it had been exciting catching for even the briefest moment that exquisite tingle of success. It had seemed so possible then.

But he, the publisher, was the man with the enthusiasm based on book one. He hadn't read the manuscript of book two yet. Good Lord, I had written it, but I still couldn't sustain the glow. It was too rough. It needed cutting, weeding, some parts even called for excavation. Would he see any good in it? Was there any good in it?

"Ah Rob," I finally answered, "I don't know. I try not to think about it. You remember what an ordeal it was before. All those months, hoping, praying, desperately feeling the longer it took the surer it was. And then the refusal. How killing that had been. Like Marcus had said, just send the damned thing off and forget about it. Let's take his advice. Let's do that. We've sent it, now let's forget about it. Who knows, maybe we'll come up winners."

"You've always been a winner with me, darling," she breathed in my ear.

"What do we do when this mattress goes flat?" I asked.

"Stand up."

"Animal.

CHAPTER EIGHTEEN
Who?

"I'm Dryer."

Bobbye and I had been chipping mortar, lost in our individual thoughts when that voice from behind us made its sudden and simple announcement. "I'm Dryer." What did that mean? A cop? But no uniform, just gray work clothes. Could he be some thug from Madlock's office? But this was not a big man. In fact, he was small, somewhat dumpy and rumpled. Board of health? (Didn't look that healthy). Newspaper man? (No fedora with a chit in the hat band). Plumber? (But we had no plumbing). Devilish thing about it was that he said the name as if it should ring a bell for us.

"I'm from over the hill."

"Oh DRYER! Yes," I finally recalled Ralph Babonas having mentioned his name plus he'd shown up a fortnight ago at the townhall. "What do you say, Henry? I'm Ken and this is Bobbye, my wife. We haven't had a chance to get together, but I do want to thank you for standing up for us at the townhall the way you did. You and the whole bunch who came forward when Ralph spoke up, that was impressive. Thank you and all the people with you. It was terrific."

This was our first real get together with him. And he turned out to be a gentleman, but one we found, over time, to be very sad, very troubled. Then I went on about his well and what he might add to the discussion.

"So, you said you're from over the hill. I think Ralph was talking about your place the other day."

At first, he didn't seem to be terribly talkative. He had a distance about him. He wore glasses and seemed to maneuver them into a position where the sun reflected off them making him seem pupil-less, blank eyed, like a character out of Little Orphan Annie or something.

"Have you always been in the area, locally I mean?"

"Have I always been in the area?" he repeated, shaking his head. "You know that big bridge over to New London? That ain't always been there. Had a ferry before. My people didn't believe in ferries. Believed less in bridges, but sure as hell they believed in state lines. I'd say, conservatively, that I've rarely if ever been more than twenty miles from where we're sitting this minute." Which he said with an aggressive thump of his fist against his thigh. He really seemed to mean it.

"New London, Ledyard, Westerly, and the shore. That's it. And everybody inside that box I figure I'm half-assed ah, excuse me

Mrs. McAdams, I mean I'm related to almost all of them. We are old here. My people were probably Hessian deserters back in 1776. Last war we were ever interested in. Critical industries. I'm a dumb-assed, excuse me Mrs. McAdams, I'm a dumb-assed machinist. Fought the last war at Electric Boat. This side of the Housatonic."

"It must be good to be so firmly rooted in an area. I mean..."

"Some good but mostly bullshit, excuse me Mrs. McAdams..."

"Call me, Bobbye, and forget it. I'm used to Ken's mouth too," she offered smiling.

"You can't make a move what the whole family gets the word, then everybody has to give you advice. I sure'd like to get out of here, but if that damned bridge did collapse with me halfway across, the family'd all say 'see, see! So, to hell with it. I'll just sit here and rot."

Overall, Dryer didn't seem very happy on that subject. So, I switched to get the word on his well-drilling experience.

"Ah Henry," I started, "Ralph Babonas mentioned you when I was asking him where to put my well."

"Ralph's a good man. His kids drive him nuts, but mine sure don't stroke my brow either."

"Right, great guy," I nodded. "But anyway, looking around here, where would you figure to put a well?"

"I'm the last person to ask. I picked the spot at my place and the crazy bastard who did the drillin... I'm sorry Bobbye, I'm just not a nice man."

"Oh Henry, don't be a worrywart. You wouldn't believe what that man," and she pointed at me, "what he lets out when he gets going. Just forget that I'm here," she said with a soothing smile.

"Well, I guess I always got going on something myself," Henry said kicking a pebble with his stubby work boot. "But like

I said, I picked a spot, had Petini with his old piledriver in for the job. That damned thing banged and snorted for two weeks gettin' no place. So, we pulled up and tried another spot I figured on. Same damn thing. Both times, about, I don't know fifty feet maybe, we ran into a rocker..."

"What's that?" I asked.

"A big damn boulder that your drill bit hits right in the center, and all it does is wobble around. The bit never gets into it, nor by it. It just keeps slamming into the thing and going nowhere. 'Two in a row, so I said to hell with it and never went back 'till Petini called, Christ, must have been two months later with a bill to choke a cow. But what can I say? That's my kind of luck anyway. So, you do your own well. I'll stay out of it."

Then we heard the roar of Ralph's big dump truck starting up the drive with a load of gravel and his tractor on its trailer towing behind. Carl Bausche and his beautiful South-African Ridgeback were walking along behind for a kibitz too. And behind them it looked like Moody coming home from work. Now we had an army to talk to. With this gang, I was sure we'd get a well-drilling consensus.

Bobbye had other things to do so said goodbye to Henry, then was gone before I could ask her to put some coffee on over the Coleman.

As it turned out, Henry continued to refuse to give any opinion, and Moody, since he was renting from Carl, and hadn't had to drill a well himself, took a pass, too. Then he and Dryer got off and into a side conversation. And as so often happened, Ralph got into a frisky mood and decided to start baiting Carl, who sure was totally baitable. Ralph needled him about being such a rich old fart again, and Carl started to get hot. He didn't like talking money or even joking about money in front of one guy he'd sold land to, me, and another he was renting a house to, Isaiah. So, rather than have Carl swing on Ralph, I said something about this friend of mine coming in to drill the well probably the next day.

"What kind of equipment?" Carl asked.

"Hell, I don't know," I said. "What do you mean by equipment?"

"Pile-driver or rotary? Pile-driver gives you the most water without drilling to China," he said testily. "All a damned rotary drill does is give you a nice deep clean hole and no water to speak of. 'Costs like hell and's no damn good."

Oh no. I had one of those sinking feelings again. We'd already made the deal with Duffard, who was a colonel in my reserve squadron.

"Come on Carl," Babonas chided, sneaking a wink my way, "what do you know about wells anyway?"

"Now listen here, Babonas, you think you're so damned smart..."

Oh, oh. I could just picture these two rolling around on the ground kicking and biting. What was Ralph up to?

"I'll have you know," Carl continued, "I dug my own well by hand in my basement, and it's the best damned well in Ledge Rock. And I had Petini in to do the one Moody uses, that feeds his house and the garden too and it practically overflows it's so good. That well, Ralph Babonas, was pile-driven which is the best if you can't get by with a shallow hand-dug well."

"It gives the water all right," Moody agreed.

"Well, Carl," Henry offered, "Petini did my well too and it stinks. Took forever, cost like hell, had to go deep, and I'm not too damned sure of it during droughts either."

"I have no idea what kind of rig my guy has," I mused aloud.

"How long did he say it would take him?" asked Ralph.

"Didn't say exactly, that I can recall. Couple of days I guess."

"Rotary! That's one of those new-fangled rotary drills," Carl shouted. "No good. Nope. No good at all."

I wished I was rich and successful, then I could tell the whole world to go shove their drills.

"What's the difference? I don't understand," I said, almost pleading for help.

Carl took the podium. "The rotaries just make a clean screw hole in the ground..."

My unscientific mind played a few games with that one. The others, but for Carl, chuckled too, which made him think they were laughing at him. He started to get furious, kind of puffing and hopping around.

"Damn you, Babonas!" he half-shouted and started to head away through the bushes, when Robby rounded the corner of the construction again, kind of sneaky with a roll of something under her arm.

"Here's Rob!" I called out, hoping to keep Carl from storming off angry. "Hi, Babe."

I wasn't doing her any favors. She'd apparently figured to just slip by unnoticed ... her parcel, I now realized, was toilet paper. So, there the poor girl was, stopped dead in her tracks, red faced with surprise, considering where she had just been up to, (or down to) with four near strange men gaping at her, and her idiot husband yelling and pointing so nobody would miss every detail. Oh, my big mouth.

So, Bobbye gave an agonized half smile, did a quick about-face, and disappeared.

Everybody laughed. Carl came back a few steps. "You can sleep over to my place tonight," he offered with a smile. "I think you fixed your wagon with Bobbye for a while."

More chuckles, then Isaiah and Henry said they'd have to be going, as did Carl. And Ralph went back down to his tractor to spread the gravel. In the heat of the jousting with Ralph, I think Carl had forgotten about his prize Ridgeback, which had run off with Macintosh through the woods. This was going to make him mad when he got back to his place and found the dog still out. I got a feeling there'd be another besides Rob peeved at me before long.

After Ralph got through running his truck up and down over the gravel rock he'd dumped and spread with the scoop, (rock and some sand mixed in I learned was known as "ledge gravel", as opposed to the expensive crushed and washed "dress gravel".

I asked him about this drilling business, what it all meant?

"Well, Ken," he began. In his easy style, half a cigarette in the corner of his mouth with smoke curling into his squinting right eye, "the usual tale about the new rotary drills is that they cut fast and deep, but the old timers feel the spinning blades seal off the fissures that the water would trickle through. Some feel the spinning of those blades, plasters mud, chips, and sand into the cracks, pluggin' them. Then it takes a big enough seem to have enough opening to give an acceptable flow rate. This usually means a deep hole...... relative to what a pile-driven operation would give.

"There could be some truth to it, but that ain't all necessarily bad," he went on, picking at the sharp edge of his only thumb nail, which was another story I'd get to down the road. "You see, the old pile driver goes down slowly, in jerks, being hammered down from above. This has a shattering affect and gives time for the water to push through. 'Might be something to a shallower well this way, but then there's another way to look at it. Them pile drivers take time, and time is money, and inconvenience. You want your water fast, if Bobbye's face was sayin' anything a minute ago," he smiled.

"I'll bet she could kill me right now," I said, shaking my head.

"And Ken, even if rotaries go some deeper, you can't help but figure the natural water pressure working against all those little plugged cracks are going to open up over time. Plus, the depth of the drilling amounts to a reservoir of water over time. So, I'd figure you might end up going deeper with the new rig, but your well's only going to get better. And being deeper, you'll have more protection against a dropping water table. If this well man's a friend of yours and gives you a good price, then you're ahead of the game. So, I wouldn't worry about what anybody says against the rotaries. If they weren't any good, they wouldn't be replacing so much of the old equipment."

"Ah Ralph, I love ya, man. You're such a voice of reason to my troubled ears. Why don't you stay for a cup of coffee or a beer or something? Help me face Bobbye."

"No thanks," he smiled. "I got enough troubles to last me in my own house. Don't need yours too. I'll check back in a couple of days. Oh, and by the way, when I chipped at my tooth with my thumb nail, I said I had a story for you there."

"I guess," I said with a thoughtful nod, what do you want to tell me?"

"Well, so you won't be embarrassed down the road, I don't know if you've noticed but I only have one thumb, on my right hand. Well, when you meet my son, you sure as hell will notice he has only one thumb, too. Same as me, one on the right hand. But it isn't a genetic thing but the product of a long day and working late at night. It was on an engine fix up deal, very late, when I was tired and not paying attention when I let my left hand get into the generator pulley and it yanked and I reflexed back, the result was off came that thumb. Neat as it could be. Hardly that painful, just pop and it was gone. After I got it sewed up, I said to my boy that it was good he had been there to see what can happen when you are tired, late at night and not paying attention to what you're doing. I know he paid the whole affair attention because about a month later he did exactly the same thing. Left thumb gone for him too. Now we are father and son twins."

"Wow," was about all I got out. Some story. But I don't know what to say.

"Just don't say anything to my son when you see him. He is pretty embarrassed about the whole thing."

"Got cha," I said and wrapped an arm around his shoulder. "Thumb or no thumb, Ralph, you're the best." Then I walked down to the truck with him and watched him back his big backhoe up onto the trailer with the shovel hanging into the dump truck. Ralph was a pro. I liked the hell out of the guy.

"Hi Robbye, darling, darling, darling gorgeous wonder lady," I jabbered through her lovely brown hair as I hugged her close and personal, pressing my cheek against her head, my arms sneaking around her, hands locking in the front of her waist. I had slipped up from behind my sweet darling while she labored over her propped-up Coleman stovetop, stirring another glob of our eternal stew. "I love you, love you, love you. 'Can't live without you. Ummramm," I mumbled trying heavy neck nibbles... but she wasn't having any of it.

"Oh, come on Rob," I pleaded, backing away, then dumping heavily down on a crate, "I just didn't notice the toilet paper. I was trying to keep Carl from going away angry with Ralph.

Then you came around the corner, I shouted to get everybody's attention off their squabbling."

"You did that all right," she cut in. "That was awfully embarrassing. Kenny. There are some things women just hate to have publicized, and when a woman has to potty all bare-bottomed in the woods, that is one of them. She doesn't like having the whole world practically see her doing it."

"Ah Rob, I know. I ... "

"We have got to get the water in. I have *got* to have a bathroom," she proclaimed. "Ken, a woman without a bathroom is... is... no woman at all," she sputtered. "Look at France."

"Exactly," I muttered confusedly, "yes."

"France is a female nation," she announced without paying me any attention. "La belle France, feminine."

Her accent was lousy, but I still loved her.

"And what is the symbol of France?"

"Eifel Tower," I shouted, "Arc de Triomphe," I tried again with a terrific accent. "Charrllll DeGaulle." God, I'd make a sexy Frenchman.

"No, the *bidet*. French people rarely take baths, but French women surely keep their bottoms scrubbed. And in private. And I am a female, a woman, and I'm not even asking for a bidet. I simply want some privacy. I want a bathroom, with walls, water, running, flushing water, and a door to lock. Oh, Kenny..."

She turned, tears spilling from her big gold-flecked brown eyes. Utterly destroyed by those great moist eyes, I jumped up, and hugged her to me.. I felt like crying too, but not for exactly the same reasons. Her tears nearly killed me, but I couldn't help thinking of my first boy scout trip, and watching a friend trying to potty, squat-style in God's green forest, and what a mess the poor kid had gotten into. He'd first peed and dumped straight into his own drawn down drawers, then realizing his miscalculation, tried to adjust himself, teetered, and fell into his own mess. I don't know what badge he got for that trick, but he could have it. That scene stuck in my mind bringing me close to tears too. And yes, I was terrified I'd burst out laughing.

CHAPTER EIGHTEEN: WHO?

Three days later, our well was in. At the bottom of the hill, down toward the pond. I found the whole drilling thing an interesting experience. Once the bit was in the ground and had started to make its way down, I got dizzy with fantasies. After about ten or twenty feet, I started thinking—screw the water. How about oil? And the further down we went the more convinced I became, though I wouldn't dare breath a word of it, that we might, in fact, hit oil! By 100 feet it seemed a certainty. It was simply a matter of time, 'must be. At 110 feet I had difficulty looking and acting like only a regular, middle class guy. Five feet later, I began to feel that I understood, in a sense, or intimately knew Howard Hughes and his multiplicity of problems. At 120 feet ,my mind began to compose a letter I felt I simply had to write...

Dear Mr.Hughes, If I may, Howard,

As you've no doubt have heard, my well is now at the 120-foot mark. By sunset,
    perhaps by mid-afternoon next, what difference does it make, really, she'll be in. Of course, we both realize what this means. We will be in competition with each other...

At 125 feet, even before I'd finished my letter to Howard Hughes, we hit—water. Shit. And rather than raking in oil money, we had to shell out $843.00 for our drilling. Again, more than anticipated. Another chunk out of our borrowed bank account.

It was a terrific temptation to tell the driller guy to just keep on going. Water of all things. Damn. Let's go deeper for the oil we know is down there!

Nevertheless, that evening we decided to celebrate anyway. Water is better than nothing. We figured to go to another auction.

This one was in the parking lot at the townhall. It brought back memories of past triumphs, so I felt strong, tall, and tough not to be intimidated by the rapid-fire inside jargon of the auctioneer. And through this feeling of strength from being on home turf, so to speak, I gained inspiration. I saw, I bid, I won at 25 cents each, a set of ancient wicker-bottomed dining room chairs.

At first Bobbye thought I was "some reckless," as they said around there, but for an investment of $1.50 we had half sealed a serious domestic impasse.

Bringing the chairs triumphantly back to our spot by Old Gal the pickup, I set one down before my lovely darling. She looked at me questioningly, then sat on it.

"No dear," I whispered helping her ceremoniously to her feet. "Stand back, love," I said, then, lifting my work-booted foot high, I jammed it with gusto down through the wicker, leaving me standing, one foot in, and one foot out of the chair.

Bobbye seemed properly impressed by my show of strength, but still didn't looked to have captured the magic of it all. Nor did those around, as people nearby watched this strangely destructive man ram his foot through the bottom of his new old chair. "Fanatic," their eyes seemed to say. "Deviant," and worse.

Hah. I read all their insinuations, but as a great inventor, humanitarian, and dedicated loving husband, but I paid them no mind. Removing my foot again, I stood aside and indicating the seemingly ruined chair with a cavalier gesture, I announced," Madam, la toilette."

Bobbye looked at me, at the bottomed-out chair, back at me, and broke into peals of laughter. She jumped into my arms, both of us hugging and laughing. At last, we would know some comfort. I could hardly wait till the next morning.

Before leaving, we managed one more coup. Bobbye spotted a large old Victorian mirror on a bureau. It originally had little platforms halfway up both sides, I imagined, for lamps or candle sticks. It was a heavy sturdy thing, with good glass, and a strong frame. Rob figured to strip the old gook off, side pieces too, then paint it all a flat colonial black. With carriage lamps on either of the sides, it would be something special. Particularly when she set it up in the bathroom-to-be, of all places. Would be, that is, if it wasn't still attached to the bureau that was commanding... "Forty dollars, forty dollars, do I hear forty-five? There is the five. Who says fifty? Fifty dollars..." in the bidding.

Rob was sick watching that mirror and its flats going, going, gone for $60.00. But I had an idea which, happily, worked. It turned out that the fellow who bought the bureau really had no use for the mirror and mounting sides. We offered him five dollars. He was delighted. So, with the help of a screwdriver, Bobbye got her mirror and all, the bureau-buyer got rid of the unused portion at a profit, making everybody's evening a success.

Then, back home again, we modified another chair, setting the two by the back of the house. We painted HIS on one, HER'S on the other. we figured nothing but easy living ahead for us for now on.

The next morning, I met our local minister for the first time. It was another of those disconcerting situations, like us and the Moody's and our outdoor bathing embarrassment. Having a fierce call by Mother Nature, I grabbed "HIS" on the run and headed toward the back woods. I didn't go far enough though. Didn't have time. But at least I had a newspaper in my lap when Reverend Thomas drove up, and there I sat. 'Letting it all hang out, so to speak. Gawd. But I don't think he even knew what I was actually doing out there, in the bottomless chair with the NY Times in my lap.

Later, over coffee, the Reverend told us of a church in a nearby place called Noank, that might have a used pump at a cheap price. He had heard that right after their new well went in, the town put in its own water system making the church's hook up superfluous. Bad for them, good for us. We decided to go for a look. Noank. Funny. Who'd ever have thought that God was alive and well in a place called Noank?

Before going to the church to check out their equipment, I dropped by one of the big merchandise stores to talk with their plumbing "expert." I wanted an idea of how much to offer for the church pump. He told me though, that it just so happened they had one on sale at that very moment. The exact pump I needed, he said. Why pay more? Just say, "Charge it!" and all that crap. I looked at it. Hell, I didn't know a darned thing about pumps, wells, depths, horsepower required or anything else, so I jotted all the specs that he gave me down and drove by Babonas' place. Good thing I did as Ralph said forget it. The specs our friendly "expert" had given were for a shallow depth pump that would have burned itself out in short order seeing that it had to go so deep. You know, as a pilot, that's something I liked about aviation. Everybody who claims to be a flyer or a mechanic has to pass a whole variety of written, oral, and actual flight or engine-overhaul examinations to prove it. There are good pilots and poor pilots, but they are all signed and sealed real pilots. Mechanics too. I hope someday the world of "experts" will be the same. But as it stands now, any jerk can, through the simple feat of continuous respiration, qualify as an "expert" on any subject of his choosing.

The plumbing department of the New London store seemed to be blessed with one of these, to say nothing of the reservoir of similar talent we know abounds in Washington, D.C. I would get a kick out of meeting our Southeast Asian expert. I might recommend that he and the New London plumbing expert swap assignments for a year or so. 'Surely neither could do any more harm either way. Might work to the good. Then we could run a few transmission experts over to the Pentagon, freeing those stout lads for slots in the frozen custard industry where they could still get some wear out of their uniforms. There certainly is no end of swapping possibilities in the "expert" ranks. Heaven knows, it could mean the difference between war and peace, life and death.

So, Bobbye and I took the pickup over to the church. It was a reflex action. We do so much second-hand buying and bargain-hunting that we instinctively put on our seediest clothes and crank up the worst looking vehicle we own. Nevertheless, as we drove to Noank, my mind was troubled as to how in good conscience I could chisel a church? The usual methods of bluffing, badgering, and bludgeoning didn't seem fitting. Booze was probably out too. And sex. It looked as if we were stuck with only the long shot stuff like faith, hope, love, charity, along with groveling, wheedling, you know. Maybe tears. If Bobbye cried, I'd feel so awful I could probably sprinkle a few tears myself.

But at least we did have some information. With a price perspective and having picked Ralph's brain, I felt we might be able to dazzle them with our bargaining footwork in the end.

After we hallooed around some, hitching up trousers, Reverend Whatsit, a very young pink scrubby sort of fellow who looked to have family money, led me down cellar. Rob stayed back up with the Mrs.

One look at their pump told me the thing was perfect, a fact that was never to be mentioned. If anything, the pump was bigger than what we needed.

"Ah, son of a gun, this hasn't the horsepower I'd had in mind."

"I really wouldn't know anything about that, Ken. But, well, if you can't use it, you can't use it." He started to turn up the stairs.

" Oh well, dang it." Turning back, I offered, "Let me check something." Then, with great bluster and busyness, I mumbled,"Ummmm. Ah. Hmmmm."Pause. A headshake. "Well, there is a chance for it. The Jet could be changed. Might make the difference. Of course, I could just be taking something off your hands to get stuck with it myself."

"Yes, that's true. I don't know what to say. I know nothing at all about such things."

Splendid.

"Looks like it's been here a while. Rust there," pointing, commencing a gentle wheedle.

"Strange, yes, I see it," the Rev affirmed, adding, "but the whole apparatus has only been in for six months. By the time we got the appropriation approved and it put in, the town went on public water."

"You mean it hasn't run for six months?" I gasped, scrooching my face into a true Dickens-of-disbelief. "Why, as I am sure you are aware Reverend, the very worst thing for any mechanical device is inactivity. And for a water pump, oh my goodness. They built-up corrosion." So, I tsk, tsked and hmmmmed quite a bit, rather impressively really. All I had said was actually true, of course, but I was perhaps making a bit much of it.

I wiggled the impeller shaft back and forth gingerly. Frankly it was free as the air and the bearings, as best I could tell, felt tight. The pump seemed brand new. I threw the switch, a bit dramatically of course, and she purred into action. A real hummer. Just the ticket.

CHAPTER EIGHTEEN: WHO? • 213

"Ummm. Well, we got by that hurdle," I mumbled in consulting-physician fashion, "is this the tank over here? Ummm. Ah huh." If I'd had a beard, I'd have been pensively stroking it. "Okay. I guess I've seen enough," and up the stairs I went. Briskly. Keeping him guessing.

At the door I turned and summarized: "As I see it, the pump looks okay. I need one immediately. There might be problems with this one from sitting around like it has that I don't know about. But that's the chance I take. I'm not totally sure of the capacity," (true, but inversely so. It was more than we needed, and it would merely be a matter of stepping it down, I hoped), "but I believe a change of jets could adjust that. They cost money, of course. All of this is a shot in the dark for us without a guarantee, even though it hasn't run much. Second owners don't get that value. With all this in mind then, we'll offer you ... ah ... eighty dollars for the whole works. Pump and tank."

"Yes. I see. Well, I will consult the deacons and get back to you in a week or so."

"Then I withdraw the offer," I said bluntly and started off, hoping against hope he'd stop me.

"My goodness. No. Why?" he asked with some agitation.

"Sir, we need a pump now, today. Bobbye and I are bathing out of gallon jugs, pots, and pans. Today is Saturday. We have a lot ahead of us to get this thing hooked up. I need your yes or no right now. If it's no, then we have to go looking some more and fast."

"I see, yes, but I can't release it to you without the approval of the deacons. I'd have to call them each for that and I might miss some. Hmmm. Oh well, look," he said, seeming to tire of the whole thing. "1 think $80 is fine. I'll call as many as I can, and you call me back in an hour or so. You probably could come back and be on your way within two hours. How is that?"

"Hmmm," I mused, counting to ten slowly, trying to contain myself. "Okay. It's a bargain." Out went my hand on it. "I'll call in one hour. Good luck."

Rattling off, we waved goodbye. I was sure we had the deal. How could they search around for other bids in just an hour? And I'll bet $80 in the till before Sunday morning looked better than nothing, after having had the thing just sitting there for most of a year.

So, off we went to Perini's well man's place. He was in the pipe business too. We figured not to waste the hour and get our order in, pending the church's decision.

Since Ledge Rock was pretty rural, there wasn't a whole straight jacket of building codes for us to deal with. Petini told us about this new P.V.C. plastic pipe and how easy it was to use. What the hell. We could do the cold-water half with that. We'd be using it for the well pipe anyway, so why not get it all now?

It was fascinating stuff to work with. Just brush the special cement on the pipe ends to be joined, a coupler T or l or whatever, then press the one firmly into the other, twist a half turn and hold. At first there would be an odd sort of polar rejection between the two pieces, then it would start to take and finally it would set in a super strong bond. Another tinker toy for Kenny. I couldn't wait to get started.

Using Petini's phone, we called the church. Yes, the deal was on. Great. For $80 we had gotten at least $200 worth of equipment. It was a Scotsman's holiday.

I dropped Rob at home, sped by the church, hacksawed the pump off its old hook up, hauled the tank to the truck and barreled over to the Burke's pump place just before closing. They knew the pump, 'had installed it. We'd made a hell of a deal, they said as they fixed up the jet after checking everything. For $21.75. Couldn't beat that. The whole lot coming in under the big box store's expert's price on the inadequate pump alone. Beautiful.

It had been a fast and successful day up to that point. We should have expected getting bogged down by sunset, however, things always work that way it seemed.

Once back at the house with all the pipe, pump, tank, jet, joints, and goop laid out on the ground, the obvious next step became too large to ignore. A pumphouse.

Ah hell. There was the hooker in having drilled at the bottom of the hill. Now we had to get Ralph back to dig a hole for the damned thing, plus a trench all the way up to the house for the supply and electrical lines. Had I been conned? Ah, Ralph wouldn't do that. Come on Ralph, say it ain't so.

And now it was too late for concrete block. They'd closed at noon. So, yes, yes, down the drain went our weekend of water.

We tried not to do a damned thing on Sunday, besides listening to Reverend Thomas and reading the newspaper. Which nearly drove us both nuts; finally driving me back down to the well.

I dug enough out around the pipe to get a hacksaw to it. For four hours I sawed back and forth, back and forth. Good Lord what a miserable, moronic, mind-smashing idiot's job sawing back and forth, back and forth it seemed bloody forever. By the time the sucker was cut through, Carl had been by and Dryer, Florence. Ralph even came along, too. Which was fortunate. He promised to do the trenching in the morning. And he gave his solemn pledge that that was not why he'd recommended the lower place to drill, down by the pond. I knew it wasn't, but I had to pull his chain anyway.

On Monday, while Babonas' backhoe was roaring and snorting, I took the pickup over to the cement plant for some block. It was on this very trip that Old Gal, Old Beauty herself went through her change of life and even sex too, becoming and forever remaining to me, that "Old Sonofabitch."

I can't say I was blameless. I overloaded the hell out of her. Maybe a hundred block, cement, near a half yard of sand. It was too much. The truck was never really the same after that. Not directly damaged from it, only pissed off, mean, and spiteful. It spent the full remainder of our time together just busting my chops.

First the battery went dead at the block place, but I'd had trouble starting it up, so I figured it was only that. 'Got a recharge and headed back with the load.

What a trip. Between there and our place was one nasty hill and several close cousins. Naturally, it wasn't until we'd started up that first beauty, that I noticed the amp-meter sitting on the pucker side of zero. Why hadn't I noticed that before? Idiot. Either the generator or the voltage regulator was bad. And there we were, loaded to the axles, halfway up that damned Everest, running on battery alone.

As third gear lugged out, I looked behind and saw an ever-lengthening line of cars. The load was getting too much for second gear too. First gear wasn't synchromesh. I'd have to double-clutch and hope I didn't jam it. Oh boy, no time nor speed enough for double-clutching. Which made me think of the brake line that had burst a day or two before. Sure, I had fixed that one, but how about the others? If I missed first, man we'd be quickly whistling backwards waiting for the brakes blow too. Even if they held, we'd probably burn the clutch up trying to get underway again after slap-shifting into first gear. Oh Lord, please have mercy on that first gear. But, wow, with a grind, I did get in it and we were still rolling forward. Barely. Come on battery. Come on baby. Then, what the hell, of all things, out went the gas gauge. What did that have to do with it? Maybe the poor thing was straining so hard the gas tank just fell out on the road or something.

"Keep going," I pleaded. "Please, baby, twenty more feet."

I was drenched in sweat. The engine was starting to run hot, too. The gas gauge was pegged the wrong way, the temp gauge the other way, while the amps just sat in the red saying, "Screw you, pal."

I felt like William Bendix in another crappy old Seabee's movie. Would we make the top of the hill with the load of dynamite, or would the whole thing blow sky-high first?

The line of cars behind was up to an easy ten now and crawling. Pissed off. I believed I could see fists shaking out of the windows. They all hated me. I felt like a State Department man on a South American goodwill tour. Just ten more feet. We were going so slowly the speedometer had even said to hell with it. 8 feet, 7, 6, 4.... "Mission Control, John "Shorty" Powers pushing sick pills against the worry that the whole friggin' truck would blow up at, Zero.

Why did I do these things? Why didn't I make two small-load trips? Or pay for a delivery? Why push it? Why commit suicide like this and blow the truck up too?

Two, one ... blast off! But, wow! Over the top. We made it! Hey man, no sweat. I'd had it whipped from the start. Charley Potatoes, baby. And now look at how we're flying. Faster and faster down that other side. Down, down, faster. Oh shit! Could I slow it? Eeeeyow! We were Hi-balling!

Yes, it had been a bad trip, but then finally we were turning into our lane, a beam of Moody's house when it all let go. The battery quit, the ignition quit, the motor knocked out, and the whole parade ground to a halt right next to our new water pump station which was waiting to be built.

Kablaaam, the radiator cap blew up and off as I felt myself disappear from sight in clouds of hissing, pissing steam. Son of a bitch.

From that day on, every day, before I could drive the truck anywhere, I had to do repair- penance. The starter motor would jam. The transmission would hang up. The other brake lines went one by one and had to be replaced. Then a headlight here and a regulator there. I had to buy, clean up and install two more junkyard generators. Flat tires. Oh man, did that truck make me pay for my abuse. From that day on, it had become known to me as that son-of-a-bitch, my nemesis till the day it all came to an end. In time I rebuilt the sucker and sold it to, of all people, the Chief of Police. Good hunting, my man, and good luck with your Motor Vehicle Inspection.

The pump house took a couple of days. I was glad of the experience anyway. Kind of a warm-up before laying the fireplace brick. I sure needed it. 'Had forgotten the feel of mortar, the proper mix, the trowel work, just making the whole thing hang and stick together.

Then, with Rob helping and Carl directing, we had the 120-feet of plastic pipe sections all goop-locked together and connected to the jet pump at the bottom end. One pipe down to the jet, then the long return unit back up to the house. We had these laid out on the ground from the pump house on up the hill.

I hopped down in and started lining the jet end up with the well hole. On Carl's command, Rob began to walk her end forward. Carl took the middle, and I helped feed it all down the well hole as the two others approached.

It was a nervous job. I could just see that double gray snake slipping loose and clattering down the hole, to be ever-gone. And since I was nervous about it all happening, I was shouting too many "Easy, easy, hold it, come on, easy, hold it's..." it was bugging them for sure. Then I called, "Hey Rob," this is like giving the whole world an enema," which got the both of them laughing too, shutting down action for a minute or two.

Finally, we did get it all down. Straight into the bowels of the earth. What a weird feeling, just feeding 120 feet of pipe into a hole in the ground. It was almost obscene. Then, while Carl and Bobbye each held the end of the pipe, we slipped the casing cap over, threading the two ends through it, and we gooped two "L" fittings on tight. We let them set a couple of minutes, then that was it. The guts of the well were in. At last. After accomplishing so little for so long, we had finally gotten a lick in for the home team. We felt we'd screwed the world!

Ken Medley attached the electrical once we had the pump in place, the tank in, and all the pipes laid up to the house. We ran that to the water heater and one cellar spigot, all of which gave us WATER! Fantastic. And everything worked. Really! Turn the handle - on. Turn the handle - off. All that with the pump going whirr, and the storage tank filling to the preset level and pressure. Magic. And we were the magicians.

"So, Ralph, I guess you can back-fill the foundation now."

"No way."

"What do you mean?"

"No sense."

"Come on. Why not?"

"You're on a hill. No sense in taking chances on a wet basement. The best bet now is to lay perforated pipe on a gravel bed all around the foundation. Then tie the standpipes to where your gutter drains will come down to them. You'll control your runoff and create flushing for the foundation pipes as well. To say nothing of running a cellar drain downhill out the front where I've lain all those big rocks, building the wall for the house and yard to sit on. You always want to be able to pump out a cellar. Maybe your oil tank will rupture creating another need for cellar draining. Who knows? And look, you might figure as well to get all your plumbing in too. Then test the whole system. Make sure it's tight. Covering it all is easy and cheap. Uncovering to patch leaks after the fact takes time, terrific time, and that costs like hell. This will avoid it all.

"So, laddie, call me when you've got that done, then I'll come over to dig out your septic system and drywell at the same time. Save you even more money."

"Gawd. Septic system, dry well," I muttered, "Ralph I'm a suburban boy. I don't know anything about that kind of stuff. Sounds like a lot of crap to me."

"Exactly," he smiled. "Call me when everything's in and ready to go."

"Yeah, next year sometime," I mumbled. Why did everything have to be so complicated? And probably expensive too. 'Hadn't thought much about all this drainage business in the budget. Like I said, to use the truck for the gravel, and tar paper, and pipe, and joints, all the plumbing mess and God only knew what else; I had to get it running better. And that meant Old SOB wasn't going to work for me anymore without a fight. So, every morning, under it I went to fix whatever new breakdown it had decided to have the night before.

Thinking back on it, I'll bet an awful lot of people around town thought I was one real miserable SOB since they only saw me first thing in the morning. Isaiah Moody for instance. I know he'd heard a lot of me, like trailer-trash cussing and kicking my damned truck. And remember, this was still before we knew they could see our naked wash ups through the bushes each afternoon.

So, a raving cursing maniac each sunup, and a snow-white skinny-dipper each night. How often must he have asked, "Why me, Lord? Wasn't being black in Mississippi bad enough?"

It was rough on old Rob, too. Poor girl was just finishing her long-term sentence on the brick pile and had to listen to me besides that. And don't underestimate those bricks. She'd tackled nearly four thousand in all. Taking each in one hand, the awkward brick hammer in the other, she'd chip endlessly. Physically it was hard work. Mentally it was catastrophic. Chip, chip, chip, turn the brick around, chip, chip, then drop it. Pick up another. Chip, chip, on and on. It was much like my having to saw the well pipe on and on for hours, but for her, weeks.

Bobbye did have a radio anyway. 'Heard every talk show from Westerly, Rhode Island to the upper West Side of Manhattan, all day long. One conciliation, anyway, was how she took everything so stoically. She's an incredibly good creature. 'Puts up with more misery than the world can imagine. Her biggest misery, more than not, of course was angry, grumpy me.

So now, we had advanced into the plumbing stage of things. Outside, inside, literally all around the house. The place looked like a movie set. Trouble lights blazing everywhere. Extension cords feeding these, heavier cords for the power tools. Butane torches, solder, flux, hacksaws, files and filings, copper for the hot stuff laying everywhere under foot too; PVC and goop for the cold-water pipes everywhere else, even cast iron for the last leg of the poop-shoot. Did we ever look industrious? Busy, busy. Work all day, half the night, read our manuals the rest of the time. We were a whirlwind.

CHAPTER NINETEEN
Swaps For a Friend

Naturally we hadn't had any time to pay attention to old MacIntosh, but somewhere along the line we became conscious of how mopey, draggy, and devilishly depressed our good dog was becoming again. But what could we do about it? We couldn't take time to pal around with him and, unlike in Wakefield, there weren't many other pooches that weren't tied or penned for him to roam with. So, we figured that Tosh just needed a friend, and when we had a moment, we began a search for a pooch-pal for our dear dog.

The local radio station had a program called "Swaps," that Florence told us about. It broadcast goods, services, pets, anything people were willing to put up for free, at a price or even to trade. We listened to that and hit the dog-pounds hoping to save a hound from the labs if we could; but nothing. Then "Swaps" came through with a character named Clem. Ah yes, noble Clem. And with him began a very humorous era around the blue patch on our hill, yet one which in the end brought us great sadness, too.

Ever heard of a Beagle/Basset? I hope I never do again. People say it's a breed put together for small game hunting-- rabbits, and the like. They're supposed to have terrific noses. My personal opinion is that they're bred exclusively for the thickness of their skulls. I suspect the dog breeding community had in mind to codify a dumb baseline, a kind of brain power dead low or flatline. In this way all other breeds could be awarded quotients from that point, the Beagle/Basset base or, as it might well now be known as the "Clem Line."

When we arrived at the advertiser's house, we had no idea of the Clem Line. We'd never met a Beagle/Basset before. And when we did, we were delighted.

This character was the funniest looking thing we'd ever seen. He had the same coat coloring as a Beagle, but was much stockier, and lower, and horrendously long. He was really just a long Basset in Beagle clothing. He had sad, lonely, forlorn, droopy eyes, goofy dragging ears, a long skinny straight-back tail, the works. But if his Beagle blood had made him somewhat less sloppy, it had also made him even more clumsy. For instance, his male unit was so long and his legs so short that it would drag on the ground if he didn't swing his back legs high and lurch left to right. In short, Clem was an irresistible clown whose loving smiles said to us, "Take me."

We never thought to ask, why was this dog's price set at zero? It was just too good a deal to mess up with any reasonable questions.

Even as we drove away in our VW, Clem standing nobly in the back seat, his former owners called out, "Clem doesn't care for car trips much." They shouted out to us, smiling and waving.

CHAPTER TWENTY
Trips from, Hell

T*rips?* Hah. We'd traveled only a block when Clem showed us what he thought of rides in cars. You know how a VW Bug is. No back windows that roll down, so the backseat was encased only in high walls of glass, left side, right side. Clem didn't buy this at all. First, he made a wild lunge, seemingly at the back of my head. I didn't know if I was under attack or what, so I just shoved him back on to the rear seat. Where he immediately started throwing up all over the place. God, could he regurgitate. So, we stopped and cleaned up his mess as best we could. We'd had the front windows down from the beginning against the rain just starting. We figured our error had been keeping Clem from hanging his head out a window. So, for the second try, I allowed him to nuzzle over my shoulder with his head hanging out my window.

There are several breeds of dog that might be classified as Significant Slobberers. The boxer is one, the St. Bernard is the king of them all out of their sheer size alone, pound for pound, I believe it is hard to top the Beagle/Basset. I say this because Clem became a living speed governor. With his head out the window, 45 MPH became the maximum allowable velocity. Anything over that seemed to enter the car into an open-mouthed buffet-boundary throwing saliva in all directions, mostly over me and the front seat. Below 45 his mouth merely streamed out onto the outside of the car, which didn't particularly bother me till the next morning. I hadn't known what Beagle/Bassets have in their saliva, but one ingredient for sure seems to be German paint remover. Where the saliva streamlines had dried overnight, the red paint job was no longer red, but a kind of orange, several shades lighter than the factory color. I had always taken great pride in my vehicles, and this decolorization was, in my book, about as bad as it could get. Which begged the question, what the hell were we going to do about Clem?

Macintosh wasn't sold on Clem either. He took one look at this new "friend," and gave me the most scathing regard any dog ever leveled at his master or mistress. And from then on, oh how Mac ignored Clem. 'Didn't so much as sniff him at all. Macintosh only turned and strode to the nearest tree to hike a leg. But I didn't pay attention to any of this. I clung to the idiotic self-deception that old Tosh would finally find that there was hope for Clem to be considered loveable.

The next day I inaugurated a campaign to ease Clem into better traveling skills. I decided to take him with me on my short runs. The campaign lasted one trip. I thought of it as, "My Trip from Hell." There has never before been a four-mile drive to match this one.

Going down our dirt lane to the main road, I pushed Clem back further into the back seat, explaining to him that he simply had to learn to travel. I informed him clearly and concisely that I would have all available windows open to cool his tender self. He, rather surprisingly, seemed to accept this as reasonable, since it was being promoted as a short trip. So, he sat back there, in the rear, much like any regular dog would.

I was encouraged. I really felt we were a long way to solving the problem, when I heard his stomach start its pre-retch overture. I hit the brakes, veering off to the side of the road. We stopped. I threw open the door and flopped the seat forward to let Clem out. But he was in the process of picking himself up off the floor from the somersault tumble I had caused with my jammed brakes. He gave me an accusing look, ignored the open door, and reseated himself as regally as his preposterous body would allow. This gave me another glimmer of hope. Perhaps the sudden stop had had a shock affect much as a scare has on hiccoughs. I drove off again sensing a modicum of possibility.

My euphoria was short-lived. The end was very near. Pulling out onto busy Route 1, we turned right toward Bill Nelson's lumber yard. Some distance behind I saw a huge trailer truck steadily closing on us. From the other direction a fat black tanker rumbled our way too. Clem was very quiet and that was making me feel good –kind of like I was intelligent and in control of things, that is until I glanced into the back to give a wink and a word of encouragement to my new pal.

Good God! I had never seen anything like it! An Atrocity. My panicky reflexes veered us to the side of the road again. I jammed on the brakes hard as before, only compounding the disaster.

The entire back seat of the car was a horror show. Awful. There was Clem, glassy-eyed, hunched up in the classic dog fashion, defecating smack in the center of the back seat. And that put us into another panic stop that sent Clem, and his deposits, rocketing my way. Blam! He hit the back of the seat. Thump, thump came his droppings. In an unthinking frenzy I flung the door open, on the highway side, and leapt out. Then, out of the corner of my eye, I realized my mistake as the huge tractor-trailer bore down on me.

Clem had been right behind and took it on his own to dash over my back straight into the road. I grabbed for him. Thank God for that long straight tail. I caught it, pulling hard to stop him, but he was strong. And I was off balance, which caused me to flop along behind him, allowing Clem to make it into the road, just slightly short of the center line.

Then all hell broke loose. The big trucks coming from two directions locked their air brakes as one. There was a horrendous screeching racket from left and right. Skidding tires. Both big-rigs damned near jackknifed and there I was, in the middle of the frigging road looking eyeball to eyeball with the face of the bulldog ornament of one of the truck's grills as it skidded toward me and Clem, whom I held by the end of his tail as he strained to reach the other side of the road which then put him blocking the reverse-direction of the roadway as the great tanker skidded and shrieked to avoid him. And Clem, at full strain was now hunched-over vomiting, oblivious to the chaos all around him.

That is how Clem, the champion of Beagle/Bassets, single handedly closed one of America's busiest state highways, and damned near got me killed in the bargain.

Out of total cowardice, not daring to face like-a-man the havoc I'd caused, I got a better grip on that damned tail and laureated Clem back into the car. Then I sped from the scene, suffering as briefly as possible the shouts and curses of the enraged truckers. It was a miracle no one was killed, and I wasn't about to stay around to give those guys a chance to alter that score.

But I paid, paid through the nose all the way to the lumberyard and back to our place where I dumped the idiot hound, shoveled out the backseat mess, and borrowed Moody's hose to power-spray the interior of our sad car. There was no other way to spruce it up short of putting a match to the gas tank and writing the whole bloody mess off to spontaneous combustion.

"He doesn't care for car trips much," should stand as one of the eternal highs in benign understatements. God save us from beagle/bassets.

CHAPTER TWENTY-ONE
Backfilling

We finally backfilled around the foundation. The plumbing was now in, too, and we'd passed the water pressure test with only one quickly soldered leak.

Man, our plumbing work was fantastic, if I do say so myself. Cleanouts everywhere. Extra-large pipe diameters, PVC cold and copper hot, wall to wall. Extra vents, stack pipes, more and bigger than required, traps all over the place too. And shutoffs. We could isolate every section, every unit in the system. Pressure shock-absorbers before the clothes and dish washers and elsewhere to protect future valves and motors. We had the hot water tank and washing area elevated against flooding, in addition to the cellar drains. I mean, baby, this was space-age stuff all the way. We had moon-ship potential. Three, two, one, blast off.

And the bathroom toilet flushed! Enormous implications here, though use of it was still postponed until we got townhall approval. The rest of the plumbing was in, the kitchen roughed out, same for the bathroom john, sink, and tub; besides the back-filling Ralph promised, and had dug the septic tank and drywell holes, but these weren't in yet, so the glories of our own flush toilet were still denied. The anticipation, the gnawing grinding obsession to poop in our own pot was mind-shattering. We had to watch each other almost like reforming alcoholics.

The fact everything did work gave us a wonderful feeling. Having watched that toilet gurgle and swirl just once was an almost mystical experience. Because of it we knew the world couldn't be all bad. We knew there must be more to Christmas than department store windows. And we knew with certainty that God must truly be alive and well in other places than just there on our hill in Connecticut.

We were so happy that day just on the far edge of August, the peak of summer heat, but marvelously sunny clear days every day fell in place for work. Rob and I were feeling pretty confident. All the plumbing was in and the insulation would be Bobbye's task once we picked it up from Bill Williams. We could move on with a few more of the electrical steps, then with the insulation in, I could help plaster-boarding some walls and hit a few ceilings too. The Montgomery Ward boxes full of kitchen cabinet parts were also neatly stacked ready to be whacked together now that the water works were hooked up. Rob was going to tackle that on her own.

We really felt good. Not exactly like we knew specifically what we were doing since every successive job was new and strange; but we were coping and felt confident that none of it was too big for us to handle. So, as ever, when one feels her/himself getting the handle on everything, that's just about the time it all blows up. Anyway, that's what happened on the sad afternoon of our most happy morning.

The next problem started when Henry Dryer dropped by from work, as he was doing more and more, almost every day lately. Ever since the first time he appeared from out of nowhere announcing "I'm Dryer," Henry had established himself as something of a character. But with time, with seeing him more and getting to know him better, we began to realize that there was an edge of sadness, a kind of deep bitterness creeping more and more into his conversations.

Understand though, Henry was always an entertaining sort. He could tell us a story of misery and woe that would tickle our hearts. He had a sort of whipped manner about him, whipped but not beaten. And a genuine warmth. We could sense in his coming over and chatting each day that he somehow identified with what we were doing. That he had watched us come in from another state, another city, light years away from his circle. The way we just busted a road in, chopped some trees, and squatted. The brashness of it I think attracted him to us and caused him to spiritually, at least, join us in sharing the whole adventure.

CHAPTER TWENTY-TWO
Bombs, Bowling Balls and a Yam

But that particular day, the day of our toilet triumph, I walked out to the mailbox, feeling damned good. I was later than usual, past quitting time at Electric Boat. Even the homeward rush was past. Only one car was headed our way, coming over the crest of the hill from town. It was Henry's car. As I pulled the few letters and a grocery store flyer out of the box, I waved to him. He pulled up and parked by the box. We walked down the dirt lane past Moody's together, waving to Loraine who was taking in sheets from the line.

Henry really seemed to be in a bum mood. The machine shop was closing in on him. They'd landed some kind of big order, and for the past several weeks he'd been making the same part, one with very tight tolerances that only he, personally, could handle. Over and over and over endlessly again. To make one of these bastards, was apparently bad enough, but to make thousands was excruciatingly tedious for him. He was about to go nuts, he said.

Which got him off on how nuts he'd gone under such pressure in the past. Nuts for the bottle. Henry confided that he was an alcoholic, but one who hadn't had a drink in seven years. "Seven miserable Goddamned years," he said, kind of hunched over, leaning beside me against one of the huge boulders Ralph had plucked up while digging our basement.

"Ken, I want a drink so bad right now it's churnin' my guts. I got a lump right here," he thumped high on his stomach, "so Goddamned big I can hardly swallow. And there's only one fucking thing that would melt it. Booze."

I knew Henry pretty well, but not long-term-understandingly well. I was a little embarrassed, kind of ill at ease hearing his confession like this, so I looked away and down at the mail in my lap... and saw it.

Oh God. Now I had a lump to match Henry's surer than hell. The envelope had Farrar, Strauss, & Cudihy on the upper left corner. But what built the lump, what was so miserably ominous about it was the regular, no air mail, no special delivery, no registered mail, nothing not even a stamp, just one of those cold, shitty, machine red ink run 'em through 5 or 6 or 8 cent or whatever the hell price of it was, office posted letters. Congratulations' and contracts didn't come in envelopes like that. Refusals did.

So, there I sat, a bomb in my hands about to go off as soon as I tore back the flap, a bomb announcing my failure and goddamned doom as a writer. Shit man, I knew I had no chance on the first

CHAPTER TWENTY-TWO: BOMBS, BOWLING BALLS AND A YAM

book off at the contest. I hadn't even been able to get ahold of it to up-date and edit it. And outsiders didn't win those contests, I figured anyway. You stood one hell of a lot better chance as one of their family.

I felt impaled on this unopened letter in my lap, listening to another man confessing his inability to cope with the miserable fucking world he was caught up in ready, so damned ready to grab himself his first drink in seven years, never to return to the human race again. And I felt at that moment exactly the man to buy the two of us that first round, me going along for the ride.

Oh Jesus. How could I help Henry when the world had its foot planted on the back of my neck too?

So, I tried being reasonable and casual, at least while I was opening the letter. Maybe Farrar just wanted some clarification or a change of address or ... oh shit, just open it.

It was kind of a blur. I hadn't had a chance of recalling the specific phrases, only the gist that said -- Refused. Bad. Forget it. But the real gut buster, the true groin shot suggested that I quit trying to write and get a Job. Shit. To refuse a guy is one thing, okay, but to tell him to go get a job, Jesus H. Christ. And this man had been my hope and encouragement, along with Marcus' original impetus. Now Farrar tells me to get a job. And he wouldn't even suggest a field, the son of a bitch. If he had, I would at least have left me feeling I was suited for something. That I actually had some value.

If I could have talked around the bowling ball in my throat, I would have read the letter to Henry and explained the circumstances. It might have been of some encouragement to him. Wasn't he qualified to endlessly make those miserable friggin' parts over and over again? That nobody else had the talent to do. I couldn't say that. He thought he had problems. Good Lord, I was now a writer who didn't have the time to write because I was up to my ass trying to put a roof over our heads, all the while having no job, no income, no goddamned future that I could see and a wife who was getting ill so often. I'd always had boys, brothers and Marines around, so I had no feel for the peculiarities of women. Which was only more concerning with winter coming on. What lay ahead for a total lousy failure like me?

And while I was trying to deal with that, on Henry went telling the bum beside him (me) how he and another guy, way back when he was a kid in high school, got started on the booze. How they had been painting a church interior and tried the sacramental wine. And when winter came, they'd work a pint of bourbon between them to keep the chill out. Then, when he finally got going as a machinist, how necessary the bottle had been for so many of the guys just to get through the crushing monotony of each day.

But I didn't say anything. If I had, we might both have formed a suicide pact. I don't know. He was such a good guy I didn't want to make him feel any worse on account of my miseries. So, I just sat and listened and felt like the bottom had dropped out of my life, out of the whole damned world. And even the thought of our flushing toilet couldn't cheer me since it, like me, was being flushed to nowhere and gone. I still had the septic tank to put in, and the dry well to build, and another government official to face, the county health examiner or inspector or whatever the hell he called himself. I figured he must be a crook too, so I just decided to sit and hate him till Henry left and it was time to eat.

Bobbye has a soothing way about her. Whether I was cranking off in loud noisy shouts about some evil perpetrated against my person by a hammer, a nail, or by society in general; or whether I'm

CHAPTER TWENTY-TWO: BOMBS, BOWLING BALLS AND A YAM • 241

just enormously depressed, feeling whipped, feeling beaten by such things as publisher's refusals, she can calm me. The basic ingredient of her calming potion is simple, quiet, loving understanding. She'll let me rant and rave, curse, and shout, bang my head on the floor to the point of shattering both, then she will simply touch my hand or kiss me or move close to be hugged and held. I always end up jabbering love messages in her ear, hugging her tight, loving her with VIGGAH as JFK would say. She's such a good ole girl. Exactly suited to me, her strength meshing perfectly with my weaknesses, my masculinity with her femininity, her practicality with my romanticism. Such a woman. What hell marriage must be when one has the wrong mate. How wonderfully warm it is with the right girl, side-by-side with you, one like dear Bobbye.

She got me back in shape to face the new day and our next adventure. The book was put in a box for the future. It had never been more than a first draft anyway. Taking it to Farrar so soon had been a long shot. There was no sense in sending the thing out again as it was. So, it was decided, we had to forget about it for now. Build the house. Build the house.

The next morning, after doing my usual wiggle-jig to get old SOB running, we hauled 110 concrete blocks up that same huge hill, in first gear again, but without any further problem. It was a bit shocking to have done that so well, and as before, this alone should have put me on my guard as I spent the rest of the day down in the second of the two monster holes stacking the blocks around me ten feet high, building the dry well.

Working alone, since Bobbye finally was taking time off to check with the local doctor about her early day sicknesses, I'd loaded these 110 heavy mothers onto the truck by hand and unloaded them again the same way at the house. Then to get each block down the hole and intact just tossing them was ruled out. And I'm not ten feet tall. So, it was a lot of up and down, up and down, till about half those beauties were stacked below. I had already done the first row all neatly level forming a full circle around me. Then I just kept dry-laying rows and rows on top of this, no mortar, just stacking, till I'd used up all I'd hauled down. I was able to finish the second half by working from above, hanging down in, figuring to be pulled in head-first at any minute by the weight of each block.

Finally, it was done, and I felt good. It really was satisfying, believe me. Probably mostly because it was one of those rare jobs that was started and finished in one day. They are real jewels for impatient people like me. When Ralph rolled up with the septic tank, he had a good laugh. I didn't join him. I asked him what was so funny, but he wouldn't tell me until he'd gotten some of Bobbye's good coffee still on the Coleman, then he explained that I'd be so damned mad when he told me what I'd done wrong, that I'd chase him off the place and he'd miss his coffee.

He was right. "Eeeeyow shit!" I shouldn't have stacked the blocks with the holes up but I should have laid them on their sides. Then, when the well would be filled with gravel, the water overflowing from the septic tank would wash down over the gravel and out into the leaching field, through the openings of the blocks, to start the whole water cycle over again. But my having set the blocks holes up... there would be no lateral flow.

But hell, I'd never even seen a dry well before, much less built one, so screw it. Now, of course, I was hopping mad, but there was nothing I could do besides crawl back down into the damned excavation and start tearing it apart, then to put it all back together again. Each one of those blocks weighed maybe 20 pounds. That works out to be 20 pounds X 110, 2,200 foot pounds moved vertically 10 feet or 22,000-foot pounds expended. Three times. Once down the hole, then up and out, then down in the hole again. That makes 66,000 ft/pounds of energy. To say nothing of loading and unloading the truck, another 10 or so foot jobs for an additional 44,000 ft/pounds, totaling 110,000 or 55 foot/tons of effort. That is a lot of grits. No wonder I'd blown an extra few more tons yelling, "Sheeeeit!"

    The next day Ralph came back and gave my rework his blessing. The septic tank had fit like a jewel into its setting, and now good man Babonas dumped his two or three yards of washed gravel down into my gloriously and now properly, blocked dry well. Then we laid Orangeburg from the end of the required cast iron line to the foundation and its septic tank and from that on to the dry well. It was, in all due humility, a magnificent system. I was half crazy to poop in it but had to settle for simply running into the house, flushing the magic johnny, then running back around again to listen to its gurgle and splash. What a great sensation of accomplishment! I recall standing on the septic tank cover and mumbling something about one small poop for mankind, which another guy later more or less stole, as far as I'm concerned.

    But still, we couldn't yet use our glorious life support system. Regulations had it that no toilet would be flushed in anger until the local health inspector came out and gave his blessing to the hook up. Nor could Ralph cover over any of it till then either. And from time to time, I'd catch Rob kind of staring at it all longingly which made me wonder if I might be losing my wife to a working toilet if I didn't get it working and signed off damn quick.

    Early on I believe you got a feel for my attitudes concerning government bureaucracies at all levels. Well, needless to say, they were not altered by the services rendered at this point in our project either. Yes, I found our next go-around with city hall incredible. Keep in mind that before this we had been through the motor vehicle struggle, then the attempted Madlock heist, and the zoning board's flabby part in it, and of course the local legal commission's active roles in the overall realm of the inane.

So now, to legally flush our toilet, we first had to have it properly inspected by the health officer. A sound principle. Nevertheless, to get that distinguished gentleman of science to the site of one's humble potty is quite another story indeed.

Why is it that when you call some office theoretically dedicated to public service, you are somehow made to feel small, greedy, ungrateful, and downright presumptuous for intruding on that bureau's busy day? I find myself feeling apologetic for being a nag. To a point, that is. And in this case, after more than a week of being a nice chap inquiring as to where the officer was and having had Rob brought nearly to tears from a secretary's telephone rudeness on the matter, I finally started returning it in kind.

"1 don't give a darn, lady, I simply want to know where the hell he is?"

Which I am sure accounted for the next week's delay before Himself, Mr. Science finally appeared in the flesh. Also, I learned that this medical character was the evil Madlock's brother-law. I could only anticipate more ugliness, anger, and deceit.

His name was, Yam. Dr. Jeremy M. Yam. When this august vegetable finally made an appearance, Rob and I were half out of our minds. His car, with the Haut Official medical medallion on the side, pulled up in front of our place. (The car just kind of slowly quit moving down at the bottom of the hill, a few feet short of the beginning of the drive.) We sneaked a look out the front

CHAPTER TWENTY-TWO: BOMBS, BOWLING BALLS AND A YAM

window at it, giggling and hopping around some, so tickled the guy had finally shown up. We were admittedly timid, fearing we might scare him off if we appeared too eager, so we respectfully waited. And waited. And waited some more, but nothing happened. The car just sat there. No one got out. The object in the front driver's seat whom we assumed had guided the car in, made no move to burst from its cocoon.

Then, gradually, we got more courageous. We first stood openly in our own front window and looked down the hill directly at the super official vehicle. (In most government agency offices like the Registry of Motor Vehicles, for instance, that would have earned us a "This Window Closed" sign. One does not intimidate officialdom.) Still no action. No sign of life.

"Oh Kenny, could he be dead?" questioned Bobbye.

"'Be just our luck, wouldn't it? Then think how long it would take to get another one of these guys out to inspect his body, much less our septic system," I muttered.

"And that awful secretary would probably accuse us of murder," she whispered, a little over-cautiously. "You'd better go down and see what is going on."

"Yeah," I said but without enthusiasm, as I toddled out front door and down the hill.

When I got to the car, an old gentleman was sitting in the drivers' seat, staring straight ahead. The motor was off, so I figured carbon monoxide hadn't done him in. I rapped on the window. He slowly turned his head, and looked more or less at me. So far, so good.

"I'm Ken McAdams, sir, are you looking for me?" I asked hopefully.

"Yam."

That's all he said. Sesame Street, of course, has a cookie monster who says "Cookie" a lot, but this was before all that. Otherwise, I might have written him off as a harmless old potato monster. Frankly he had me stumped. Was this a password deal or something? Part of a secret phrase? Skull and Bones maybe. Was I supposed to blurt out, "Grits" or "Chitlin's" or... what the hell?

Then he sort-of lurched against the door. Hopefully, I reached out and opened it for him. He nearly toppled onto the ground, but I caught him. He was very frail. There was no hint of alcohol.

As I helped him from the car, the answer became clear. Dr. Jeremy Yam was suffering mainly from having lived for decades in memorial. I concluded he was perhaps the oldest self-propelled living object I have ever encountered.

Getting him up our hill took a cool thirty minutes on a hot day. I doubt cold weather would have cut his time any. For that matter there's reason to wager that any real chill would have shut him down all together. He was a very fragile piece of work, in an extremely delicate biological balance.

He did, nevertheless, succeed in topping our hill. Bobbye had had time to see the problem and rushed to the doctor's side with a cup of cool ice water. He accepted it, drank it, and let the plastic container slip from his hand to the ground seemingly oblivious to where it had come from or gone to.

Again, he was more or less motoring slowly ahead, slightly that was, and had seemed to have spotted something on the ground he was intent on erratically stabbing with his cane. All I could see there was a large rectangular blue tarp I had laid out to dry earlier in the day.

I had no idea where he was headed, but I wasn't fighting it. He was on to something. I glanced at Bobbye. She clearly was holding her breath. The suspense was nerve wracking.

CHAPTER TWENTY-TWO: BOMBS, BOWLING BALLS AND A YAM • 247

Finally, Jeremy M. Yam M.D., man of municipal science and authority, stopped in front of the large polyethylene blue tarp drying there, poked it twice and mumbled, "Fine. Ummmm. Good. Good job McArrr... mmmm. Fine." Then he used his cane to indicate a coming turn as he started back down the hill toward his car again.

And that was it. Our septic tank, lead-in lines, and dry well, all of which lay on the other side of the house, proudly open for his official inspection, yes over these two weeks, had in this, to me, curious manner been approved! I will make no further comment on the event other than to say that if I had known how simple this whole process would be, I'd have offered to bring the blue tarp down to Dr. Yam's office on my own for his approval and saved him the trip.

One postscript. Our bill for the inspection service rendered did not take two weeks to arrive. It came in the next day's post. At least something, other than doctor Yam, moved quickly at the department of health. And yes, it was three times more than we had budgeted. Which was more than worth it, as Bobbye and I walked into the bathroom, admiring the toilet like it was a new member of our family. Neither of us said a word. Bobbye took my hand. I turned to her and smiled. She was crying which told me that you knew you were doing a bang-up good job as a husband when your wife cries because she gets to use a potty.

Dear Rob returned to the cabinets. The directions laid out on the floor like the schematics for diffusing a bomb. I know I would have exploded the sucker if I had tried to follow them. She went step by step, making steady progress with no mistakes. No swearing either. Not even a self-serving bizarre justification for one drawer not quite shut all the way, about which she just said that it added character to it all. That told me that I had married a grown up.

The next morning, I did my half hour's startup-penance on Ole SOBi, then drove it down to the lumber yard for the insulation. The insulation came in big rolls which looked kind of like those telephone cables on the giant spools you see around sometimes which meant for the trip back Clem and MacIntosh would have to ride in the cab with me. So, bingo! Banana Head barfed all over the seat and out the window. MacIntosh gave him a deserved growl and snuggled over closer to me. If nothing else, Clem was solidifying our MacIntosh / Kenny loving, man-to-dog and dog-to-man relationship which frankly had no room for dorky Beagle-Bassets.

After Rob's work on the kitchen cabinets, she decided to start on the insulation we had picked up. That sounded like a good idea to me. Putting it in place was one of those non-building-type building jobs. No real banging and hammering, grunting, and cursing to it. I figured it demanded taste and art appreciation, i.e.. a woman's touch, so I chauvinistically passed it on to my beloved.

Luckily Nelson at the yard knew the job we had ahead of us so issued a pair of mighty staple guns, along with boxes of their ammunition. Somehow Rob seemed to have expected this, all of which saved us from embarrassment if I had failed to return with them.

The studding was 16 on center. Admittedly it wasn't until we came to installing the insulation that I had any clear idea of what 16-on-center meant, nor how important it was. The "on center" part meant that there were sixteen inches separating each 2 X 4 inch stud, measured from the center of one to the center of the

CHAPTER TWENTY-TWO: BOMBS, BOWLING BALLS AND A YAM • 249

next one to it. It didn't mean that there were 16 inches of space between each stud. If 2 X 4's were actually close to 2 inches thick, that would make 16 inches between studs, 18 inches on center. See?

So, what if you don't? What it did mean though, was that all insulation for such general construction was made to fit nicely into that space between the studs, with borders on each side to staple to. Hell, I didn't know this. Bobbye showed it to me. This is when I discovered I had not only a wife, but a full-fledged partner to help build our house. Someone I should probably think of as... my boss.

And that she was. Mercilessly so. She worked so damned fast in every task, it was embarrassing. Remember, I'm the guy who works a little and dreams a lot. Not Bobbye, she's wham, bang, work, work, work. And on top of all that, she was always smiling, except when she was under the weather some mornings. Something we had to talk about.

Naturally Rob ended having to work around me or wait impatiently, pinching my fanny, tickling me, or jawboning my slow work, pushing me to finish whatever was the next job waiting. Humiliating. But she was so beautiful and could think so smartly ahead I only smiled, nodded, and pressed on as best I could. Lord, with the electrical, she went all through the place marking the studs for the light switches, plugs, and Junction boxes, then stapling the insulation not on the forward faces of these studs but on the inside edges indenting where necessary. This way she made it possible for me to drill our electrical holes up from the cellar through the flat 2 X 4 baseplates, clear of the insulation, making them more accessible if we had to get to those wires after the walls were finished. This process also allowed her to get the whole job done, out of phase perhaps, but free of having to wait for me to finish all the plumbing and wiring first. I was still called in to lay sheets of the insulation overhead though, and that was one son of a gun job. Hot? Gawd. With the late summer sun beating down on the roof, up in the eaves with those big rolls of insulation, like doing a juggling act on a high wire trying to keep from falling between the locked-in joists. Then trying to staple the suckers had me deep into Bad Words Country.

I soon learned what Bobbye had been through with this stuff, but without complaint I must add. Fiberglass insulation is awful. It has little strands, bits, and chips that get into your hair, your eyes, mouth, down the back of your neck, all the way down to your knickers. You could work yourself into St. Vitus Dance itching, scratching, grabbing, bitching, and moaning. That was my style anyway. Rob was now through with all that, having moved over onto hammering some shelves together and mounting them on the back entry mudroom walls. She'd held off attacking them till she was finished with the insulation, but when she got rolling, bang, bang, bang; that was it. My dear, sweet, adorable, soft spoken, non-cursing, loving, darling built them all herself after she'd finished the cabinets. I was starting to get embarrassed. Thank goodness there weren't any bricks left to be done or she'd have had me out chipping mortar off them next.

So, at this point a whole mess of half-finished jobs were rushing to completion. While Ralph was plowing dirt over the sewage system and roughing out a side and front yard, Ken Medley was going over our wiring plan, and Rob was hammering the switch and plug boxes into place. After drilling a thousand or so holes all over, I felt like a giant mouse lost in a huge cheese. We strung the wires through the basement joists, then up through the floor studs to the boxes Bobbye had positioned. We both ran around connecting the wiring, but left the electrical boxes open so Ken could inspect and officially approve them.

Next, we roughed the rest of the kitchen in, laying heavy ¾-inch plywood over the subfloor, and mounting the lower cabinets and counters on this and to the wall studs. We laid on a quick coat of paint, too, to hold down the grease and splatter. The sink itself, and plumbing of course, were already in place. We held off on the Formica counter tops till the walls, ceilings, and upper cabinets were hung. We'd bought a refrigerator early on which was in place and cranking away. The electric stove had fitted into the counter next to it nicely, completing the basics.

What a good feeling this much gave us. Yes, so much had come together so quickly we could hardly believe it. Bobbye had a sink to wash in, I had a john to do my thing in. And lights to light our way. We could even read in there now too. It all was a matter of Today the bathroom, Tomorrow the world.

CHAPTER TWENTY-THREE
A Drill Weekend

My next Marine drill weekend, the second weekend in September, I bought a washing machine. We couldn't afford it, money was leaking out everywhere, but Bobbye needed the thing badly.

The supplier was again the friend of my dad, the Armenian who had lined us up for so much of our other equipment—power tools, stove, kitchen, and bath mess. He was a beautiful, heavy bearded gentleman known only, and mysteriously throughout my childhood, as "*Chabook*." I was told that meant "Stick" in Armenian, he being tall and slim, but as a kid I figured the word meant something more like Shazam in our language.

So, armed with the washer we couldn't afford, I rumbled up our twisting drive through the slip-and-slide-mud of that rainy Monday. My plan was to surprise dear Rob and fill her heart with joyover the new device I'd purchased to make even more work possible for her. Husbands can be most thoughtful.

Juggling the big cardboard boxed sucker down to the cellar was another of my usual snorting, cursing, ill-tempered struggles. No steps down yet, just a long, wide board rigged to slide heavy stuff down on. But once there, I connected the thing in no time, Bobbye having already made those gorgeous plumbing and electrical provisions. When I plugged it in and pushed the button. Wow, it worked.

With that struggle over, my mood changed to serene. The house was really coming together. The roof on and rain proof, the foundation backfilled, structural walls up all around, along with those of the interior awaiting wall and ceiling plasterboard. Next would be the exterior siding and finally that magnificent old Boston brick chimney that would grace the first observed wall as one drove up to the house.

On top of all that progress, I surprised Bobbye with the new washer. Everything felt cozy and warmly cheerful inside. Coffee perking, chowder smells. I love rainy, chilly, drizzly days anyway. Only God knows why. I liked to wear sweaters and tweed jackets and smoke my pipe feeling warm and snug in from the wet and cold outside. I detest endlessly beautiful days. Living in Hawaii had been the pits for me. Every day was perfect. I ached for the fog, drizzle, and the chill of Boston. 'Scottish blood. Sweating can be a smelly process. To say nothing of the flies it attracts, fleas, and mosquitos. Worst of all, I hate sweating Santa Clauses.

Unfortunately, my wellbeing was shortly to be jolted. When Bobbye came back from her damp trudge out to the mailbox, she

CHAPTER TWENTY-THREE: A DRILL WEEKEND

stood in the doorway, looking much sadder than what just a mucky day would have made for her. She had a single letter in her hand. This one wasn't registered nor special delivery or anything else important like that either. It was from the First Novel Contest. Without even opening it we knew what it said, "Sorry Charlie."

But they didn't leave it at that. It was even worse. Like John Farrar's "Get a job," these charcaters even wanted me to send them some money just to get the manuscript back. In retrospect I guess it was reasonable, return postage with the entry and all, but at the time it seemed such a kick. They wouldn't even let me fail with dignity. It was still going to cost something like a buck eighty to get the manuscript returned. Hadn't Farrar had the decency to spring twice for postage? These people, gawd. No critique either. Just something like, "Fee on you." So, I wrote them saying to either keep the manuscript and publish it or send it back at their own expense; whichever they felt was more appropriate.

Eventually they did send it back. No imagination. But in a sense, it wasn't a total loss. I was now armed with the argument for the Internal Revenue Service that my writing had produced income, something like 3 X $1.80. Which wasn't totally satisfying, but it did indicate to the IRS that I was no longer just a simple amateur failure; now I was a professional failure!

I don't know how many readers have ever failed in life, but I find it a very unsatisfying experience. No matter what you try to say, to explain, it sounds empty, hollow. You find yourself regarded as very boring since you have gone over and over it all a thousand times to yourself -- before sleeping at night; in your dreams; before the house wakes in the morning; every lonely moment of the day no matter how busy you have been, there it is in your face. Not satisfying at all.

And, on top of this, MacIntosh started gobbling down Ralph's gravel which I think was his reaction to Clem's eating as much of the leftover bits of insulation Bobbye had left lying on the floor. Clem had been getting so much attention from us for doing that, that Mac started feeling left out. At first, I hadn't noticed MacIntosh's gravel consumption until his belly looked to be swelling daily and his jogging had lots of jingling to it. Dear Mac, he always wanted our love and attention and he'd seemed to elect gravel-gobbling as a means of winning us back from Clem, the banana-headed Basset, who'd been so involved in gobbling down insulation. So, the vet bill for two stomach-pumps cost us most of my next Reserve check.

As I moped around that rainy afternoon, with our vet bill plus my second refusal in as many weeks around my neck, it was like a scarlet letter added there. Nevertheless, I could not escape a certain irony in the whole situation. When I was discharged from active duty with the Marine Corps in San Francisco, for the hell of it, I did some wandering around the City-by-the-Bay before driving back to Boston. One quiet Sunday afternoon I happened into a bookstore in Sausalito and got chatting with the youngish fellow behind the counter. I don't know how these things happen, but this guy was from the same suburb of Boston as I was, and had gone to the same high school, though in a class with one of my older brothers. His family owned a lumber yard only a few blocks from where my parents live today. And he was a writer.

Naturally we talked for quite a while. I told him of the book I had started in the Marines and how I was on my way to get married, and to finish writing the book while my wife kept us afloat teaching school.

He and his wife had been doing the same thing. Actually, it had taken some digging to get this out, but the coincidence of hometowns loosened him up. He went on to explain that he never liked telling people he was a writer since he was not published. I sympathized saying that now, with my discharge, I was in the same boat. He said no, not so, because I was just beginning and hadn't been refused yet. (Hah.)

I had no intention of being refused, of course, but luckily, I failed to mention it. Thank heaven, since with the next breath he told how his first book bombed for no reason other than he didn't know how to edit or rewrite it. He said that a publisher was interested, but it required a rewrite before a contract could be discussed. He confessed that he simply hadn't been able to do that, short of writing a whole new novel, which he did, and which just plain got sent back. But he said he was still trying and would go on trying. He had some kind of a deal, living in a house free for the winter on Nantucket Island that he was going to take. His wife had a job lined up there already and she was agreeable.

"She's got a lot of guts," he said, "I don't know how she takes it."

At the time, I thought the guy must be nuts, besides being a loser. Anyone who could fail on two books must be some clown at the typewriter, to say nothing of his plugging on so long. I wrote him off as grossly insensitive for living off his wife all that time.

These were my thoughts then, two years earlier, practically to the day. And there I stood, in a half-finished barn, rain pouring down making great sucking glop holes outside our unpainted door … double zeroed myself. No jobs for the two us. Who was the jerk now?

I had to ask myself, was I simply dazzling myself with romantic thoughts and images of the Impressionist artist as the writer? What the hell made me figure I should even try to write? Maybe all that sounded colorful; or perhaps I thought I looked like a writer with the pipe, the tweeds, the prematurely graying hair.

But was that enough? Did a broken nose make a boxer? I hadn't dared ask myself such a revealing question.

But I'd always had a technique for making myself do things. I'd talk about them, whatever they were - like driving wild motorcycles, joining the Marine Corps, flying jet fighters... all kinds of stuff like that which basically scared the hell out of me. So long as I would sound off about doing them, I'd trap myself into actually doing them, forcing myself to keep from looking the fool by not doing them.

I guess I'd done this now with writing. It had been necessary to set myself apart from the other pilots in my squadron. I had decided there had to be more than chasing rich sweethearts around Waikiki beach. Nor could I be another drone-like regular officer covered with boredom's dust, lugging the attaché case around with only Approach Magazine in it, along with a resplendent egg salad sandwich, tennis sneakers, and a jockstrap. I would have gone nuts if I hadn't been able to see myself as something different and beyond such mundane pursuits.

But was seeing believing? Did I really have anything to believe in, anything that truly said, you can be a writer? Bits and scraps, maybe a nod from a professor at Yale and later kind words from Marcus Aurelius Goodrich and later John Farrar. But now it was time to face how hollow that past really was; how cold the present; how empty the future was shaping up to be.

Thunder! The day had turned dark. I was standing very still, staring unseeingly through the living room window at the falling sheets of rain. I felt so beaten, lost, and alone ... until I felt Bobbye's arms sneak from my back around me, and her sad voice whisper in my ear, "I love you, Kenny."

CHAPTER TWENTY-FOUR
An Editor?

I knew I needed an editor. I think subconsciously I had assumed that I could write any sort of crap, my innate genius being what I presumed it to be, and this noble toiler would make it right. I had heard so much about Thomas Wolfe's editor, Maxwell Perkins, it seemed that if only I could capture such a creature I would rise again from the ashes. My reasoning in this wasn't that unsound. We were building a house from sun up till well past sunset, which didn't leave one me a hell of a lot of time or energy for thrashing at the typewriter. In fact, more than an editor, at that moment, a ghost writer would have been more realistic. Some talented, selfless simple soul who wanted to make me rich and renown while he or she remained poor and anonymous. Where to find this silly creature? How to advertise for such a fool? Oh, to be a king, statesman, or President to whom such wordsmiths flow.

About a week later, Carl mentioned a New York lady he and Florence knew, a writer, published, the works, first cabin, who had a weekend cottage not far away. If only I could get an interview with her, have her read the first book, and get her advice on how to attack straightening it out. That might be the answer. Hell, at least it was something in the way of hope. God knows, these few short months had reduced my final great experiment to a near rout. There seemed no hope now for income beyond my Marine Reserve checks. Unless something got cracking, I'd be sitting on some miserable commuter train-to-nowhere, probably in the bar car, with my hands full of Alka-Seltzer, as I tried to make the going great. Failure was shocking, cold and icy-real as my empty future looked to be ahead.

If I'd had any way of knowing what the next job facing us in our house-building project would be like, I might have clamored to get to that railroad station instead. Walls and ceilings. Innocuous sounding, but how on earth did you attack them? Ceilings in particular.

"Furring strips, Ken," said Henry Dryer.

"What are furring strips and what are they for, Henry?"

"Well, what you do is nail these long skinny strips of wood, furring strips, to the underside of the joists at ninety-degree angles, using spacers to get the strips level so your plasterboard nailed to them will give you a flat, level ceiling. Once your four-by-eight sheets of plasterboard are nailed to the strips with each sheet butted up tight against the first, then you'll tape over those seams with the rolls of tape designed for the job, set in damp plaster. Troweling that over the taped seams to later be sanded, gives you a continuously smooth flat ceiling. You'll need Bobbye to hold up the far end of the plasterboard while you nail your end, moving from there on down toward her end. Sink the nails slightly so when you plaster over their indentations and later sand those spots, your ceiling will look flat and seamless."

"Hello," I replied staring at him with my mouth hanging open. Sometimes Henry could talk really fast, when he assumes whomever he is talking to has his same depth of knowledge on whatever he is talking about. I, of course, had none of the above and was left with the configuration of my mouth as just mentioned.

"How do you mean, Henry? How do the strips run?"

"Across your ceiling joists at right angles, but set with shims for leveling."

"Hunh?"

Clearly, I wasn't getting the picture, so Henry took me by the hand over to Nelson's lumber yard where we picked up ten or twenty miles of these furring strips. Then, back home, he held one up across the joists, and simple me saw what he meant. They would cross the joists at right angles, yes ah hah; be nailed to each joist, using shims here and there to make them totally flat, level along each strip's length, as well as cross-wise in relation to each other, wall to wall. And again, 16 inches on center.

Sure, it sounds bad, but it really was much worse. The shims were of different thicknesses. Some joists even drooped having to be hacked out rather than shimmed up. Then you'd cut too deep, and have to shim the cut anyway. And that levelling! There's where I really screwed up.

In the evening after dinner, Bobbye and I started doing our first furring. Since the bath was the smallest room, we figured we could screw it up the least. I doubt, however, that I could have screwed it up anymore. I didn't listen to Rob till it was too late. Yes, I had been blustery, pompous, condescending, arrogant, chauvinistic, in short... manly. Swept aside, Bobbye waited till all my strips were up, carefully leveled their individual lengths, then said, "Now check them crossways, each to the other."

The late Phillip Wiley described strong women in our country as "Strident American bitches." But, of course, this dear lady was my wife — and even worse, she was right! Dang it. I didn't have to lay the level across them. Even I could see it was a claptrap mess. Each was on its own plane. If I'd put the plaster board up, the ceiling would have waved like ocean swells.

Which made me uncomfortable. Perhaps testy. Irritated. Angry. Goddamned mad!

Bobbye had stood there all that time and let me make a mess of it. Incredible. Quiet as a mouse, smugly and probably enjoying my coming kick in the pants. Secretly relishing the fact that I would have to tear the whole thing down again, every strip but one that is, to use it as my cardinal unit, redoing all the others in relation to it. My wife! My wife had let me do that. And it was late. Damned late. Which also upset me. So, I told her that and cussed some for emphasis, (Actually a lot, for a lot of emphasis), and she said she wouldn't stay around and listen to such language, and that got me angrier which made her very, very, mad, which automatically caused her to cry which made me frustratedly angry and sad all at the same time. When I tried to snuggle her back to putting this behind us, she pulled away and went to bed alone. I kicked Clem while going outside, which made me feel a little better. So then both dogs and I peed together out on a rock, then went back in to wash up and go to bed where Bobbye and I made up and loved each other very much despite my rotten temper and her not volunteering that I was screwing up the ceiling while I was screwing up the ceiling.

The next day I redid the bathroom-strips and finally did get the ceiling up properly. It was a brilliant job. Then Bobbye came in with the plaster, which we also called goop, for smoothing over the joints and seams. It was a very tedious job. A dusty smelly sort of job. It struck me as a woman's kind of job. Men were better at the bigger stuff. Right?

At the tapered seam of two boards butting each other, you had to slap on a layer of goop, smooth it, then apply a length of non-adhesive perforated tape to that. Add another goop layer; let it dry, and goop again. When all that had dried, you sanded it smooth to blend the two flat board surfaces you'd just joined and masked. Simple. Sure. You were working over your head. The goop oozed and dripped onto your head and into your face. Until it dried. Then, as you sanded it, your eyes, ears, hair, nose, and throat disappeared in a cloud of dust. A stinging, gagging experience. So, you had to turban your face with a mask over your nose. And since you were working close to the ceiling where the heat was up, up and away, the sweat tended to mix with the goop dust creating a kind of death mask. Of course, working over your head, arms up all day was exhausting, neck wrenching. A shitty job for sure.

Then, like out of a ghastly television comedy, what had to happen? Picture the scene. Bobbye was a mess, and I was making an even worse mess of myself. We were irritable, uncomfortable, and looked awful. Next, at that very moment Bobbye again threw up and then there came a knock on the door.

We looked at each other. Who could it be? We weren't expecting anybody. Since I was up a ladder struggling with a ceiling board, Bobbye went to answer it. You can't believe how she looked. An old rag turban, chalky dust all over her face, crusted, matted, pasted in the corners of her mouth and eyes, ugly dirty torn shirt buttoned tight at the neck, shapeless baggy jeans. And I didn't have the heart to tell her that she had tracks of upset down the front of her shirt. So, tugging the door open like some kind of haggard old crone, she was met with…

"Avon calling!"

For the longest time Bobbye could only gape at the inanely smiling beauty peddler. Finally, though she did muster, "Come back next year," and took her card reflexively before leaning out the door and saying "Please" to the retreating salesgirl.

The plasterboard sheets were four by eight feet, 5/8 inch thick. They weighed quite a bit, but worse, they were unwieldy as hell. Well, like a real hammerhead, I was balancing them on my skull, walking a step or two up a small ladder, and trying to jiggle and wedge them into place, holding them still till I got a nail out of my mouth and hammered it into one of the unseen furring strips the sheet was supposed to attached to.

Sure Charlie. I soon learned that the nail had better be going in where the strip crossed the joist, or I'd vibrate myself half to death. But I'd often gotten so intent on this, that the sheet would slip a little, and though the nail got in okay, the whole damned thing was cockeyed. Like I was. And my neck and legs trembled with fatigue from being bent over trying to nail the sucker home.

My job was no piece of cake. Though it could have been if I'd thought about it. By the last room I finally figured out how to build a "T" brace to hold one end of the sheet up while I nailed the other. I had been too stupid not to make such a "T" earlier. And too darned lazy, making the job ten times as hard and time-consuming as it should have been.

But you know, I learned, from all this that there are some jobs you can do all wrong, really botch, but still get them done. I think of them as "Liberal arts" kinds of jobs.

The next to last ceiling section was to go up in the living room, but 1 was in a spectacularly foul mood from finally doing it. We had wanted that room to be perfect, but so far it was pretty-well botched. Sloppy joints, some bad nailing, all depressing. Hopefully Bobbye's gooping would cover and blend things out, but this didn't save my frame of mind. Of course, I can be perfectly miserable without half trying at times like this, maybe even thrive on it, but the room was getting to me.

I needed a change. There was a little patch of subfloor in the hall closet I wanted to work on anyway. I figured to cool off with that.

It was a simple enough job, just put a couple of nails into an extra 2 X 4 added for support. Having recently laid the beefed-up kitchen subfloor, I'd become adept at blasting-in nails. I'd averaged just three whacks—one to set the nail, the next to drive it, the last to finish it flush.

But that was a couple of weeks earlier. I guess I was a shade rusty. My first mighty blast started the nail all right. The second smashed the bejeezus out of my left thumb, and with the third I put the whole goddamned hammer through the subfloor into the basement. Then I crouched and waited for my numb, smashed thumb to do its thing.

Good God Almighty, son of a bitch oh, shit! Lord it started to hurt! But that first throb was only openers. I went into a jig. Up the walls, down the walls, straight up in the air. I went through such a fit the dogs cleared out on the run. Bobbye didn't know what to make of it. 'Scared her half to death. So, she flopped, swooning flat down on her back on the kitchen floor. Good grief. That struck me as damned silly. Irritating really. But she said something about palpitations. Whose palpitations? My thumb looked like a balloon. 'Felt like an elephant was stamping on it. Palpitations, no one cared about mine. I was hopping around bellowing, moaning, and cursing while Bobbye just took a break on her back, all spread-eagled on the floor looking ridiculous. What if someone walked in? Like Avon again.

Then the miseries subsided some, but I still had to face the ignominy of climbing down through the cellar hole to go grubbing for the hammer down below. Damned little light. I had forgotten a flashlight, so I bumbled about cursing in the dark, walking into support columns, getting myself fit to be tied even though I did find the damned hammer and then struggled to finally climb back up to civilization. And whose faces were the first I would see once I was up again? My mother's and my father's.

"Well, Kenneth, aren't you even going to say hello and thank your parents for remembering this date and driving hours down here to deliver our best wishes in person on your wedding anniversary?"

Our anniversary, of no, say it isn't so. I had forgotten the date and I had not even thought of a gift. To say nothing of the fact we had no money to buy a gift anyway. Beautiful.

"I am sorry mom We've been so loaded down with all kinds of crap, and Bobbye has been on and off sick. At times we've even been totally out of water. Everything has been a mess, very difficult, so my fuse is a little short. Please forgive me."

"I'd prefer you shy away from that kind of wording. Your father has adequately covered those bad bases for decades. And remember, Kenneth, Bobbye is a southern belle, not used to such language."

I looked over to my darling who only smiled and threw me a slow big-girl wink and nod.

So, it was from this generally negative frame of reference that we approached the next scene, twenty or thirty minutes later, after our parental visit was well underway.

My thumb was still hot and throbbing, which only allowed me a grumbling hello and a hug for each parent, before I tip-toed up the little ladder I'd set on the main room floor to get started balancing the last 4 X 8 ceiling sheet on my head, I was doing my Charlie Chaplin best to get the damned thing up the wrong way. Then mother chimed in with a loud, 'Bobbye, how are you? I hear you have some morning sicknesses. My goodness. What do you know about that? And Macintosh, good doggy. And who is this other odd looking fellow?" breezed Mother as she came swooping on to stage center in her TV Loretta Young way. Dad was behind struggling with his canes, his aching knees the reminder of an auto accident he was in with old Patsy Taverna the construction man, years before.

"Get the hell out of there, damned dog," dad growled, bouncing a cane neatly off Clem's head. Pater cursed a lot. He was no politician. You knew where he stood, whether or not you wished to be anywhere near the area yourself. He owned a small cookie/cracker factory which he'd been able to keep nonunion. To do that, he'd even won a fistfight with a Teamster organizer,--something I'd witnessed as a kid. Dad had knocked the thug out flat on his back with a mighty right uppercut. All his employees cheered as the union boss toppled off the loading platform where the battle had started.

So, with those kinds of hands-on positions in business, my dad's politics were straightforward as well. For instance, his solution to the difficult Cold War situation vis- a-vis Comrade Stalin was: "Take an Atomic bomb to Moscow and shove it up his ass." Of Harry Truman, he was recorded as having said, "All bullshit." He often applied that short, crisp, aphorism to a whole spectrum of world opinion makers, whether they realized it or not. Included in these were NPR, Charles de Gaulle, the Pope (name and number your option), Eleanor Roosevelt, Adlai Stevenson, and anyone named Kennedy. But his reactions to these were as a spring breeze when compared to the paroxysms he went into at the mention of names like: John L. Lewis, George Meany, or the ultimate bugaboo, Walter Ruether. All of which defined my Dad's politics. Yes, Barry G. was his boy, along with "Tail Gunner Joe," George S. Patton, Winston Churchill, Douglas MacArthur, J. Edgar Hoover, and Fulton Louis, Jr. every night at seven. You see, Dad had fought his way up, sometimes with his own fists, and so naturally the men he respected were those who also displayed the same kind of fighting spirit. I think secretly he really did like old Harry Truman. They shared a lot of the same vocabulary.

Mother was a strong lady, equally as strong as dad, and consequently always in mortal conflict with him. Which seemed to delight him. Certainly, he would make sure to give her enough of a needle to keep their Greco-Roman tussle going Infinitum. Every time I was with these two, I understood better, the essential nature of my own personality flaws.

So, in they came --my, Mother breezy and bubbling, Dad blustery and smiling as he thrust and parried to get the dogs out of his way. They were happy to be there, to see us, and anxious to help. I knew immediately it was going to be a disaster.

In any family, the relationships between parents and children are difficult, but when the child somehow becomes grown, i.e.

leaves the nest, marries, and starts his own home, tensions rise. It's that the old relationships are breaking down and new ones are forming. Their boy is a man now. The complications of this are obvious and age-old. The entire interplay becomes extremely brittle ... and amongst three people of a family with very similar personalities, it becomes traumatic.

Even under the most normal circumstances, the relationship was testy, but man, when Kenny was doing his life-or-death balancing act on that small ladder, the plaster board on his head, and the splattered thumb crooked tenderly away from further misery, the possibilities were A-tomic, nuclear for sure.

"Oh, let me help!" A rush.

"No, no, no thanks." A wobbly toe-dance.

"Damned dogs."

"Please, Mother, I can manage."

"We came to help, not just get in the way."

Insanely I kept mumbling, "No, Mother, I'd rather do it myself!"

My head was tilted back, neck red, straining, sweat riveting down my back. I was struggling to balance the heavy damned sheet on my head as a fulcrum and hold it as close to the furring strips as I could, while my hands and one huge thumb labored mightily, almost in panic, to get a nail planted before Mother made contact.

But all in vain. She got to the drooping edge of the sheet behind me before the nail had fully taken hold. Her upward thrust then, working across my head as a fulcrum, popped the other end down and out. Naturally the swing of my hammer was altered, managing a glancing blow off that poor pitiful thumb again. I let out one of my coveted JESUS CHRIST's!

Dad saw the problem of the falling edge of the sheet and rammed a cane up to reverse it. For an instant, then, the whole thing was off my head, his cane propping up on one end, Mother's arms on the other. During this brief intermission I shouted, "Goddamn it!" hugging that poor jellied thumb to my chest.

"1 will not stand for that language from you, young man. I had a lifetime of it from your father," announced Mother releasing her end of the sheet.

"Damn it, can't you ..." was as far as Dad got, one arm and a cane not being enough to hold the two ends up either. So down, splat, on my head came the 4 X 8 foot section, toppling me off the ladder, bang down on my face in a cloud of dust, the forgotten-man-with-thumb.

Dad had harassed Mother for 35 years over this-and-that. She'd always fired back with a neat broadside of her own. Bobbye, not used to such loud family conflict, was tempted to fall flat on her back on the floor again. All this made my head spin and only Clem, of all creatures, seemed concerned enough about me to shove his big wet nose under the debris to see if 1 was still breathing. I was. Beloved MacIntosh only went out the front door to stand guard. Like Bobbye, he wasn't used to such hubbub, either.

Once on my feet, waving my quivering thumb like a bloodied battle flag, I read the family a harsh, clipped, undignified riot act, driving them all, mother, father, wife, dogs, mice, the whole lot out of the room. At an elevated volume I forbade them, on threat of their very lives, to take one step back in before I got the last piece of ceiling up. Thank God, they took me at my red-faced value, or I'd probably still be up for manslaughter.

Thirty minutes went by. As I finished the job through the throbbing pain, I couldn't escape the humor of the scene. Though I had banished them from the living room to the kitchen, where mother huffed, dad cussed, and Bobbye occasionally grimaced at being caught in the middle, Macintosh howled at the backdoor, all while Clem was sleeping serenely in the center of the floor, exactly in everyone's way. There was no solid wall between us. Only the interior studs. We hadn't put the plaster board walls up yet.

So, in effect we were all still in the same room, huffing and puffing and muttering, stealing furtive, fuming glances at each other all the while. It was ludicrous. And so typical, perhaps of many families. Good Lord, a mother and a father had driven two hundred some odd miles to visit their son and daughter-in-law on their anniversary. And what had come of it? A brawl. The son floored in the first round. Howling dogs. Teary-eyed daughter-law, shouts, curses, accusations, dust, din, and roar. A regular Jack London event.

Finally, I got the section in and stepped through the studs, returning humbly to the family fold. We all tried very hard to be pleasant. To some extent the remainder of the afternoon till the folks left was a more reasonable reunion. And their departure, of course, was large with hurry-backs, so-good-to-see-you's, great-to-have-you-come-down-and-help's. You know, but in my heart, I knew that the next gathering, be it in Boston or there on our hill of blueberry bushes, would still be the same. We were a turbulent family. It was our way. But, after all that, Mother took me aside and whispered, Bobbye is pregnant!

Oh, good Lord. And that was her anniversary gift to us both along with Mom and Dad coming down to be there when I learned of it all.

The next major event in our endless drama was Clem's falling in love, but with a huge great Dane. There can be little doubt that this had a great bearing on his later lifestyle. He suffered intense frustration. Such a short, but very long dog was he, and such a long-tall dog was she. And all gal. Clem hopped, jumped, leapt, barked, whined, but to no avail. Short of coming upon her while she slept, there was no way for love to conquer all. And she was a light sleeper. Just think of the consequences otherwise!

Clem's first symptom of true-love-spurned was a continuous, daily 5 AM howling. Before the sun, perhaps up with the cock, that absurd animal bayed, driving us to distraction. Our day had started early enough as it was. And it was always a tough day. But to have that idiot dog crack it over our heads each A.M. like a champagne bottle smashing off a boat's bow, was sheer hell. We couldn't explain this to him, just as he couldn't explain the other to us. MacIntosh wanted none of it, and just wandered off on his own, looking sadly back at us, the family he seemed to feel was emotionally disserting him.

Then Clem's diet was affected. Pregnant women have their ways, as I was learning. But Horny beagle/bassets have theirs too. At first, we thought Clem had simply taken to eating bushes. Odd, but not out of the question. Dogs ate grass for their tummies. Why not bushes for their Johnsons? Maybe the crisp autumn air had something to do with it along with the Indian summer that had set in.

Bobbye saw him at this first. She commented a few times, but I was busy with other things. Finally, she dragged me by the hand down the hill to see the phenomena for myself.

Incredible. Even more so, because it was blueberries, not bushes that he was eating. We hadn't known they were so abundant all around us. We hadn't had the time to see anything but plain bushes there until Clem came along. Now we saw the fact of the matter was that blueberry bushes covered most of our hill.

Clem was a sight eating them. That fat-but-long dog would curl his lips back, gently encase his small front dentures over and under the berry clusters, then walk backwards, popping the purple juicy devils into his mouth. But being the drooler he was, his whole muzzle, chin, even down his white vested chest got stained blue. And his sides would swell. He ate so many at a crack, he looked to becoming a regular mobile wine barrel. Naturally the fermentation got to him. He belched like a lord, broke wind like a buffalo. Ah, and all of it over a very tall girl dog he had fallen for. This long-tall-sally was a full-grown great Dane. But bottom line here, the fact was she seemed to have driven Clem to drink. Each morning he would trudge off through the brush to his field of blueberry dreams. There he would do his coveted berry field-stripping procedure, then, once his belly was packed full, he would lay down on a large flat rock, in the returned summer sun, and fall asleep. As time passed, the hot sun would ferment the belly-load of berries, totally intoxicating Lord Clem. Then, by late afternoon, he would pick up some dinner smells and decide to head back up the hill to the house. Of course, as drunk as he now was lent his short stubby legs poor control, added to by his side-to-side sway required to allow his large unit to clear the ground as it swayed from side to side. Accordingly, from time to time, his tipsiness would lead to his stepping on his side-swinging wiener, causing him to stumble and fall over. Then, shaking his head to try to stabilize his woozy brain, he would set off as before, but still miss-stepping again and again. It was something to see. My own sides ached from watching the whole stumbling ballet.

Sometimes, Bobbye and I and MacIntosh would take our lunches down to watch Clem. It was quite a show. We'd be sitting on a huge round tree stump side by side, with Tosh at our feet feeling love and happiness despite all the negatives we had working against us. Cost cutting had us eating day-old bread and leftovers, but our Clem Show was worth every penny of it. We were super conscious that we two were slowly becoming three, and our hearts and minds were filled with joy, thinking of what was ahead for us.

But that was only the beginning. Clem's overall conduct was nothing but downhill from there. Through the boozy blur of his blueberrying, Clem even ate the buttons off Bobbye's favorite sweater. They were blue. They were dark. They were round. Clem decided they must also be blueberries. He should have checked with Tosher dog first. Mac had all kinds of smarts, and he could speak and understand Dog Talk too.

During this time when Clem was missing in action, lying in state if you will, MacIntosh seemed to feel that it was just him and me again, like it was in Wakefield, so he was ever close by my side, snuggled up against my leg at lunch, or ever-close while I worked. We were close pals again, a lost relationship I'm sure we both missed.

Of course, Clem had been the cause. I had thought, months before, that moving away from suburban Wakefield where there were so many pals for MacIntosh to run and play with, he would need a pal for running around in the woods at our new place. Then came Clem, but that was my error. I was so charmed with the goofiness of Clem, that I thought he would be right. MacIntosh was not convinced, so he shied away from his new "pal." And that led to the sad tragedy that Clem's nose brought to MacIntosh.

Somehow Ledge Rock and its forests, fields and streams had never seemed to be right for our beloved and super smart Scottish Border Collie. That was a huge surprise. And clearly Clem had not provided the answer to the problem.

Then, one day, Clem's nose picked up some new scents. Since his nose seemed to have a brain of its own, Clem started off up our hill, even forsaking his blueberries. MacIntosh picked up on something too, and dashed in behind Clem in hot pursuit of whatever the basset hound's nose was on to.

Seeing the two dashing off into the high forest together, I breathed a sigh of satisfaction that Clem had finally been accepted and the two were now pals. They were gone for the rest of the afternoon, for at least three hours. Excellent... I thought.

As the autumn sun was setting, a pickup truck arrived, displaying some kind of official looking lettering on the side door, right below a state seal. Who could this be? Clem and MacIntosh were in the back, roped and collared. What on earth?

As it worked out, Clem's super sniffing brought only sorrow. That day Clem had picked up a new scent. He made such a fuss over it, dear Macintosh chased after him to see what it was all about.

Sheep. Way back in through the woods beyond the power lane where MacIntosh, Bobbye, and I had once seen a great long antlered stag at sunrise calmly taking the morning air; beyond that, up over the next hill, is where Clem found the sheep. Which Macintosh thought were great fun to run after... till they would eventually drop over-stressed and finally die.

The shepherd, also the dog warden, was able to find us after checking MacIntosh's collar. He stopped by late that afternoon and explained that the sheep were his livelihood. He had a lot of money invested in them and could not allow them to be threatened. He recognized that Mac was a large part Scottish Border Collie and running sheep was in his blood. He said though, that he had come by to warn us that we would have to deal with MacIntosh's breeding. If dear Tosh was caught running his sheep again, he'd be shot. The law was on his side, he pointed out. He knew we loved our dog, but that did not allow our dog to kill his sheep.

I thanked him for the warning and promised I would do all I could to keep Mac away from his sheep.

My first move was to set up a heavy wire between several trees that would act as a run for Mac when I had his lead attached to it. I did the same for Clem, but Banana Head didn't even seem to notice it as he flopped on his back and went to sleep. This worked for about a month until MacIntosh slipped his lead and headed up over the hill and off toward the call of the sheep. All I could do was get in a car and head the long way around to the shepherd's place, but by the time I got there I heard a rifle shot... which told the story.

By the time I arrived, Mac's body was already in a small crate. The shepherd seemed as sad as we were, but could only shake his head and help me load the crate with MacIntosh in it into our pickup.

I dug a grave and set a cross with his name on it back by one of the tumbled-down walls near our special quiet place on the edge of the woods. Bobbye and I both cried as we said goodbye to our dear friend, a dog so smart that he seemed to understand all that I said to him. That is, except for those times when what I said conflicted with his ingrained instincts relating to basics like the attractive power of lady dogs as well as that of chasable sheep.

Too much to deal with. Our hearts were devastated with Tosh's demise. We could not handle such a heartbreaking loss. In a way he was the breathing symbol of our marriage and quest for accomplishment. Such a loving friend and companion... always smiling his precious dog-smiles with that special twinkle in his eye. Oh, such a painful passing, such a devastating loss. And now all we had was Clem.

CHAPTER TWENTY-FIVE
Another Down

These thoughts came to our minds about the same time Clem lurched out into Route 1 and got smacked by a trailer truck. Had he become suicidal having lost his pal who did not think of him as a pal at all?

Florence Bausche, had observed the whole thing. Screeching brakes, a ghastly hollow thud and then her rushing up the lane to tell us that Clem stumbled into the road and was hit by a truck. She had just gone out to her mailbox and the event took place right in front of her there. She knew we had lost our beloved MacIntosh, and now she, too, was teary-eyed bringing this news on top of that.

She told us how the driver was wild-eyed and handwringing in distress as he ran toward Clem who was sprawled on the road with his eyes bulging and his breath coming in choking, short spurts. At least by the time he got there, Clem was still more or less alive.

We got in our bug and drove over to the Bausche's where the truckdriver lifted the length of Clem into our car as I was ready to speed off to the vet's. Even if he died, I reasoned, at least he would have made his last auto trip a success being unconscious and accordingly not barfing or messing all over the backseat.

"Clem will live!" the vet said smiling. For me, mixed emotions. Clem did, however, have a broken shoulder and a cast would be too awkward and inhibiting for much mobility. So, he'd be confined to quarters, kind of lying-in-state. Reviewing that with the vet, it meant I would have to be designated senior combat nurse to keep him off the booze and to do all I could to lift him to keep pressure off that shoulder. It also meant this situation would totally negate his endless attempts to rise up to mount the very tall babe of his dreams.

My veterinary role, long-term in all this, was for me to be Clem's medical valet, 24/7. For weeks, I'd have to lift that clown off his bed (of roses), carry him outside, and gently support his front end while his back end peed and pooped. Ridiculous. Goodness-knows, many a colonial President's mother emptied bed pans sure, but how many American patriots struggled with such an ignominious burden as did I with Lord Clem? So much for our colonial house-building days in rural Connecticut.

What really hurt most was when we discovered, after weeks of all this, that Clem had long been conning us. For some time now he had established in our minds that he was truly suffering, and his crisis was being faced with a pioneering spirit and stiff-

CHAPTER TWENTY-FIVE: ANOTHER DOWN

upper-lipped colonial resourcefulness, putting pain aside and just... carrying on.

After weeks of our recuperative accommodations for Lord Clem, it happened that Bobbye and I risked enjoying a movie-evening one day, leaving him on a nest of cushions and blankets on the living room floor where he would be comfortable while we were gone. Well, when we returned about three hours later, we found Clem stretched full-length on his back, up on our bed, his head sunken into a pillow, tongue dangling obscenely out the side of his wide-open mouth, contentedly snoring the evening away. Which also commented on his watchdog instincts. He never cracked an eyelid no matter how much racket Macintosh made to warn of something threatening from outside.

At least it seemed his shoulder and his heart were now healed. His senses had come back to him with a rush as well. His nose once again was a veritable vacuum cleaner of information processing... which also had its deficiencies. Times when we would call him, "Clem, Clem boy, here Clem." Then through the forest he'd come crashing, snorting out our scent, tracing our last ten days of movement all around the area, growing closer, ever-closer yet never raising his head-of-stone to just look, and see, and run directly to us. No. Snort-snout would collide with my foot and then that turkey would look up and joyously wag his tail seeing he had located me... for the first time.

During this period there had been reports of car thieves in the area. Unhappily I was away at the Reserves and Lord Clem was out for the night visiting ladies. Bobbye told me how that night Clem suddenly burst into a howling uproar. Was it the call of his woman lost or something else? Bobbye was very concerned. She took our revolver in hand, put a lead on Clem and with a flashlight, down the hall they went. It was evident Clem's golden snout was hot onto tracking something. Bobbye said she had kept the light off, the gun levelled.

The showdown came in the kitchen. Clem snarled into action. Rob flipped on the light, ready to blast away but, as it turned out, her bullets would only have threatened the life of one small field mouse frozen in wide-eyed terror as it sat next to Clem's prized hambone. I swear that was the only time that dog ever sounded an alarm as long as he was with us. But wow! To hear a tiny mouse licking a ham bone two rooms away spoke legions of Lord Clem's peak level of sensitivity. Perhaps when all was said and done, after his shattered love life having ended due to his lady friend's height, he had been left at least with that level of nose power.

Whatever, now our good friend Tosh was gone. He had never seemed to like our woods as much as he enjoyed the people and dog friends of Wakefield. He had suburbia in his blood, and he never seemed as much at home in Ledge Rock, as he had been back in Massachusetts.

Of course, we had gotten Clem to be his friend, but neither had taken to the other. Perhaps Tosh had felt betrayed. Something I could understand. Clem was a loner and somewhat of a drunk. And now we were stuck with him alone. It was sad. I know many would say that we should reach out to Clem, train him, school him to become a full replacement for dear old Tosh whom we had loved so much. However, the reality of the situation was that Clem had only a nose and a large Johnson with legs too short for him to rise up to whatever the occasion might be. On top of that was the over-riding fact that his skull seemed somewhat empty. No matter how hard I'd worked trying to train him, he would still poop on our car seats or barf out any open or even closed window. So, as I saw it, the only way to deal with the problem was to let Clem go. Of course, that was not going to be anything easily done. Never forget that we were told – "Clem doesn't like long car rides very much" so we'd have to find a nearby buyer for sure.

Carl and Florence Bausche finally were able to get me an interview with their lady writer friend. Maybe we weren't out of the writing business after all. With a manuscript tucked under one arm, Rob under the other, we dashed off for another crack at our destiny.

I must say we allowed ourselves some optimism at this point. The favorable reviews we had gotten of manuscript #1 had come from people with writing backgrounds. Certainly, I was aware of weaknesses in my work, but I was eager to tackle the editing if only I could find someone willing to direct me. I wasn't proud. No illusions. I just wanted a chance at some guidance. Perhaps this encounter would lead to that relationship.

Astaire Ashley or Mrs. Ashley as everyone seemed to call her, including Tony, the youngish man, her constant-companion who clearly recognized how her gravitas augmented the aura of the Grande Dame she happily accepted. Her appearance, her manner, her carriage cried out for the "Dame" rather than just "Mrs." She was stunning. An ageless creature so perfectly preserved that one could only gape at her. Yes, ageless, not a particularly flattering term, but one somehow applicable to Mrs. Ashley. Her complexion was flawless, her waist diminutive, her breasts intriguingly ample and emphasized by her dark turtleneck sweater and the wide waist-pinching belt she wore. Astaire Ashley seemed a Coco Chanel confidant, yet perfect in her own style. And strong, it was like visiting royalty. Bobbye felt it too. The Duchess was granting an audience. Her consort Tony, too old to be Tony except in her presence, was hovering about, seating and serving, busy. We were intimidated ... but not negatively, nor antagonized. It was somewhat of a treat. I had never experienced such a person before. Such self-possession, dignity, and command. Yet you knew, if no other way than simply by the fact of Tony, that she was a deeply passionate woman as well. She gave me tingles and shivers, and God knows she must have been at least sixty perhaps seventy years old.

It felt awfully good speaking to a professional, seemingly successful, working writer. So decent, kind perhaps, to reflexively take my side against the "miserable bastards," as she surprisingly put it, who ran their publishing empires, treating all writers as beggars at the gate. What a delicious feeling to be awarded a place in that queue.

She was sure my manuscript was good simply by looking at how neatly done and well laid out it was. She had to be right, of course, because she was who she was. Though her remark smacked a bit of Oz, I shook off the heresy. Dame Ashley could not be unreal, particularly if she was unreal in my favor.

Departing, she promised to give the book a reading as soon as convenient, but not to expect anything for a good month or two anyway. She was just finishing a novel of her own and was naturally harried. But she would help me. She was willing to help!

The beginning of October saw us finish the wall-boarding. All the ceilings were done, but for the far back bedroom with our junk in it, which would remain that way till the rest of the house was completed. Ah yes, those walls went up like a dream. We used a heavier than standard plasterboard throughout. It cost more, of course, but made a real house of it. Substantial. So many new places are cracker boxes. Lean against a wall and feel it flex. If the price were cracker box too, that would be one thing, but modern economics don't seem to work that way.

We installed soundproofing in the bathroom by insulating between its interior walls. I hate sitting at the dinner table with guests all having to shout over those very definitive noises produced there. And it's so embarrassing for everyone when the performer returns to the table. Somehow you feel you know too much about the person, more than you really want to know.

So, we did it up right, and fast, compared to the ceiling horrors. Perhaps I was progressing as a human being too, not having blown my stack once during that period. It was probably a comforting thought, though, an inaccurate one, truth be known. But at least Bobbye now had a private room. One day, down the road, she'd be changing diapers there.

Then my attention scurried outside to the clapboarding. At last, as those bleak middle wall composition panels would start to be covered with siding and the real look of a new house would begin to appear in their place, we were encouraged. Admittedly I had some feelings of guilt leaving dear Rob with so many interior goopings, and sanding miseries addressing the remaining joints and nail dents to fill, but what the hell, we were moving better now. The house, though unfinished, was at least "tight." When winter winds started to swirl, all we would need was heat on the inside pressing against the cold embracing the house on the outside.

Gleefully we dashed out into the clean sunny outside world to start giving the house its real look, it's soft, warm, rich redwood clapboard-siding-look. Yes, together we felt some original sin here too, regretfully thinking of those gorgeous forest giants being felled just to make our modest little house tight and beautiful; but then there were rumors that only the little redwoods were cut for commercial use. 'We didn't dare check that out. 'Didn't dare. Please you dying trees, forgive us. We wanted your beauty so badly. And we had a baby on the way.

As seemed to be my custom, I got to this new work late one afternoon when there was really no chance of beginning it in earnest. But maybe it was better that way, considering how I was at the start of a new phase with all my usual staring, wandering about, gaping at the thing perhaps for hours before actually getting started doing much of anything. I disliked all the calculating, and measuring, and setting up guidelines that everything depended on. It wasn't liberal arts kind of stuff. I preferred by-gosh and by-golly with lots of body English and Jesus-factors thrown in as one's bottom line. That other was too engineeringly bureaucratic for me.

So, there I was, staring like an idiot at the blank far back wall of the house, (Figured again that was the best place to make the usual early mistakes), when up the drive came an old friend from long before, a guy named John Reilly, and his father.

CHAPTER TWENTY-SIX
He Comes

B ig John, baby, what the hell! Son of a gun. Straight from a Peace Corps hitch in deepest remote Africa. All 6' 4" of large John had returned, across an entire ocean to help his regular-sized friend Kenny, and economy-sized, but starting to grow Bobbye, to build their tiny-sized castle in Connecticut. What a nice fellow indeed. John's dad at that time was the school superintendent in New London. Another huge guy, but much like our minister, Reverend Thomas, whom we never got a lick of work out of around the place any time he showed up. A talker. Constantly challenging me for the larynx championship of the world. And as ever, that day, though talking bigtime while neither of us listened to the other. So, before we realized it, it was dinner time. Which made the Reilly's our first official dinner guests.

Our table was a door laid across two sawhorses. For chairs, the old "his" and "Hers" plus two others found for free by the side of the road. It was just right. The two Reilly's were a pair of characters perfect for this scene. And man could they eat! By the time they got done, the place looked like a reclamation center. Cans, bottles, stuff everywhere, followed by burps and belly pats for a soundtrack. The Reilly's had eaten.

John's arrival at that particular time was for us a tonic. Though Rob and I were making solid progress on the house, it was now early October. In past years, her classes would have been underway again, and I'd have been buckling harder down on a book. A nip was coming into the morning air. For the first time we heard a school bus stop at the end of the lane. For Bobbye the teacher, this was the first autumn since she was five years old, that she wouldn't be getting on a bus or driving herself to a school. No new shoes. No new books. This year there was none of that. Things were different. Just sawdust and nails lying around, dirt to be swept up to say nothing of a tiny one growing in dear Bobbye.

Other realities were pressing on us too. Money, the dimming hopes for my writing, even the coming winter hung over us. Growing doubts. Uneasiness as friends wrote of this promotion, that new job, medical school finished, a law partnership agreed to.

Were we fools? Were we kidding ourselves? Was the chucking of the everyday scramble just adolescent idealism soon to be set straight by reality's ruler cracking across our knuckles? Was that incredible new spirit we had felt grow with Camelot, now to die in us this autumn as it had through the nation the year before? Miserable questions, because it could mean cutting the heart and guts, the spirit out of the two of us for a long time to come.

After my parents and Bobbye's family had gone, we had a quiet moment together to feel the reality of our two-plus years together. I had squirreled away a few dollars from the Reserves, so I formally asked my darling finally to have an anniversary dinner out!

John's coming was a big deal. He was a disciple of the New Spirit returned as a New Frontier warrior. Here was a dreamer who had travelled much further than we had from the everyday, and who was behind further still in the self-promoting young executive scramble all around us. Here was empathy. Here came a guy who knew what we were talking about even if we couldn't say the words yet or say them right. In the world of seeing past or through the petty crap, big John was years ahead.

Yes, it was a joy and a surprise to see this guy again. He'd been away with the Peace Corps a couple of years after serving with me in the Marine Corps after Dartmouth College. He always was the idealist. One couldn't help thinking of those whorehouses from Havana to Tijuana he'd only drunk beer in, while the rest of us were doing naughty-boy things. This character was some-principled, but not embarrassingly so. One of the guys all the way to the point where he drew the line which he did not cross, and nobody jazzed him about it.

John had some great African tales to tell. Meeting Albert Sweitzer, showing off his team's work to Sargent Shriver out in the middle of nowhere; working with the kids and men of Gabon, West Africa building homes with little more than the sweat off their brows. Few tools. Laying block, brick, even mortaring with their bare hands. Building schools!

"Good Heavens, John, you didn't need to go all the way to Africa for that kind of work. We offer it right here. Yes, you have come to the right place! Our place is your place. Just bring tools."

So, the poor guy was recruited and with the next sunrise he returned. Wow. With a big dude like that around for a few days, Bobbye and I could sure make some headway, speculated my corrupt greedy mind. If this guy had worked for nothing for two years in Africa for people he didn't even know, think how he'd put out for an old Marine buddy in Ledge Rock, Connecticut!

Damn it, wouldn't you know the big fellow wasn't working out as we had envisioned? He had this ugly habit of doing things his way as opposed to my way. Perhaps Tom Sawyer could abide something like that for a price, but not me? Being somewhat of an imperiously egotistical turkey, I simply could not bear to have a guy work himself half to death gratuitously for my exclusive benefit without having the decency of going all the way by subjecting his own ego to mine as well.

In other words, I didn't like the way he cut the butt ends of the clapboard, nor how he over-drove the aluminum nails, denting the soft redwood. So, as the day progressed, a tiny level of friction developed between us driving me toward the horrible realization that I was the kind who had to do his own work. Damn it. This was going to be no good for me. My shoulders sagged just looking around at how much more of that house there was to do. Unless I shaped up, growing docile enough to keep my big fat mouth shut, I'd have the house strapped to my back, moving Bobbye and me both rearward, ever farther from the mystical Land of Completion. And I wasn't as big as Big John.

"John Reilly!" came Bobbye's anguished cry from inside the unfinished back bedroom. She slid up the window and stretched her head out adding, in a strong unladylike voice, 'John, you get in here this minute and look at what you've done." She spoke with command in her voice. It was a voice I knew well.

CHAPTER TWENTY-SIX: HE COMES

I don't know how his belly felt as we trudged in to inspect whatever the horror was, but mine seemed totally missing, like my bottom had fallen out and off. What could be the problem?

Redwood siding has to be done right the first time or not at all. Screwing up regular clapboard is no problem. You can always pull out the bad nails and putty the holes knowing a coat of paint would cover the error anyway. Wood to be left natural or stained, such as redwood, was strictly a one-shot deal. Right or wrong.

So, could you believe it? Could anyone believe how many places right up neatly, straight as an arrow, from the floor line to the roof, went a row of nails, perfectly parallel to the vertical studs, but never, or only occasionally, into the damned wood stringers! It was the most skillfully botched job I had ever seen.

"Reilly!" At first that was all I could say, then finally, "Oh, John."

I sat down on a box. "John, Jesus John." But I couldn't help being awed by how straight that row was. All the way to the peak of the roof. Incredible. Man, he had an eye like a hawk. I started to giggle; kind of a marginally deranged snickering giggle that built finally to a sobbing, snorting whiney sort of thing.

"Oh John, Jesus John." I choked, "you certainly have built a monument to Murphy's Law which now should be renamed Reilly's Law. Oh man." If I wasn't laughing so hard, I would have been banging a nail through my forehead.

"What is Murphy's Law?" asked Bobbye.

"You tell her pal, you're the only guy who should be named Murphy around here," I laughed in a moist sucking sort of way.

"Ah, umm, well Bobbye Lou," he began with a bashful smile, "in the military a principle has been established over the years that goes something like: 'If a job can be done wrong, no matter how difficult, expensive, or time-consuming it might be to do it wrong, someone, somewhere, sometime will do it that way.' That is the, ah, substance of umm, Murphy's Law."

"Oh come on John, don't be so modest, you know you wrote the damned thing." I was smiling, but I'll have to admit there was an edge to my remark.

"Now Kenny-Wenny, these little things happen. No real harm done. That was kind of an extra row of nails anyway. The others will hold it tight," he comforted me, putting an arm around my shoulder.

"Sure," I mumbled. "Next high wind, I'll let you know how it holds up."

And so concluded Murphy's days as a carpenter on our house on blueberry hill.

As he drove off down the drive at the end of that day, we exchanged warm waves and the usual rude gestures of long-term friends, but the thought kept creeping back into my mind ... should I wire Gabon, Africa and tell them to evacuate those schools next time there are high winds coming before somebody really gets hurt?

As we had worked together that day, John had said stuff which was to stay with me. Things which seemed germane to Bobbye and my struggles, meaningful too. Hell, I don't know how you'd phrased it, maybe addressing life itself. Meaningful to my own search for identity, if you will; or better, for my own, for all of our searching for an individual relationship to living. Yes, the trite reason for living, our own raison d'être; but in simpler measure, each of our accommodations and explanations to ourselves, conscious or otherwise, as to just to find what we are bothering to live for anyway.

John had said how difficult he had found it returning to everyday American life. Most of the Peace Corps people had experienced this to some degree as well. The focus of the situation was on the vast materialism of our lives back here. Stop and think for a moment. Guys like John had gone off for two years, marched right out of everything they had always known, to try to make substance out of a young, vague, idealistic urge to give themselves to something of value.

I'm not bringing this up to get into a row over the pros and cons of the Peace Corps, I'm just talking about guys and girls who want to try an act of selfless idealism for a bit, before their lives get too tied up in the usual complications of family, career, ambition, accomplishment, and gain. They are simply the products of the good principles once taught in our schools and houses of religion, mouthed by our politicians, emblazoned, and perhaps now lost from our Constitution, its Preamble, the Declaration of Independence; all those great documents that originally launched an entire new nation on the very same kind of experiment in new ideals and positive action. They are regular people like Bobbye and me, but for the one difference; they have actually gone out and done what each of us merely dreams about. And, I might add, gone out for those couple of years while the rest of their friends were back getting a head start on climbing the money tree.

So, John had said how he had come back home and felt an awesome disappointment in our society. It was like walking from a clean fresh autumn day into a saturated steam bath. He had been out where everyone's major concern was with helping other people who were struggling at least for survival. He had come back to a hot, sweaty, jostling rat race that seemed to reek of greed and self-promotion. You know the feeling you get in a really greasy, greasy spoon. How the countertop is slick with the stuff your finger is able to draw pictures in. How even the air has a film of sour/

sweet sweat in it. How your shoes want to stick to the floor, and how edged your fingertips feel after they've been drug along the gum globs plastered under the counter. The way you find yourself almost panicking in a place like that is, I guess, similar to the trauma a guy like John experienced re-entering the day-to-day of American life.

Here was the idealist, the philosopher returning to civilization from the wilderness. From the clarity of self-sacrifice to the murk and swamp of self-interest. How was he to adjust? How was he to find a working relationship again with the society around him, yet retain enough of his humanism to continue to work within that society to bring it more closely in line with its own founding principles? How to remain untainted by it; to resist simply diving back in feet first to kick, claw and carve out of someone else's hide his own. 'Piece of blighted turf? And how tempting that could be for the returnee since his fellows already had that two-year jump on him.

In John's case, happily, he seemed in-route to a decision for law school and perhaps politics afterwards. Oh man, how good it would be if he could pull it off. Think of what a big son of a bitch full of the grand old Irish charm, the sense of humor and the sense of timing that went with it; what he might be able to do as an idealist capable of action, self-proven. Think of all the cages he might rattle. Think of the Madlocks and mayors and zoning boards and town councils he might rap by the side of the head. Think too of all those vegetable Yams he might plant. What more appropriate chore for a very big smiling Irishman?

But the more I thought of it, the more I began to realize how real John's dilemma of return actually was. How universal it was, in one sense or another. Look at Henry Dryer, for instance. His struggle was the antithesis of John's, yet so closely akin. Henry was at the other end of the line, the other side of the coin, however the hell you want to describe it. Henry was up to his mustache in the mundanity, the shattering, gut-grinding oppression of the common place. Of plain and simple lifelong boredom, from which he couldn't extract himself. He was the eternal prisoner of the provincialism that had defined from birth the economic, territorial, intellectual, spiritual, and occupational boundaries of his prison. How, at fifty, he had to continue to be the super-capable machinist. There was the house, the kids, the car, the wife, the family, the bread, the butter, the community, the schooling, the long apprenticeship, the very simple lack of anything else possible for him, Henry Dryer, that made this irrevocable. A life's sentence, if you will, that was just about to drive him nuts. His very talent was his curse. The lead machinist, the only one at the shop who could perform the certain disciplines that had landed the new 4,000-unit contract. Four thousand goddamned units which he alone would have to make because he was so good at it. Over and over, over and over, seventy times seven, times seven again, plus five hundred and seventy more! Not even Jesus Christ had asked that of a man. But society asked it of Henry.

How then could this man spring his idealism free from its prison of endless, repetitive, crushing, drudgery? The only answer his mind and the very chemicals of his body had come up with was alcohol. But, damn it, that was another prison at the other end of the spectrum whose guards were not machines, bills, babies, endless production, but all the flotsam and jetsam of delirium tremors.

What the hell? Sitting on one of our big rocks strewn around the front by Ralph, and watching the dust from John's departure gently settling, I began to feel I was catching a glimpse, an elusive glimpse of life's true dilemma. And God knows, we, Bobbye and I, were caught up in it just as Henry was. But how to focus on it? How to bring it into sharp definition to cope with it; live it with some sense of understanding, dignity and grace?

There had to be answers here. For instance, John, back from the Peace Corps and finding the adjustment difficult. Henry locked into the middle of Middle America ready to blow his brains out. Bobbye and I in a struggle, succeeding and failing at the same time, wondering what the hell we were going to accomplish in the end anyway? And from my vantage point sitting on that rock, watching Moody roll in from one job, only to eat and roll out again to start the next. All true, all his reality, but a true triumph of his and Loraine's applying their special brand of grace and dignity.

Bobbye's folks showed up next. Her long-tall basketball playing brother, later to distinguish himself as one of the world's hairiest men, her super-calm father, able to leap tall buildings in a single bound with his total imperturbability. Her mother, a woman who could out-talk a television set with endless histories of people many times totally unknown to anybody listening. A hard-working bunch they were, Godfearing Southern folk who didn't drink, smoke, or cuss, which made it pure hell for me. Sometimes I'd want to yell *SHIT* so badly, I'd have to put down my tools and go off into the woods to shout it, just for sanity's sake.

But they did work hard. Rob's mother broom-swept a ton or two of the shavings, plaster, putty, sand, and cement the site perpetually filled with, freeing Bobbye to ceramic-tile the bath walls, get a shower curtain up, and finally put us in business as totally clean-livers. Which all inspired me to spend the evenings building the world's sturdiest sink cabinet and spiffy countertop all inlaid with marble-like Formica. Being built out of left over 2

X 4's and inch thick plywood, it was a some strong construct, but gloriously set off with colonial louvred cabinet doors which went handsomely with that big old-fashioned mirror we had wrangled for five bucks from the man at the auction.

We were so enthusiastic over pushing ahead this far with the kitchen and bath, we ran out and got a pair of carriage lamps from Monky-Wards to go on either side of the mirror frame. Then we got a pair of shaving mugs mounted on the little candlestick platforms and we had one damned fine-looking bathroom. So, we painted it, and even laid the tile floor in big black and white squares.

Son of a gun. The room was done! Our first. Now only what? Five more to go.

"Kenny," Bobbye burst out all full of smiles, "We have actually finished, completely finished, one room of our house. Just look at it," she continued waving her hands in from the door, kind of like a magician would as the rabbit hopped out of his tall hat, "and look how beautiful it is... really is." And that gave me a wonderful, weird, shivery feeling which Bobbye got too. We could do it! We could finish the whole damned house! What was it but just a series of rooms, and none more complicated than a bath with all its plumbing, hot and cold water in; sinks and drains out; tubs, showers, bowls, electrical fixtures, walls, floors, cabinetry, so much! To have done that one room was in effect to have done the whole house. We felt cocky and self-assured. We felt good.... at least until father-in-law, brother-in-law, and I would finish the clapboarding, which, because of John Reilly's screw ups, was miss-matched by about an inch at the back of the house's last corner. Damn, damn, damn!

An, here's what had happened. You've got to be awfully careful with clapboard since it is nothing but a series of wooden parallel lines. This means that you must make absolutely sure your guidelines on every side of the house are absolutely positively horizontal i.e. bubble in the dead center of your level. If you don't, and if you fudge the bubble a hair this way or that, by the end of all those hundreds of running board feet around the outside of the house; when the final piece of clapboard goes on completing the full-around girdling of the house, then your final bottom skirt comes around to meet your first bottom skirt and they don't match evenly. It's nothing more than a crooked hemline on a woman's dress.

If only I wasn't so damned impatient most of the time, I would have done a level chalk line around the house to prevent this. Certainly. But I didn't feel I would be that clumsy anyway. And I didn't figure in my ballgame that there'd be a Big John, standing beside me looking at the bubble, along with his father, also along with my own hairy brother-in-law all deciding when the bubble was centered at the midpoint. And I was too polite to keep checking their work every five minutes, particularly since their price tag was zero. What is that about a gift horse? But never lose sight of the fact that any horse can kick you in the backside pretty hard too, gift horse or not.

"My stars, it doesn't look so bad," Bobbye said just as her mother, Nova, would have, cocking her head as she spoke.

"No one would ever notice it," John said.

"It's only one inch in thousands," my reasoning heart cried out, adding, "Besides, it's at the far back corner of the house. You can put a bush there."

All true. But till the day I died, I knew I would see nothing but that cockeyed inch.

"Kenny," Bobbye said, "you're such a perfectionist, you'll never be satisfied with anything you ever do anyway. You should try to be more philosophical about that one little inch. Heaven only knows, you are the only man on earth who will ever see it. And didn't rug-weavers in Turkey, India, all over the world, put a missed knot in everything they work on since only God can weave perfectly?"

True enough, but that still didn't help. I never should let others assist unless I was spiritually, intellectually, and philosophically prepared to accept errors made by them. Of course, through all this I was seeing how different Bobbye's family was from mine. As the youngest of four boys, I had known conflict, even combat. Pushing, shoving, wrestling, shouting and heated arguments were the tools of my growing up. And I saw, well, witnessed the near combat resolutions of disagreements between my parents and older brothers. Yet none of that seemed to be the process for disagreement resolution in Rob's family. With the dominance of her mother, she had become the Shaman of her tribe unchallenged by any of the others, Warren, the father, Bobbye or Frank the son. And because of Nova's dominance, all was dealt with silently. Yes, there might have been bitten lips, rolling eyes, and strides out a door, but Nova was never directly challenged. Because of this, in their house quiet reigned, whereas in mine, the clash of steel was dominant. Certainly, these were two different worlds, but I will say in defense of my upbringing, the explosions were noisy, but brief. Having been blessed with more than two years of living with dear Rob, it took at least that amount of time to get the smallest scratch below the surface of her family's upsets, angers, and animosities. From these realities, I have been fortunate enough to have a loving wife who quietly oversees my bluster and bombast, while she has gained a knight in shining armor, sword in hand when needed.

So, I did grit my teeth, let my eyes run up, down and all around and then I gently bit my tongue.

Bobbye's family stayed for several days. We pulled beds, cots, and sleeping bags out of our side storeroom to comfort all as best we could. However, all this activity worked out to be a smidgin too much for Nova. She came down with a cold. Bobbye put her to bed and had to turn her attention from house building to health caring. Fortunately, Rob's parents had the money for us to call in our local doctor. He was concerned about Nova being ill and having Bobbye nursing her, "In her present condition."

The entire time they were with us, Bobbye felt she had to look after her mother, and she did bring her back to health in just a few days. Those were days marked by brother Frank and Clem becoming fast friends. They got so mutually cuddly that Clem took to snuggling with him all through the night.

When Frank proposed adopting the odd-looking pooch, I had to struggle with my conscience. I really wanted to get rid of Banana Head, certainly with a baby on the way, but I could not deal with the guilt I might feel if Bobbye's brother and parents were saddled by a two-day car ride back to Tennessee with a barfing, seat-dumping odd-looking hound. Nova would be her dominating self, and husband, Warren, would be giving in, mile after mile of listening to Nova giving directions,-- it all would have been way too difficult.

As Rob's folks drove off to waves and smiling goodbyes (without Clem), I turned back to the house and realized with some shock that the time had finally come to build the chimney. I had no idea what an ordeal that would ultimately turn out to be, though it was clear that the very success or failure of the entire house would ride on this one task. So much depended on it. The chimney would constitute about half of one wall of the living room. Until it was built, there wouldn't even be a central heating system, since the furnace required one of the chimney flues for exhaust. To say nothing of the interim job of heating the house with wood fires while the oil burner was being hooked up. But then there were the aesthetics of the matter, too. Externally, that six or seven foot facing of beautiful old Boston brick would so perfectly set off the gentle redwood hues of the siding, making a true gem out of a basically simple sort of place; a little house which could so easily slide into ugly tackiness with just the right/wrong touches ... like less than seven-foot plus ceilings and such. As with any work of art -- the thin line dividing great beauty from basic ugliness had to be meticulously guarded. The line here was the brick work about to begin. If it was shabbily done, or if the chimney was put up out of, say, concrete block, the whole place would be a tacky mess. If great care wasn't used laying that gorgeous cache of hand-molded colonial brick, the living room would become an overpowering eye sore, a dominating disaster. So, it was understandable that we had left this near the end of it all. It was awesome. I had needed to count on a growing confidence and increased skills over the long summer before tackling it. Nevertheless, there was still one haunting reality chilling my confidence. I had never actually laid a line of brick in my life, only assisted experts.

Before beginning this finale challenge, I called Merriweather, telling him that the exterior siding was "Essentially on," (a small fudge) making the house officially tight, which meant we were into the last financial stage. Which also meant we were into the reality of having a livable house. Which meant the final check should be freed up. I've got to admit, however, that I didn't say too much about the wall I'd have to take out for putting the whole chimney in. The fireplace was an extra anyway. But I don't think Ed sweated it too much either way. Bless him, he had faith.

In truth we had built up an awful lot of debt waiting for this moment, though nothing yet was overdue. Our credit was good around town, but still things were getting tight. Costs had gone up considerably over what our original estimates had been based on. Building materials and copper especially had increased significantly, plus the fact that we were living and eating off the bank loan too. I had very little coming in. I was nervous. As the money dwindled, I began to see that I'd counted on my submitted books for something. When there had been money on hand it was easy to pretend otherwise, but now it all was coming home, as they say.

Getting started on the outside again, I began my usual stare at the wall, the brick pile, the trowel held awkwardly in one hand, the brick hammer resting equally uneasily in the other, and one phrase kept whispering through my head, "May God have mercy on my soul." Over and over, it went. "May God have mercy on my soul." Bobbye's too.

The next morning, I began the fireplace in earnest. Hearth and broadfaced outside chimney effacement from the bottom up, based on the foundation surfaces up, all the way to the roof-top and above for a good draw. My timetable was for completion in two weeks. Carl Bausche had told me earlier that it had taken him and a friend three days to do his. I estimated that I could probably do the job in five, but I doubled my calculation to ten working days, to be on the safe side.

In the end, my figuring turned out to be faulty. The whole job took me five weeks! Five whole f-ing weeks. Not days. Thirty days on the overrun side. Even by liberal arts standards, that was a fairly wild error of Pentagon-level screw up.

The first major hurdle was how to be sure the fireplace would draw. How many people have had beautiful fireplaces put in their homes, only to find the living room filled with smoke rather than heat? Or the reciprocal dilemma of a fireplace that drew so effectively it sucked everything up and out, warming only the sky above rather than the room below? Knowing nothing about fireplaces, Bobbye and I were very uncomfortable. Just the thought of breaking my back to build the thing to have it useless one way or the other scared the daylights out of me.

Which, in conversation with Carl, brought me around to one of those *Heatilator* units. The Bausche's had one in their fireplace and it drew well and heated the room like a champ. And since it was nothing more really than a heavy gauge steel fire chamber, in itself, and engineered to guarantee a proper draw, added floor level vents to throw extra heat into the room and house, so be it? If, after we got the whole thing built, it failed to work right, I'd have recourse for the manufacturer to come bail us out. Or so the guarantee said. Which made the one-hundred fifty-dollar price tag look pretty good.

That first day, then, was spent picking the unit up, reading the instructions, and overhauling the busted brake drum my tired old truck tore up in-route when the emergency brake actuator fell off inside one rear hub sending me skidding, shrieking, careening, and smoke-sliding all over the road like some hapless Indy driver fighting for his life. Never did I have a sunrise nor a sunset without that frigging truck giving me a shot below the belt.

That was the first day. Nine to go to completion. The fact that not a single brick was laid yet should have told me something.

Happily, Ralph came by that evening and promised to drop off a tub I could use for mixing cement. I had figured the wheelbarrow would be adequate, but he said I'd need much more volume per batch. For once I listened. He also offered an electric mixer, but this time I didn't listen. Somehow, like cutting the trees by hand, I persisted in my half-assed Thoreauvian haze that 'wouldst be nobler to mix great batches of mortar by hand than by mundane, establishment, copout, modern electrical mixer. God knows, you'd think I'd have learned by then. Particularly with winter coming on. I mean I learned by then that it was far nobler to have a heated house for oneself and one's loved ones when the snow began to fly, than to still be mixing stupid cement with frozen fingers and a frost-bitten stupid head as the thermometer crept irrevocably below the 32° magic marker. But we were in the middle of an Indian summer at the moment, making it difficult to foresee impending doom when one was otherwise warm, fat, and glossy. (As the Aussi's would say of the natives they oversaw in Borneo.)

In the end, it took only a week of noble hand-mixing to capitulate to reality. I was learning, but slowly. 'Like so many other jobs on the house, just getting visibly started was damned difficult and frustrating. I worked for days before there was one exterior brick laid for God and man to see. Unbelievable. And how ludicrous my ten-day estimate looked by the end of that first week.

In the beginning, you see, I hadn't bothered to think about the interior cellar base that had to be added to the foundation wall to support the hearth and interior front of the chimney. At least I'd had the foresight to have provisions built into the foundation itself, but there was still a lot of block and concrete work to be added to that. I had to make a wall across the foundation cutout to act as the front support of the fireplace floor and hearth above. The space between it and the outside wall became an ash-trap with kind of a dump chute cut through the base of the fireplace floor. Our Sears Roebuck manuals again came to the rescue detailing every step. Nevertheless, the first five days were shot before I ever

CHAPTER TWENTY-SIX: HE COMES

got a regular brick in hand. Carl and his friend must have been hell on wheels was all I could say. Getting a whole fireplace up in three days! Son of a gun.

All together mine was a tough week. No piece of cake for Bobbye either. She was still struggling with gooping ceiling and wall joints. Poor lady looked like a white-haired Geisha by noon each day. She had an icky job and icky work isn't known for happy thoughts, so she started feeling low, which led to some miseries over our departed dog Macintosh and the dirt everywhere, dwindling money, all of it. Which made me feel pretty much down too. And the more we fussed over it all, the more we came to think maybe we should rustle up a replacement for dear old MacInosh. Why not? Why not get some more animals around the place, if for no other reason than to act as a buffer between us, well me, and Clem. Oh Clem. His days were numbered sure as hell as far as I was concerned. And a few more hairy but lovable faces around the place might cheer things up a bit.

So, very quickly, we added two new little guys. One a female dog and the other a male cat. The dog was very small, a mixed breed and kind of overwhelmed looking. When folks asked what breed she was, I said she's a North American Rat Hound. We named her "Tinkerbelle." Actually, she was the result of a miniature poodle breeder's inability to keep a neighboring beagle out of his bitch's britches. Tinker, then, was technically either a peagle or a boodle, depending on your allegiances. Unfortunately, like Clem, she managed to alienate my affections straight away since she had the retched yip of the poodle around the house, and the ghastly bay of the beagle outdoors. She never barked, you see, at human arrivals, only dog arrivals, which meant as a watch dog she was only effective against burglars who brought their pets.

The other addition was a truly splendid little fellow, orange in color, who became about the only cat I had ever had enthusiasm for in my adult life.. We named him "Goldfinger." And damned if he didn't live up to his 007 heritage. He was a great mouser. Too good, really. And arrogant about it. Every morning he'd stack a couple of carcasses on the doorstep just for show. But that wasn't all. During the day you'd see him strolling about with the rear section, stomach, hind legs, and tail of a chipmunk or baby red squirrel protruding from his mouth. By carrying his prey like that, he'd keep them half oxygenless, then from time to time, release them so they could catch a breath;--only to toy with them again, then pop them back into his mouth. Cats can be ghastly creatures to watch in action.

Apparently, mouse-catching alone wasn't challenging enough for his hunting blood. But what was most impressive about Goldfinger was his terrific personality. He was a lot like Jimmy Cagney in the movies long ago. Small, but a hell of a scrapper. He'd take on much bigger cats despite getting all torn up in the bargain. At breakfast, for instance, he'd jump up onto the countertop, walk up and sit directly in front of my face, low enough by way of my chin in hand, he would look up and study me for the longest time. He would sit directly in front of me, then move his face straight into mine, ending with his nose against my nose, eyeball to eyeball. Next, he'd lift a paw slowly and rest it on the end of my nose and gently run his claws out and in, out and in, quietly giving my nose a couple of double tweaks. His eyes, all the while, would stare into mine. Slowly, he'd wink first one eye, then the other, giving me the distinct feeling he was not only a hell of a lot smarter than I was, but that he could even read my mind. Scary.

Later, Bobbye discovered that Goldfinger liked to play hide and seek with her too. It was something to see. Rob would sit the three of them down in the kitchen, then go off to hide behind a door or a stack of boxes somewhere. She would then call out -- "Okay, come on" and they'd all scramble to find her. This was the only time hammer-head Clem would not use his nose, so he'd run and grunt all over the house, roaring right past Rob, not missing a step. Tinker really was too young to do well. But she did have the sense to ignore Clem and follow Goldfinger. And that cat, every time, would walk straight to Bobbye and put his paw authoritatively on her foot and look up to her as if to say, "Gotcha."

Other times that crazy animal would wait in ambush behind a carton or around a corner. We'd walk by, when suddenly out would come a paw. If I didn't trip, he'd lunge onto my ankle for a full-bodied, "Gotcha."

Goldfinger was a really neat cat. He didn't like Clem much though he adored Tinker Belle. They slept together in a basket with their paws mutually wrapped around each other. It was the cutest damn thing. He was really some character.

With a new week beginning, I was enthusiastic. Finally, all the foundation stuff was done. We were ready to lay brick. I felt we should really sail now, just fly up the side of the house on wings of brick. And I was right. I flew up the side of that house just about like one would expect of a bird with brick wings. Though a pilot, I could sometimes still be pretty stupid about things aeronautical.

The first course of brick told the tale. Sure, I had gotten a little feel for the job doing the pump house. Laying block is a lot harder than brick and quickly teaches you something about mixing mortar for moisture and consistency. But subterranean block pump houses in concrete blocks don't exactly have to be works of art. The same went for the half-sized block wall, in the basement, under the fireplace. And don't get the idea I just tossed these up either. I labored mightily over them, first using too little mortar, then too much, rarely getting a block to fit snuggly against its mate, and evenly on top of its predecessors on the row below with cement in between. I mean it could be exasperating. To think of how much block and brick laying I had watched summers with the Tavernas. How easy Frankie had made it look, flipping his trowel to fling the mortar against the edges of a block, sticking on them so neatly as he lifted and placed, then tapped the next block expertly into position, tight, level, and in line. Bam. As I tried those dimly remembered motions, if I even hit the thing with the mix, either too wet or too dry, it just seemed to rebound or ooze off. As a kid, all Patsy had had to say to me was,"*Tuo fa il chimento liscio, liscio,*" and I'd mix it right. I began to get the eerie feeling that it was impossible to lay brick or block in English only in Italian.

God knows how much cement I wasted, along with sweat and tears and hot breath seething out through long hoarse stanzas of short foul words. Maybe WASP kids just couldn't lay brick. I mean genetically.

So, that first course was a kind of a nightmare. Though each brick got into place finally, reasonably straight and in line, it took a hell of a long time. And this was only a foot or two above ground level, laying on top of a perfectly flat foundation, bubble in the middle, everything going for me. It was terrifying to consider that the next row, and the next, and the next ad infinitum would all be dependent on my own preceding work, not on that of beautiful Joey Gildea, back from his latest boat ride. Appalling. I started working slower and slower.

I think people can sense drama, impending climax, much like animals seem to pick up scents even through solid stone walls. My body was probably pumping out telepathic distress signals like fire-alarm-horns and bells. Think of it. To make way for this fireplace, I'd had to cut out most of the living room wall. Naturally we hadn't clapboarded this area, but still it was a sight to see. A big gaping hole in that wall. Coming up the drive you'd be looking through into the newly finished living room. From the outside, you'd see the inside. Unsettling. Scary.

So, people started to appear. Henry, as always, but Carl more often than before, Florence, Moody, and of course Babonas. Everyone had a word of encouragement. What a nice thing indeed. And by the end of the week good Ralph finally rolled in on his own with the electric cement mixer. He was such a compassionate kind of guy he didn't want me to have to ask for the thing after I had already refused it once. Thank goodness. I was getting hand-mixed-out. It was tough going, doing my own mortar, carrying my own bricks, building my own scaffolding. And the higher I went everything compounded. To say nothing of learning how to lay brick with each brick I laid in the first place.

By the end of the second week, though all estimates were thoroughly shot, I was still encouraged. Much of that early work had been quite intricate and challenging. The wall in the cellar, the base for the hearth, and the fireplace floor; but best of all had been the struggle to work in a flue for the future heating system. After much fore and after scratching, I'd finally found that it could be run up through the floor base, which was yet to be poured, behind the Heatilator shell, snuggly inside of the exterior brick. Then it and the regular fireplace flue would parallel each other up the chimney. Manificci! Suddenly I felt like Leonardo da Vinci.

After I'd laid ten or fifteen course of brick, the lush Indian summer suddenly quit. And the autumn rains came. And came. It had to be expected, but it somehow seemed so unexpected that coming down as hard as it did was almost cruel. It made the job miserable. Never heavy enough to scrub work altogether, just enough to slow things to a crawl. Oh man, those chilled rivulets trickling from my collar and down my back were challenging, exceptionally so when they reached my skivvies and items south.

Where had summer gone? Especially after that October's return to the warmth of August. All now gone and giving away to the reality of winter coming. There seemed to be an omen for the future in all of this.

Originally in tackling the chimney, I had kind of poo-pooed using such crutches as plumb bobs, lubber lines and such. I figured to just eyeball the verticals and horizontals. This reasoning came from my original ideas of hand-sawing down the trees necessary to open up the area for the house and drive. It was a bizarre wish to be close to nature especially since nature had no internal combustion engines. Hand-power was "greener." Closer to Mother Nature. Blah, blah, blah. But then it occurred to me, after I realized my eyes were not actually calibrated for the perfect verticals and horizontals. I became coldly aware that I wanted to build a functional and handsome chimney attached to an equally charming house. I certainly did not wish to duplicate the Leaning Tower of Pisa, no matter how "green" such a thing would ultimately finish out. Once I had my scaffolding up, I let a plumb bob run down the two front edges of what would be the chimney to counter any slants my otherwise hawk-like eyes might allow. It was a nod to Mother Earth and forces of the "green" bent. Fortunately, realities quickly took over, forcing a cop-out on the horizontal factor, but it wasn't until I discovered how hard it was to tell whether or not I was laying brick straight across, up or not, that I had finally given way to a plumb line. And, of course, I also accepted that I required a scaffolding to lug my bricks up to where my next

CHAPTER TWENTY-SIX: HE COMES • 309

course would go and all that it took to get it there. And that also meant another battle to get dear tired old truck up and running. That would be another hour under him before I even got down the drive. And down came the rain ...

Also, the higher I went up on the chimney, the more difficult it all became. Mix the cement, put it in a bucket, haul the bucket, (heavy), up the slippery ladder, pour it into a working pan. Down for another load or two. Heavy. Wet. Slippery. Then the bricks. Up the ladder, put them next to the pan and around the work area so as not to have to crawl so far once back up and laying them. Heavy. Wet. Slippery. And cold. My flight jacket was good for most of those remaining three weeks as long as I remembered to dry it at night, and the orange fire-proofed flight suit ultimately joined the costume, with its partial waterproofing. Then my flight boots. As a matter of fact, all I needed to complete the picture of aviation in action on the home front was the helmet and oxygen mask, plus the yellow leather gloves How dearly I would have liked to have had those gloves, but they and the helmet and the mask were in the locker at the air station. My hands were damned cold pushing bricks around. The mercury seemed to have locked on 36° and below, day and night. The wet made the chill cut, cut deep. But frankly the lack of money was cutting deeper still, considering there was nothing to speak of coming in. I feared even going out four or five dollars for new gloves. Which made me pause and look at those cold hands, chopped up, cracked, calloused, with winter chewing at the fingertips. Looking around me, back at my hands again and at myself, I was shocked. I felt the bottom dropping out of my life. Money, always money... to say nothing of failure.

The growing financial realities were compounded that afternoon when the card came from the oil burner people announcing the unit we had ordered was finally in stock. It took a day away from the chimney to run the truck to Massachusetts for it to save the delivery cost. I had a hell of a load onboard coming home. The burner, oil tank, and all the ducting. And what we did have on the truck, we didn't have in the bank, money. So, Merriweather's all-purpose buy-the-nails, feed-your-belly, pay-back-the-bank was easing me toward exhaustion. Alone on the wet road home I felt very uneasy. The load on the truck itself had cost us about $600. $1500 of the final money was already spent too, yet so much still lay ahead. Depressing, I thought, it might pick me up some if I had somebody to talk to, so the first hitchhiker I came to I offered a ride.

And that, as it turned out, only made things worse. This guy was even more depressed than I was. He was in the process of dropping out of college. He'd simply said screw it and walked out. He had a backpack and a few bucks he said would take him to Big Sur. Whatever the hell was at Big Sur I had no idea. He didn't really seem to care either, but he was going anyway. I tried to talk him out of it and into going back to college, but he wouldn't listen. He wanted a new life, a new start. Good luck, pal. For the hell of it, when I dropped him off, 1 gave him our address in case he needed a bunk for a night some time. I told him my name, shook his hand, and said good luck. Watching him in the rearview mirror as I drove off, I found myself thinking that Big Sur was not going to help him much. Seeing a judge would have been his best bet, not for a new start but for a new name. He'd introduced himself as Peter Suck.

CHAPTER TWENTY-SIX: HE COMES

Back home, weather still dreary, Bobbye seemed to be coughing more. I hadn't noticed it before. She said she'd had the cough for a while, but neither of us had thought much about it. Clearly, she needed a warm house. The house needed a warm house. If I didn't get the chimney built, our water lines stood to freeze as the temp slumped below freezing. Soon we could really have a mess. And the colder it got the harder it was to work, so I wasn't exactly burning rubber up the side of that chimney. Those next few days were tough. I began to question why the hell we had decided on such a wide grandiose piece of brick work in the first place. Beauty, aesthetics, just the right touch. The colder and wetter it got, the less important these seemed to be.

Each day I had to struggle with myself not to cut the chimney back to half its width for the last run up. That's how most chimneys were done anyway. What difference would it make? So much less brick laying and so much less rubble to be hauled up and dumped down around the flues, and so many fewer batches of mortar to keep locking it all together.

But hell, the chimney would be the house. If it was ticky-tacky, the house would be junk. I had committed myself to make the thing a personal monument, so, damn it, I'd have to carry on.

The end of the third week was the first time I finally talked some sense to dear Bobbye.

"Dear one, we can't go on like this," I said.

Wheezing she looked up at me and quipped, "You want a divorce?"

"Good lord, Bobbye, I'm talking about your coughing, spitting, wheezing, all that. I'm afraid you'll die some morning while I'm up on the roof and I won't even know about it for the rest of the day. We can't go on ignoring what's wrong with you. We've got to get you to a doctor."

Frankly, even if this doctor character would have made a house call, we were nervous about having him see our heatless digs with the big hole in the wall. That gave me nightmare visions of Madlock and the sinister Jeremy Yam jointly declaring we could not hebetate while we fabricate or some such crap. To have to find an apartment till we'd finished certainly would have finished us for good financially. A bank foreclosure? Under those circumstances, possible. I was developing an acid stomach.

"I think that makes sense," Bobbye whispered, then coughed big time. "Let's go right now."

I'd warmed the VW before half carrying her out to it for the ride to the doctor's office. Now this man of medicine didn't exactly dazzle us with his sage announcement that Bobbye was suffering from a "Cold. Your wife here has a cold." (He gave that report with the duty stethoscope resting shoulder to shoulder and roped behind his neck. He laid on a kind of technical intonation which I think he believed would imply that he had read all them doctor books on this kind of stuff, too."Rest, miss, drink plenty of fluids, ah water, um and juice, orange, or um ah, fluids. And take some aspirin."

On into the fourth week, past the 25th day of our ten-day struggle we trudged forward. That week the drizzle seemed to content itself with a steady 33 degrees. Bobbye bedded down for a couple more days like the man said, but finally chucked it and returned to her finish work on the interior. Which was about when my coughing began too.

I started to dream of the next drill weekend coming at the end of the month. How warm it would be at the squadron, and dry. How overheated those B.O.Q. rooms were, so incredibly stuffy, that normally I thought I'd go nuts if I couldn't get a window open. And how sticky those old windows were, and how close I so often

CHAPTER TWENTY-SIX: HE COMES • 313

came to slinging a chair through them just for a breath of fresh air. But now how I was starting to panic over the cold, bitter, wet, unconquerable kind of illness grabbing me as I went up and down the slippery frosty damned ladder. Oh, how I wanted to load Rob and the dogs and Goldfinger all into the VW and cut out to the folks' place near Boston. It would be like a Florida vacation just being locked snuggly inside a real house.

Then Bobbye got a temperature and we telephoned Dr. Science again. I think he plugged me into a rerun of one of his turn-of-the-century favorites ---"Bed, Fluids, Aspirin, and Me." My cough was stone hard by then too, but I just couldn't bear that song again.

The weather had been too rotten over the last week for our cheering section to come by much. Between Moody's place and our driveway, the ruts were running axle deep in muck. So, along with the gray days and early night darkness, it was getting kind of lonely miserable around there too. I had old Rob back under a huge pile of quilts in our bedroom, a tight room, gooped and sanded, but still heatless. She was so damned brave and cheery about things, I guess 1 let myself hear what I wanted to hear, rather than pay attention to the increasing severity of her cough and the wheeziness of her breathing. It's so tragically easy to be cruel to a brave person.

Standing on the scaffolding, a brick in one hand, the trowel in the other, rain running down my neck, sick, broke, jobless, a failure, my wife hacking away in a moldy damp unfinished house below, and me up on a ladder freezing my ass off, I began to ask myself just what the hell I had in mind? Just what the hell did I think I was doing; and if I could think of an answer to that, then ... why? Why was I continuing this ever-expanding, ever-deteriorating, freaking farce?

"Ken. Oooh, Ken."

It was Florence's voice through the fog and splatter that brought me back. Turning I saw her wrapped in an old tweed coat pulled tight to her neck with one hand, the other struggling with a man's black umbrella as it kept catching in the over-hanging branches. Her shoes were soaked. Her stockings and the hem of her dress were sodden too.

She hadn't wanted to telephone for fear of disturbing Bobbye, so she'd slogged through the wet to say that Lady Ashley was summoning me to her salon for the final verdict on my manuscript. Two o'clock. Don't be late. Two o'clock sharp! Yeah. I didn't dare look at her eyes for fear of knowing bad news too soon.

I got Rob some soup; saw the dark rings around her eyes, listened to her wheeze and cough, then had the gall to tell her about the appointment. God, I couldn't believe the sniveling weakness forcing me to open my mouth about it to my sick darling. No matter how sick and miserable she was, I couldn't leave her at peace. I still had to lean on her and beg her sympathy and encouragement. I felt totally worthless.

Finally there, Tony, her Matre D'Amour, let me in. I kept my head down. Executions, I mused, are like that. The executionee just can't stand the phony looks of pity, the none too well guarded looks of superiority, the whole aura of condescension exuded by the executioners and their staffs. And so, in kind of bumbling fashion, Tony directed me toward Dame Ashley with tugs and pushes on my arm. I came to stand, literally with my wet hat-in-hand before her Eminence.

There was a momentary pause. I had forgotten to say hello. Now it was too late. I gave a slight jerky nod, then coughed a huge whack of phlegm, and had to content myself with trying to gag it down without retching.

CHAPTER TWENTY-SIX: HE COMES • 315

She looked at me hard, with slightly narrowed eye as if to discern whether or not there was any substance at all to me. Then she said, quite simply:

"It is God awful."

If the scene had been from an English play, a UK drama, my part would have returned,

"Indeed" or, "I say" or something of the sort indicating that though smitten, I was, nevertheless, still in control of all my body parts and upper lip as well.

"Are you really serious about writing?" she asked with the suggestion of a physical therapist eyeing a legless man who was requesting assignment to the track team.

My answer never really got beyond a fit of coughing, but no matter, she went on anyway.

"If yes, you are going to have to work like a black to straighten this out."

I found some secret amusement in this. Usually the much-maligned black fellow is abused for supposed indolence and lack of performance. Here, however, a very white lady was suggesting the very opposite, still without implying any merit for one of the brothers at all. I immediately thought of how incredibly hard Isaiah Moody worked helping others and even fighting overseas for us all.

She handed me the box of manuscript. "Frankly I didn't read the whole thing," she said, "only a sampling here and there because of my eyes. They have only so much sight left to them, and I have so much writing to do before they go completely. I am working on the galleys of my latest book, you see. I must say, though, that your section on the Irish fellow … Doogan, no Duggan, you must throw out that abominable dialect. 'Much too difficult to read. Oh, there is so much work to be done on the thing." (1 wished she'd used a less general term there. Something like book, or manuscript, or a novel. To spend two years of one's existence hatching a thing could be a blow to even the coarsest mother bird.) "Like the way she said I had to "Work like a black to make anything of it."

1 hacked and gagged a bit, which seemed to be accepted as farewell. She turned back to her desk and Tony took my arm again, nursing me to the door.

If I had thought to drive old Sad Truck to her place, I would probably have put the manuscript in the open rear with the tools and sand. Because I had the VW on this trip, the manuscript sat beside me. On the death seat. 'Seemed appropriate. That thing sure as hell was dead now.

On the way home, between coughs and spitting out of the window, I found myself laughing, yes laughing like a goddamned loon. It had just occurred to me. Throughout the entire inquest ,I had never produced a single word. I'd said absolutely nothing. I'd simply marched up the scaffold, had Tony fasten the noose around my neck, the Thing handed to me for ballast, and then I felt the floor go out from under my own ineffective gags and gasps of acceptance. Not a word. I had died in silence. For the first time in my life, I had done something without opening my big fat mouth. I had failed.

From the deep ruts and zigzag tire tracks all over the drive, I knew some kind of horror show had taken place in my absence. Jumping from the car and hurrying into the house, my fears were confirmed.

Though Rob was safely in bed, she was really a damp bedraggled mess, and through her labored breathing she recounted the ghastly tale of Henry's visit of doom.

CHAPTER TWENTY-SIX: HE COMES

"Oh Kenny, it was horrible. After seven years on the wagon, Henry had, as he told it, simply said 'piss on it' and done exactly that. Thoroughly intoxicated, he roared and lurched up here in his new car, banging it roughly in the direction of our house, finally coming to a stop up on a boulder, which was jammed into the fender.

"I wrapped my blanket around myself, and a tarp on top of that, and went down to help. Kenny, Kenny it was awful. I found him swimming in a sea of throw-up and urine. I didn't know what to do, as sick myself as I was. So, I started honking his horn, over and over until dear Isaiah came to his door and my waving and flashing Henry's headlights brought him over. If he hadn't been home, I don't know what I would have done."

And frankly it all was a little much for dear Bobbye to handle considering her "cold," her temperature, a growing little one, the rain, muck, and the weight of Henry's near dead body. So, Isaiah supplied the muscle and Christ-like compassion needed since Henry's wife was away. He sent Rob back up to our place and he wrestled the wheel from Henry's grip, getting him more-or- less across the seat, somewhat cleaned up, then he drove him home where he got him into a shower, washed and pajamaed him and got him into bed. Then he walked all the way back through the woods just in time to go off to his second job of the day. What a strong, fine, good man he is.

If only I were such a man.

The whole scene had left Bobbye a wreck, so I bundled her up and ran her back to the Great Practitioner. This time, thank God, rather than cranking out the same old tune, he figured to take x-rays and do other doctor things too. After I got Rob back home and in bed, he called to announce that she had pneumonia. He'd phoned a penicillin prescription in for her at the drugstore.

As an extra kind of a package deal, to soothe his conscience I guess, by confiding that 1 had a rousing case of bronchitis myself. But this time, anyway, he popped up with a second prescription for me as well.

The fact that my literary career had finally been shot in the forehead was kind of lost in the shuffle of Henry's crashing fall from the wagon, and the sudden realization that if Rob and I didn't apply ourselves medicinally we might just die there in our sawdust filled, unheated, partially wall-less freezing damned dream house. A dead book was one thing, a dead wife was something else again.

I drove the VW to the pharmacy and then over to Montgomery Wards. All cold chills and sweaty, coughing and phlegm-producing like a champ, I presented my magic charge card, backed by a fictional bank account, and bought an electric space heater. This way I figured we'd at least get that back bedroom warm. It would be a hedge, our last hope for getting the house enough together to get the wall sealed and the fireplace going. That would see us through till I could get the heating system in. Heat, everything now was a matter of heat.

I'm sure there are those who would cite me as a first-class ruthless, bastard for not getting Bobbye straight into a hospital. In retrospect, I guess I feel the same way. But I've got to say that in the fury and confusion of that most difficult day we hadn't really thought of it. And then later that evening, with the one room for the first time warm and toasty, it didn't seem necessary or practical. Necessary because Rob responded so well to the heat and penicillin and practical enough because we had no way of paying a hospital bill. Neither of us had ever held a job in Connecticut so there was no workmen's compensation nor health insurance or unemployment or anything like that to draw on. Short of her going into convulsions on the hospital steps, we had no idea of how to get past an admission's desk with Nurse Ratchet presiding who would want some proof of payment. We had nothing, zip, zero, nothing unless I could sell our VW to the nurse. So, we figured we'd ride it out a bit to see what happened. For the moment we seemed okay. And the heat was doing some good. If I could just keep her in bed now, keep her warm, relaxed, and comfortable, then the rest and the medicine should bring her along. Anyway Dr. Doctor thought so, too.

Keeping her in bed though, was something else. Bobbye started feeling guiltier and guiltier, hearing me coughing and cursing at the other end of the house up on the roof. So, she'd struggle up to put some soup on for us for lunch, that kind of thing. Then I'd shout, cough, and gag at her making her cry for what she felt she was doing to me. Essentially, we'd exhausted ourselves in an emotional struggle to save the other from exhaustion.

Nothing was going right, and what with the drizzle still eating into my bones, the depth of physical fatigue I was sinking into from the work and the bronchitis, coming from all directions, I think I became marginally hallucinatory towards the end. I began to grow paranoid and I guess a touch manic-depressive. I had horrible visions of us dying out there, no one knowing nor caring about it. The house finally falling in on our bones, it never having been finished. The tune "Singing in the Rain" kept running through my head, but with a new lyric. Rather than singing, my mind substituted dying. "We're just dying in the rain, everyone will forget ... "

Frozen hands, cold to the bone, sick as hell, a wife inside sicker still; little money, seemingly no hope now as a writer, we were as low as we could get. Then it started to sleet.

"Oh, shit no, God, come on. What do You want from us? "I shouted to the gray murk above, then added. "Uncle! UNCLE, for Christ's sake. I said it, UNCLE!" But no response. The sleet remained steady.

I worked along for a while building up more frustration, more rage. What the Christ had we done? Why were we getting worked over like this? I never claimed to be Job. God sure as hell couldn't prove anything to anybody by me.

I looked back up again, climbing the icy ladder and shouting, "If this is something between You and the Devil, leave us out of it!" Just the idea of a devil was a joke anyway, I mused silently to myself, then added, "And who the hell was going to want to believe in a god who kicked the shit of innocent bystanders? How about it? LEAVE US OUT Of IT, PLEASE!"

Rob, steady Rob, even she was getting a little shell-shocked. Between us we began to conjure up any number of horrors. The most recurrent, of course, was the vision of Dr. Doctor coming out on a house call, (You can see how far gone we were), taking one look at the ventilated squalor we were living in, and condemning the place. The irony of that was too macabre not to believe its possibilities. To have your house condemned before you even finished building it would be too sensationally horrible for God, fate, whoever it was calling the shots, to pass up. I worried. That night we huddled under our blankets fearful of even showing our faces out from under them ever again.

So, would you believe? Lord Almighty. The next morning, just before sunrise, we were awakened by the sounds of sirens, not out on the highway, we would have slept through those, but sirens on police cars bumping and banging-up our own sloppy, mud-rutted lane.

CHAPTER TWENTY-SIX: HE COMES

I leapt out of bed like a good laboring Black in clan country and ran to the window. My heart, beating wildly high in my throat, suddenly took a dive for the back exit at what I saw outside. Two big police cars had our little dirt road blocked where it intersected with our drive. Their big red and blue rotating beacons were whipping and whirling, flashing out the news of our condemnation to the world. And most frightening of all, coming toward the house, with a thirty-eight in his hand, was one big cop behind one big silver badge. By the cars at the bottom of the hill were many other armed cops, semi-crouched, one even with a riot gun, all ready for action.

"When they evict somebody in this county," it flashed through my mind, "they sure don't fuck around."

Running back to Bobbye in the bedroom, I considered the .22 caliber revolver in the dresser, but what was the sense? These guys obviously meant business. From the looks of it they probably had tanks out on the main road, General George S. Madlock commanding.

"This is it, Bobbye," I said totally defeated, "the police are coming up the drive right now. There's nothing we can do. There are just too many of them."

She didn't say anything, just took my hand. Then the whole house reverberated with a heavy fist on the back door. The jig was up. Both our eyes filled as I rose. We couldn't look at each other. We had tried so damned hard to make a go of it, and now, sick, cold, and miserable we were having to face the final insult being forcibly thrown out of our own home and carted off to only God knew where.

Thump! Thump! Thump!

Tinkerbelle started to bark in unison with the banging. Goldfinger only pitter-patted over to Clem, who continued to sleep, and snuggled down behind him, using the clown as a buffer against whatever was causing the racket.

Bobbye didn't say anything, she just patted my hand. Then the whole house reverberated with a heavy fist, this time on the front door.

Thump! Thump! Thump! Bark! Bark! Bark!

"Yah, yah I'm coming," I shouted, shuffling down the hall barefooted, struggling to get a second leg through my trousers.

"You the McAdams's?" demanded the belted, buckled, booted star-spangled, gun-toting ,portly defender of justice.

"Half of them, officer, why?"

"Anything strange goin' on around here?"

"Well yes," I answered testily, "policemen just banged on both my doors, front and back, at five thirty in the morning and there's a roadblock at the end of my driveway right now."

Glancing over his shoulder down the hill, much like the last bureaucrat to get the word, he muttered, "Oh yeah, that.

"Well, you see, Mr. McAdams, we was chasing a pack of car thieves who dumped a stolen veehicle," (permanent government employees seem to say veehicle more than not), "at the end of your road. They took off back this way on foot. We're goin' in after them, but I wanted to check to see if you'd seen anything."

For all we knew we might have a pump-house or cellar full of desperados, but I was hugely relieved. God, what a load off. I kind of slumped against the door jamb and let out a sigh.

"Now, nothin' to worry about Mr. McAdams. We will protect you and we will catch them for sure," he comforted, misinterpreting my heavy breathing.

"Bless you and your men, officer. Bless you all," 1 said, hardly able to contain myself. Bobbye, all bundled and pressing against me, nodded too, after coming out of our bedroom and easing up beside me.

"Thank you, sir, we need all the community support we can get. Now, where does this road here lead?"

Realizing then, that we were on the same team, and not wanting to cloud the issue, I buttoned my fly and said, "It goes pretty much straight up to the power lines, which run east and west. It gets real faint for a while, then turns into a farm road up on the hill where the dog warden has his sheep farm. There's one branch that goes through the meadow to the right toward the old cider mill. Another very faint branch just craps out in the woods. There are a lot of ways they could go back up there."

"Shit," said the badge, "ah, sorry, Mrs. McAdams, I mean that's a mess of a country to surround. 'Take a damned army."

Again, visions of Madlock mounted at the head of a column sped through my head.

"Well, better get humping," he said, turning and moving back toward the barricades. "Thanks for the info anyway."

"How about some coffee and ah, donuts?" I threw in, wondering what he'd say. He hesitated, looked down the hill again, and finally said, "Ah no. Love to but thanks, no. It was the chief's wife's car they took. He'd be some pissed if we didn't keep movin.'"

Jogging, then stumbling down our rutted drive, along with the other portly defender of democracy who must have been the backdoor thumper, he waved, and grouped his troopers by the cars for a briefing. Then, four of them went on into the woods on foot, while the remaining two took the cars back out to start circling the area. I didn't see that they had a chance, but still was impressed at how fast such heavy men could move so early in the morning and how cynically arrogant criminals were getting to be these days. The chief's wife's own car! Think of that...

It goes without saying that Bobbye and I were tremendously relieved. She confessed that while I was at the door with the officer, she had been lying in bed agonizing on what to try to take with us in the police car and what to leave behind. And the fact that she had no idea where we would be taken had made it doubly difficult. Did they have welfare hotels out there for evictees - "down the station", or did they just throw them out on the street to fend for themselves?

The picture of the old man and the old lady at the table on the rubble strewn sidewalk back in Boston came to mind. They had been evicted, forcibly, by a great steel ball that left their apartment house a simple heap of broken brick. Would the McAdams's end up the same way?

For a while, over breakfast, we felt a little better about our lot, but it didn't take too long for that tiny bubble to break dumping us moistly back into our own confusing world again. The sleet and rain hadn't really stopped. Oh, occasionally there'd be an interlude of drizzle and fog, but that was about it. If anything, it had gotten colder. So, after piling the dishes in the beautiful double dip sink, and leaving Rob wrapped and snug in bed, I trudged out to re-engage the chimney dragon.

God it's hard to get your fanny in gear on a cold miserable morning following a police raid. Though I'll admit that after so many lousy mornings in succession, I was starting to get the hang of it police or no police. Prepping mortar was just a matter of uncovering the mixer, hooking up the electrical connection, tossing in some water and sand to mix with the cement, and keep the mixer cranking.

While that was puttsy-puttsing, I banged out the five-gallon pail and put that with the big pan that holds the working mortar up on the scaffold. 'Make sure everything is free of crusted mortar from the day before. Hump a few loads of brick up to the top. Check that the trowel and brick hammer are up there too.

Make sure I hadn't forgotten the level. Take the small tarp off the top of the chimney and feed up a couple more flue sections. Leave the stones and rubble till the end of the day. Now tilt the mixer with the first batch into the big pail and struggle that crusty bastard up to dump into the pan. Go down for one or two more loads. Keep the mixer running while hosing it out so a hard build up won't crust in with the next mix. Shut it down, then crawl up the icy ladder to the work area. Blow hot breath onto your cold hands, then have a small fit of coughing and spitting before laying the first brick. I might rather have been in prison. Something for the record anyway, I was through the roof overhang, done very neatly I might add, what with all the fancy flashing on one side, and the uninterrupted facing board carrying the roof line from peak to gutter, and all that lovely brick marching up neatly behind it. Yes, yes that touch worked perfectly, the overhangs being large and equal all around the house.

So now I had only to build the chimney up above the peak of the roof to give it a proper draw. It looked to be two more days at my usual tortoise-speed pace. Thirty-two days were gone, shot completing the estimated ten-day job. Who could be happy over that? Oh, how that schedule over-run had knocked me on my Kei ster.

It had carried us into winter ... on a stretcher, and with no heating system in. That miscalculation, so gross, was the weighted straw in the end. But what was life without straws and overruns?

The next day, still raining, could you believe, I topped out! 1 laid the last brick, filling the remaining cavern around those last two flu pieces with rubble and mortar, and spread a smooth cement cap over the top, gently sloping it to the pair of flues from each side. It was a thing of beauty.

When professional brick men top-out they do something like this. They press a nickel into the wet cap. At the time I did not know of such customs, but I did know that for good T.V. reception of the Giant's games from New York, and the Red Sox from Boston, I'd need a hearty base for a tall antenna. What could have been a better base than that huge, super strong, cement chimney? So, I sank a three-foot pipe into the wet cement that would make me the football/baseball king of eastern Connecticut. Perfecto. Done!

I could hardly believe it. It seemed impossible. THE CHIMNEY WAS FINISHED! Hallelujah! Glory. Glory. And on that slippery wet, icy roof I took one step back to survey my work and ... ah yes, -- somewhere in this favored land the sun is shining bright. The band is playing somewhere, and somewhere hearts are light. Yes, true, however my foot slipped. Oh, good God in Heaven, YES, my foot slipped! And I lurched backwards, teetered, then lunged forward, wildly grabbing at my glorious antenna base pole set in the top of the wet chimney. Only it could save me ... I thought.

I did catch ahold of it ... as I went by. Straight across the front corner of the chimney, over it, off the edge of the scaffolding, through the air in a somersault, to hit, smack! flat on my back in the mud, two stories below.

There wasn't a whisper of breath left in me. I was absolutely down and out.

Finally, managing one panicky gulp of air, then another, and another, I realized if nothing else, I was still alive. I tried moving my fingers, then toes, arms, legs, back, pelvis, neck, head. All seemed in working order. Nor did I experience any great pain.

"So," I thought, "rain and soft mud are good for something, like cushioning falls from the top of roofs."

Actually, I was quite comfortable lying there. I imagined those sensations of relief directly following the terror of the fall were similar to what a prize-fighter feels coming-to, also flat on his back, to the sound of the single word, "TEN! " Surely, it's going to represent a grinding disappointment, but for the moment the luxury and delicious relaxation of his flat-out position are a great relief after the horrible beating he'd been taking.

The wet mud soaking into my trousers, my back, into my hair drove me to my feet. I staggered some, coughed a lot, but I'd been doing that before taking flight. I seemed okay. Until I looked up at the top of the chimney.

Unbelievable. Absolutely. Oh God. Words of four letters ... I didn't leave one out. That magic f-bomb and all its variations I shouted to the sky. I touched base with every part of the anatomy. 'Made up a few from the usual building blocks. Naturally none of it was enough to soften the horror and rage my seeing the five-course of brick torn out of three sides of that glorious chimney's face. And the antenna pole was at my feet. Cement oozing all over the place. It was bad. But, I just didn't have the vocabulary to cover it all. So up the ladder I went, to stand on the peak of my icy roof bellowing every horrible word I had ever heard. Until, out of sheer trembling exhaustion I roared ---"Fuck the whole damned world!"

And below me, at the door came Bobbye, all wrapped in a bundle of blankets, her nose running. Her voice was raspy as she looked up at me where I'd climbed way up on the roof, and she struggled to call, "Kenny, Kenny, what is wrong?"

I looked at her and all I could say was, "Bobbye. Darling. I fell off the roof and I... I... have... got to... get a job."

Would you believe, at that very moment the sleet stopped, and the sun came out!

The rest of that day and the next I spent patching the disaster I'd caused. It was a crushing experience in itself, to have to go back to, literally pick up the pieces and reconstruct what physically and psychologically had already been completed. But I did it, happily without further mishap. Then, as we waited several days for the cement and mortar to set prior to starting our first fire, I devoted myself to rehabilitating Rob, and looking at want-ads. I had crossed over. Now it was simply a matter of taking hold of something on that other side.

I wrote the Yale Alumni placement people in New York advising them that I was ready to take command of any of the Fortune 500 firms possibly leaderless at the time. I looked into a bookstore position at Connecticut College for Women, feeling that there might be material for a future seamy novel there. I picked up an application for social work in New London. I even did an audition for a radio show on one of the local stations, (Maybe I could have been Rush Limbaugh before Rush went national, but I didn't get a call-back.) Next, I thought of a journalism career with the New London paper after reading an intriguing article about Madlock's daughter, yes, the offspring of my archrival, and her apprehension in the backseat of a parked veehicle on lover's lane.

Then, sitting on the bare subfloor in front of our first fire, Rob and I tried to take stock of our position. She was still all bundled up, but seemingly better now that there had been a slip of sunshine at the end of the other day's rainbow, and more over the next few as well. My roof top decision to finally get a job seemed sound, even after a few days of empty job hunting. But already, I was jerking and hopping this way and that, ready to grab any old thing—yes, like a defeated man.

CHAPTER TWENTY-SIX: HE COMES

So Bobbye, sitting cross-legged in front me, my hands in hers, the flickering firelight dancing through her lovely brown hair, caressing the flicks of gold in her eyes, she decided to have a good talk with me, to make a few things clear.

"Kenny, first of all, you're not a failure," she said, "and you're never to feel guilt for these last years. We are still only beginning. You've got to see that. Believe that."

There was a long silence. I could only stare into the fire, feeling exactly like a failure, feeling very guilty for the last years; and not believing a word of what she was saying... yet loving her very much for being my dear supportive wife trying to heal my many, many wounds.

"You don't agree with that do you?" she said finally.

"Ah Rob ... I guess not," I returned, laying back down, my hands going behind my head, my eyes staring up at the shadow patterns on the beautifully finished and sanded ceiling done by my darling. At least that work had come out right after all.

"Remember when John Reilly was here, the troubles he was having getting the feel of the country again?" she asked. "And Henry. The way we could only see his mess coming on?"

"Yeah," I said, just half listening, more intent on feeling sad, feeling sorry for myself.

"Neither one of them was happy with the way things worked, but each are setting out to try to make it different, while the other just seems set on trying to kill himself," she said, her head bowed as she studied a chipped and broken set of fingernails.

"I guess," I mumbled still staring at the ceiling, "but so what?"

"Moody is the so what," she returned, then fell silent.

I lay there on my back first trying to let her remark go on its own but finding I couldn't let it just float away. "Moody, what's he got to do with it?" I asked finally.

"He and Loraine are everything, Ken, because they're the successful ones, a happy couple," she said. "Moody and Loraine found the answer. Think of it. They work harder than any others around. Henry, John, us. But they're happy, because it's all part of their cause, their particular war."

I was listening now. I rolled, onto my side, facing the fire and propped, my head on a hand. I could watch the lights and shadows dance around Bobbye's hair and cheeks, around her fabulous green/gold-flecked eyes.

"That's what happiness is, Kenny," she said with a soft smile. "The good fight," she continued, her eyes sparkling. "That's why Henry ended up at the bottom of our hill like he did. He was only surviving. New house, new cars, T.V.'s, none of it helped for long. There must be the challenge, the prize ... John Reilly thought he'd lost it coming home because it was just harder to see. Feeding starving kids, building a school where there wasn't one before; that's easy to see. And satisfying. Back here things are more complicated. The goals are less defined. Certainly, harder to reach."

She sat a moment, then took my right hand and started fiddling with it, pushing back the cuticles, picking at the nails. She knew I liked that sort of fiddling.

"So, tell me more about Moody," I prodded.

"Oh, he's happy because his goal's in sight all the time, and he's making it happen every day," she said simply. "He and Loraine are lucky in a way because their fight is so clear cut. They got out of Mississippi, they are educating and giving a chance to their nieces, and they're making a nice home and a safe way of life ,too. So, all their work is worth it. They're happy, Ken, and that's why we have been happy too, and why we will continue to be happy and really, why you are not a failure at all ... as long as you keep fighting."

"Great, Rob," I said feeling a little heat on the back of my neck, "but just what the hell can I do about things now? I can't just sit down at the typewriter … . there's no money left. I can't even continue on the house with the winter having rolled in like this. All I can do is get some stupid damned job, just to hold things together."

"I know that, but don't be angry," she soothed, "because that doesn't mean it's all over. It is only just beginning. You'll find a job and we'll finish the house, and you will get back to writing too. Because that's your fight, our fight. And, as long as we keep after it, whether or not we ever even make it, we'll still be happy. That's what is so wonderful about having a goal. Just the working for it makes life a success. Makes it good. And even gaining the prize sometimes is the worst thing of it all. Success can damage, even destroy everything. Think of all those overdoses out in Hollywood. So come on, Kenny, smile. We'll make it because we won't quit," she said snuggling close, "and let's never quit loving each other either. If we went that way, away from each other, I'd get awfully sad, too."

Ah hell. I couldn't say anything. My throat was all lumped up again, my eyes starting to swim. I eased my arms around her and held her, hugged her tight. Good dear Rob, she could always do it, could always bring me back.

So that was the night I decided to be, of all things, an airline pilot rather than any of the other things I'd been fooling with. The pilot money was good. There were blocks of time off to write, much like I'd had teaching back in Wakefield. And the more we thought about it, really, the better we felt about the whole idea. I'd be off the hook now, making the whole dollar and cents for a change. Which would ease my conscience, and perhaps keep me from rushing blindly into another book like I had with the second. It would be good for me too. Make a man out of a boy, and all that.

Which made me think back to the guy I talked to at the Sausalito bookstore. Was he still living off his wife? If he was, and still not making it, his conscience must have been eating him up. Which becomes the issue. Can the writer, any artist in good conscience, continue to press on ... at the expense of those whom he loves and who love him and sacrifice for him?

It takes a tremendously strong man, strong in his regard of his own capacities, strong faith in himself, to be able to cause his woman suffering for his sake alone.

If I was going to succeed at all, it would have to be on my own. Which left no alternative. Like the man said after junking book two, I had better get a job. Maybe he knew what he was talking about after all, and was not just kicking me in the crotch. This is what I thought, looking back on that painful night of realization and commitment.

The next day we sent off a mess of applications to various airlines. I was hoping for a New York based outfit in particular, but could do little more than wait and see.

On the house, we lined up a guy whose building crew needed a quickie indoor job for a few days, and for a good price, he agreed to hook up the heating system. While this was underway, I was able to wrangle two weeks active duty with the Reserves that would bring in some immediate cash.

Dear Bobbye had recovered by then. Between the space heater and the fireplace, her bones must have dried out. So, while I was

CHAPTER TWENTY-SIX: HE COMES • 333

at Weymouth, she stayed behind to keep an eye on the heating people. Which turned out to be hardly necessary. They were good men. Worked like hell, and had the whole thing running in two days. It would have taken us probably a month doing it ourselves. Bless them, bless them all. The blueberry patch finally had heat.

Then we got a carpenter for the last of the finish work in the kitchen and here and there throughout the house. This character was a fine craftsman but had a head like steel. He never said a word and was as gullible as they come. 1 nicknamed him, 'Hammer." Which had its ironies, since I often called the dog, Clem, Hammer Head. Well, the two of them fell in love. I could see they truly were meant for each other. 'Became inseparable. Clem would fall all over himself to greet Hammer each morning. Hammer's eyes would flood. Never before had I seen Clem take to anybody at all. I'd thought he was hardly more than a long squat body hooked to a long-wet nose. His only form of self-expression in the past had been throwing up or dumping on car seats. But now he was clearly in love.

This was too good to pass up. By the end of the week Clem was dealt off. Hammer (2) was so grateful, he did extra work. He was a hunter. Clem was a hunter too. The two of them were a marriage. Bobbye and I were free at last.

Clem's departure and my acceptance by the New York airline I'd hoped for, Pan American World Airways, was really something in itself, and apropos of the crazy elements of my professional life, dating back to Yale and my becoming a fighter-attack pilot in the United States Marine Corps.

Way back in the late '50's, it became clear that the family needed some financial help funding my college expenses as well as my living costs in New Haven. I looked into the ROTC program which would pay much of that and could send me on to flight school to become a full-fledged Naval Aviator. That looked to be the answer to everything worrying me at that time. So, I applied to enter the program and shortly after that received a directive to report to the Boston Naval Yard for a physical. Which I failed for color deficiency. I was officially tagged as color blind and with that failure on my record, I would no longer have qualified for OCS nor flight training. My color deficiency would have ended my pursuit of any program which would lead to an officer's rank, much less qualification as a fighter-pilot. My military future would have been as an enlisted E-1 and with Vietnam cranking up, I would have had only one stripe and an M-1 rifle in my hand. *C'est la guerre.*

Then, however, that Yale /Princeton football weekend I mentioned earlier came about in which I won a bare-knuckle bout against a Golden Gloves champion. That led to my passing the Navy physical, assisted by the Quantico Marine referee, who told me he was so impressed with my fight performance and its victorious ending that he was going to prep me to pass future color tests. And this led to my qualification as a Marine officer and pilot.

During my final pilot qualification physical at Quantico, I had a by-the-book Flight Surgeon who was in the process of declaring me deficient, at least until a fighter plane crashed on the runway. Being the base flight surgeon, he was required to get to the crash site immediately. As he dashed to the door and started down the stairs, he shouted over his shoulder for the corpsman to finish the test I was a hairsbreadth from failing. With the Flight Surgeon out of the room and running down to the runway, the corpsman just shut the test machine down, smiled at me and said, "You passed." That meant that my twelve years in the Marine Reserves, rising to the rank of Major, flying jet fighters on and off aircraft carriers, "Special Weapons" approved, I was technically never actually qualified to do any of it. At least I think it established color perception requirements for aviation in our era of supersonic flying was ridiculous and only related to First World War slow-flying biplane issues.

So, after calling around to the various airlines to find out which were hiring and what the process of getting on with them was, I got involved in other moments of intrigue which I feel my days getting into the Corps best prepared me for dealing with.

On discovering there were long lines of applicants to the various companies and that the process of testing and the results forwarded to each airline's headquarters taking months, I figured there must be a better way. I asked myself how would the great Pappy Boyington have handled such a situation? I thought of my days in the Corps. Even how I had become a pilot, much less a jet fighter pilot in the first place, and how I had handled the situation on the beach at Waikiki when I saw the woman of my dreams and convinced her to become my wife until death do us part... all in one day! I vowed not to become passive and give into an unrealistic system that would only negate my future. So, I applied what I feel can now be known as the *Pappy Boyington Prerogative* and never looking back, I ramrodded my application to the head of the line by calling the procurement officer of the airline I hoped to get on with. I discovered he was a pilot himself, but on medical leave and not a fulltime desk-jockey. Ah hah, I said to myself, he is not a bean-counter, nor a by-the-book-type either. It turned out he too had been a fighter pilot. He was one of us. I was sure we could talk.

The next morning I got him on the line and said, "Captain, I understand that you are running the hiring show which is not a career choice for yourself."

"You are damned right. I want to be back up on one of those big birds flying off to the faraway places I'm used to flying to. But I'm stuck here, flying a desk, having to pull-in all kinds of qualified warm pilot-bodies to do what I want to be doing myself."

"So, sir, you've got a problem similar to my problem. You have to fill cockpit seats and I need one of those seats as quickly as I can get into it. I need the job right now. How can the two of us we pull it off? I asked.

"Doesn't work that way. 'Wish it did."

"Well sir, I was a Marine jet fighter pilot, finished number one in flight school, carrier and Special Weapons qualified and was assigned to Pappy Boyington's Black Sheep squadron, VMA-214. Were you in the Corps sir?"

"VMF-232 Red Devils.'

"They shared the ramp next to us at Kaneohe Bay."

"Semper fi, my man."

"Right on, sir. So now I think we can talk real world stuff. No bullshit."

"Okay, talk to me."

"As I see it, you need people right now and the system you're riding is in slow motion. I just finished building my own house, with my own hands: while my wife is sick and pregnant. I'm running out of money, and I need the job immediately. What I want is for you to put together all the stuff you need accomplished, tests, all that crap, pull it together for me, and I'll be in your office tomorrow morning, 0800 hours and I guarantee I'll get it all done before you close shop tomorrow afternoon. That will make it possible for you to get me a seat in your next pilot class starting Monday and you get home for cocktails by 5 hours Friday evening. What do you think?"

CHAPTER TWENTY-SIX: HE COMES • 337

The recruiting officer heard all this, after first thinking I most likely was just a pain-in-the-ass who might not be right for the "World's Most Experienced Airline" anyway, but then, the more he thought about filling this sudden medically opened slot, the more he thought this guy (me) could make his job and the coming weekend easier by handing me, if I could pull off all that I'd just shot off my mouth saying I could. If so, he'd save transportation from who knew where, hotels and all that. This McAdams character was local and could be plugged in painlessly. So, rather than going nationwide for the right applicant and arranging all the details of getting him to New York, hotel setup, per diem and all, this character (me again) was ready, willing and able to bring it all home *toute de suite*. I could save him weeks. He decided to give me a shot.

"Okay, McAdams, if you got a slot in the next class here at JFK, would it be pain-free for me? I mean, would you be ready and able to commute from wherever the hell you live, back and forth to classes here with no costs to the company?"

I was tempted to say, you better believe it, but decided "Yes sir," was better for the moment. Then the recruiter went on to say, "Okay, you get yourself back here tomorrow AM for the tests we'll run you through all day, and if you manage top scores on everything, at the end of the day I'll shake your hand and offer a Semper Fi for your future with us. Sound good?"

To me it was the Boston Symphony playing the 1812 Overture! I wanted to jump across the guy's desk, hug and kiss him… but that might have been a little much for a first day with his outfit. Nevertheless, I did say "Yes sir" and jumped through all the hoops he set up for me that following day.

Then, as it worked out, I had twenty-six or more years with his airline, the magnificent

Pan Am and in that time I became Chief Pilot of two of its divisions, broke three world records, and beat a previous record set by the U. S. Air Force, flying over both north and south poles.

I was, as well, appointed to the Thomas Committee which reorganized the entire airline and became the model for other companies expanding in the jet era as had Pan Am. And, included in my later duties was my designation as personal pilot for the founder, Juan Trippe, his successor Najeeb Halaby, and the Board Membership which included Charles Lindberg.

Yes, I accomplished a lot, my Marine fighter pilot brother Randy even said, "In the cockpit, Ken is a natural." And yet, despite these plusses, I am sad that no such thing is said of my abilities at a typewriter.

"Oh, I believe in yesterday."

THE END

www.ingramcontent.com/pod-product-compliance
Lightning Source LLC
Chambersburg PA
CBHW062057280426
43673CB00085B/450/J